A Balcony in Nepal

Praise for *A Balcony in Nepal*

"Whether you explore the world in hiking boots or a comfortable chair, A Balcony in Nepal is the perfect companion. Wonderfully written, smartly illustrated, the book discovers a universe in one small village. This is a book for the mind and the heart."

—Susan Isaacs, author of *Compromising Positions* and other bestselling novels

"A wonderful account from two American women who trekked through the Himalayas to a remote mountain village, shared the primitive life of village women and their families and became 'adopted grandmothers.'"

—Evelyn Kaye, author of *Active Woman Vacation Guide* and other books about unusual travel and women travelers.

"Sally Olds and Marge Roche became part of the vibrant, exotic, and difficult life of a rural Nepalese village. They observe the life and the poignant dramas of villagers and, as participants themselves, interweave their own western-based hopes and fears. This poetically written and beautifully illustrated tale of East-meets-West raises many issues of deep personal meaning and broad international significance."

—Broughton Coburn, bestselling author of *Everest: Mountain Without Mercy* and other books about Nepal

"A rare and intimate glimpse into the lives of the Rai people in a small village in Nepal. Whether describing death practices in which a delicate bridge of flowers is built so that a dead person's spirit can cross surging waters and go to heaven, or relating how they build bridges of trust with the Rai women through photos of their own families, the words and art of Sally Olds and Marge Roche are filled with respect and affection. By frankly relating how their experiences in this village affect them personally, their words and images come to life for us and take us with them on their journey."

—Jean Smith, editor of the "Beginning Buddhist Practice" book series for *Tricycle* Magazine and author of three *Beginner's Guides* to various aspects of Buddhism.

A Balcony in Nepal

Glimpses of a Himalayan Village

Sally Wendkos Olds
Art by Margaret Roche

ASJA PRESS
San Jose New York Lincoln Shanghai

A Balcony in Nepal
Glimpses of a Himalayan Village

ASJA Press
an imprint of iUniverse, Inc.

For information address:
iUniverse, Inc.
5220 S. 16th St., Suite 200
Lincoln, NE 68512
www.iuniverse.com

Cover art by Margaret Roche
Cover design by Dorri Olds

ISBN: 0-595-24027-5

Printed in the United States of America

We dedicate this book
to all the children of Badel,

with our warmest wishes for happy and fulfilling lives

And we want to acknowledge a few special people: Mary-Scott Welch, who brought the two of us together; Peter Owens, who brought us together with Buddi; Buddi Kumar Rai, who was our tireless, knowledgeable and caring guide to, from and inside Badel; Jai Prasad Rai, who had been our capable sirdar on earlier treks and who came with us on our first visit to Badel; Jai's and Buddi's wives and parents, who made us welcome in their homes; Carolyn Krupp, who believed in us and our project; Sarah Wernick, Bonnie Remsberg, Jean Smith, Broughton Coburn and Bernie Asbell, who read parts of this manuscript in earlier stages and offered valuable advice; and of course, our husbands, David Mark Olds and Pierre Dwyer Roche, who gave their blessings to our travels and to the work that came from them.

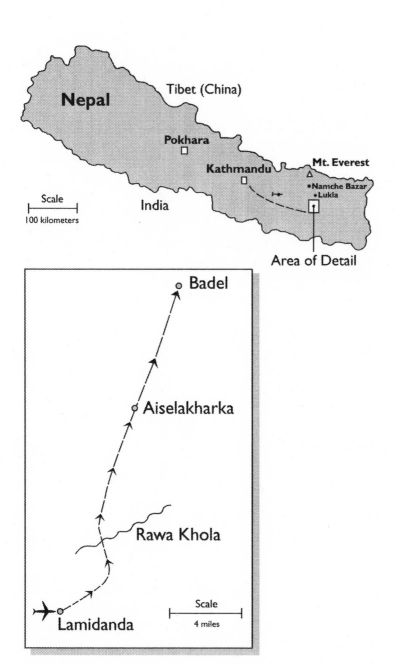

Nepal

Tibet (China)

Pokhara

Kathmandu

Mt. Everest

Namche Bazar
Lukla

India

Scale
100 kilometers

Area of Detail

Badel

Aiselakharka

Rawa Khola

Scale
4 miles

Lamidanda

Contents

Prologue:
Why I Went to Badel

March 1987

It's 1:00 a.m. and I'm unblinkingly wide awake. Mark is sleeping soundly in our double sleeping bag. I make a vain effort to be quiet as I unzip the tent flap, but despite the loud rasping sound that tears through the stillness, he doesn't wake up. I crawl out to see a sky bursting with more stars than I've ever seen in my entire life. After spotting the only constellation I can always identify, the good old faithful Big Dipper, I sit outside on the ground to write by the light of my flashlight under the dark blue canopy of glittering stars. The night is mild, the silence pierced only by the snoring of fellow trekkers, the barking of a nearby dog, the trilling of an unseen bird.

Last night, the second night of our trek in the shadow of Nepal's Annapurna Range, as I was sliding into the downy warmth of our sleeping bag, I was thunderstruck by the idea of hiking day after day and camping out night after night for two whole weeks. What insanity, I thought, to have signed up for such a trip! What is a 53-year-old tenderfoot hiker doing up here in the Himalayas? Now, in this solitude, I look forward to falling into the rhythm of the walk and enjoying more perfect moments like this.

I eventually drift back into a deep, dreamless sleep, and then the perfect moments continue when I wake up again just before dawn at 5:45. After Maila, the kitchen helper, chirps a "Good morning! Tea-time!" in front of our tent, pours Mark and me cups of black tea, and offers a plate of pineapple-filled Indian cookies, one wave of beauty follows another for the next hour and a half.

First the sky, now a pale gray dotted with dancing stars. Then a faint hazy silhouette of the mountains in the distance. Then the silhouette darkens and sharpens as a faint pink glow appears behind them. The pink deepens into rose, more mountains appear as if summoned by a wizard, and then the sun bursts from behind them in a fiery orange ball. Soon after, on the other side of camp, snow-capped summits emerge in the distance. On this side loom some of the highest, youngest mountain peaks in the world: Lamjung Himal, Nagadichuli, Himalchuli. Back on the sunrise side, Ganesh Himal (named after the god with the body of a boy and the head of an elephant) rises before us.

Moments later, the sun shines silver on the sparkling crests. Between the daybreak on the one side and the panorama of peaks on the other, I run back and forth between the two magnificences, eating my granola and toast on the move. I never dreamed mountains could move me so. Two weeks won't be nearly long enough.

No, two weeks are not long enough. The last line in my trip journal reads: "Sometime, somehow, I know I'll come back." And so I do. It takes me four years, but then, drawn by these majestic mountains, I return to Nepal.

April 1991

Every hour or two during our first night camping out on this four-week trek near the Everest range, I wake up with stabbing stomach cramps. My head throbs and a wrenching soreness across my back keeps me wakeful. Each time I eventually fell into a fitful sleep, only to awake again. This morning at 5:30 when Chamarsing comes to our tent with tea, cookies, and a cheerful "Morning, ma'am! Morning, sir!" I can barely open my stinging eyes. I feel as if I'm moving in slow motion, but still Mark and I get our tent emptied and our duffel packed sooner than our 45-minute allotment. I manage to get down some grapefruit juice, but I can't swallow the porridge and banana nut bread our talented kitchen staff have served. Even though Peter, our trek leader and solicitous "Jewish mother," stands over me urging me to eat.

We're only at about 8,000 feet, so I can't be suffering from altitude sickness, I tell myself. I've been this high many times before. Still, today's walk is *hard*— especially feeling as I do. My thighs hurt as we walk up 1800 feet and then down again—which they probably would anyway, even if I felt good. But I don't feel remotely good. I am, by turns and sometimes simultaneously, exhausted, headache-y, light-headed, nauseated. When we stop for lunch I marvel—and almost gag—to see my fellow trekkers wolfing down french fries, rice, spinach, meat and cheese. Peter diagnoses dehydration, gives me a salt pill and urges me to drink. While the others eat, I fall into a deep sleep murky with fevered dreams. Then it's time to drag myself to my feet again and go on. I wasn't sick a day on my first trek, but now I am four years older. And this trek close by Mount Everest and some of the other of the ten highest mountains in the world will be longer, harder and higher. How will I endure four weeks of this?

Helen looks like I feel, only worse—proof that these mountain ailments respect neither age nor fitness. At 57 I am the oldest woman in our 14-person group; at 36 Helen is the youngest. This prototype of the California woman— blonde, sturdy, athletic looking—seems to be feeling even sicker than I do.

Even at my lowest point I can manage to carry my daypack, but when Helen seems to bend under the light weight of hers, Kalu, one of our three sherpas, quickly steps over and relieves her of it. "Here, *Didi*, I take." Kalu Tamang, a moon-faced 22-year-old who looks like a teenager, is smaller than I am, but his ropy legs and wiry body hint at an extraordinary might. Today Kalu is our rear guide, while our other two sherpas handle the front and middle of our scraggly group. Walking a little more easily without her pack, Helen summons her strength to trudge a few steps ahead with Bob, her long-time companion. I urge Mark to walk ahead while I lag behind with little Kalu, who stays close by my side and takes my arm gently but firmly when I need help along the trail.

Knowing that he could handle my daypack too if necessary helps to give me the strength to keep going. Somehow I feel empowered by his support.

As we tread up and down through terraced fields and we skirt forests thick with sixty-foot-high trees abloom in scarlet rhododendron blossoms, Kalu talks about his life. "My mother and father, they die. I very small so I go live with my grandmother. She like mother to me. She 77 years old now. Very old. But very strong. Your mother, *Aama*? Your father? Still alive?" I shake my head. "Both dead. My father died when he was 76, my mother at 79. Both my brothers are dead too."

Kalu looks so stricken as he says, "Oh, you are all alone," that I quickly add, "Oh, I have my own family now. Mark—my husband. Our three daughters. Two grandchildren. Now *I'm* the old one." I grin. He nods. "You come visit me and my grandmother in my village some day. We had fire in our house last year, all burned down. But Peter give money to fix. All good now. Ready for you to visit. Okay?"

"As long as it's okay with your grandmother."

"Okay. No problem."

I walk along, thinking how nice it would be to take Kalu up on his invitation. Some day, maybe.

Soon we come to a stream. Exhausted, Helen has sunk down like a rag doll on the grassy bank. Bob stays with her as the others take off their hiking boots and ford the shallow waters. Kalu immediately sizes up the situation. He smiles the smile that shows his even white teeth, deepens the dimples in his brown cheeks, and makes his dark almond-shaped eyes almost disappear, as he hands Helen's backpack to Bob. Then the lithe little sherpa kneels in front of Helen, invites her to climb up on his back, and carries her piggyback as he sloshes across the little river.

Looking at them as I wait for Kalu to come back to help me wade across, I remember the Zen story of the monk who carried a beautiful young woman across a river and was berated by his fellow monk: "Brother, it was clear that you enjoyed carrying that woman." "Yes, Brother," answered the first monk. "But I put her down an hour ago. You are still carrying her."

Kalu reminds me of the first monk. Even as I feel a sense of triumph in trudging through the water on my own two feet, I know that if I needed him to, he would carry me as well across on his back. I see the generosity in his spirit, in the devotion of this sweet young man who enjoys the work that lets him serve another human being in need. I am to see this generous spirit over and over again in these four weeks on trek—in Kalu, in our other staffers, in local people we meet along the trail. There is something special in the spirit of these people—something that goes far beyond what I have experienced from other people in other lands where I have traveled. Something I warm to even as I yearn to know more about it. And as I see it—as I see the warmth and kindness the Nepali people show us, I know that if I survive this trek, I will return once more to Nepal. This time it will not be her snow peaks that draw me, but her people. I know I will have much to learn from them.

Of course, I did survive the trek. By evening of that first day I felt like my old self—but during our weeks out on the trail, I became, in some ways, a new self. Who was this new self? I wondered. And how much did the changes I felt in myself owe to the people of Nepal, this narrow crescent-shaped kingdom sandwiched between northern India and southern Tibet? The quest to answer these questions and to explore what other changes might be in store for me was the engine that would drive me back to the Himalayas. Not only once again—but four more times before the decade was out.

Part 1
Before Badel:
1992 and 1993

1

The Beginning: A Wild Idea

If the beginning is good, the end will be good.
                                              —*Nepali proverb*

In November of 1991, I received a letter that was to set the course of my life for at least the next eight years—and that laid the foundation for this book. I ripped open the envelope with the familiar return address, extracted the hand-written letter, and read: "What do you think about our going together to a village in Nepal? I think you and I could do a beautiful book on the daily life of the village families. Not an anthropological study—we would bring readers into the village with us, not inform them about village mores. Lots to think about. A wild idea but, I think, one worth pursuing."

This letter and this invitation came from a woman who, in less than a year, had become an intimate friend, even though we had seen each other in person only once four years earlier, barely exchanged hellos, and promptly forgot about the meeting. The friendship began in January of 1991 when I—sitting at my desk in my cluttered home office in Port Washington, New York—wrote to my friend and fellow writer Mary-Scott Welch in South Palm Beach, Florida, to tell her that I was going trekking in Nepal. I had no idea that her reply would change my life.

Scotty wrote back, enclosing photos of a dozen or so charming drawings and watercolors of Nepali villagers and trekking staff. The artist was her cousin, Margaret Roche, who, said Scotty, "hikes into Nepal as often as she can swing the trip." I wrote to Marge Roche at her home in Evanston, Illinois early in February. Among other things, I recommended to her, for future trips, Peter Owens, the trekking leader Mark and I had gone with earlier and who would be leading this next trip. When Marge replied, she wrote that she had trekked five times with Peter. And then her name suddenly clicked with me; I went back to my 1987 journal, and I realized that back then, Marge and I had sat at opposite ends of a dinner table in Narayan's Restaurant in Kathmandu, Nepal's capital city, when my trek was ending and hers was about to begin. I had to pick up the phone to celebrate this synchronicity. After a long, rich conversation, I asked Marge to send me the three books she had produced of her drawings and journals from her treks.

It was through these books that Marge reached into my heart. Her journals read like letters from a soul-mate, as she revealed so many feelings that I shared—her affection and respect for Nepal and the Nepalis; her embarrassment and guilt over having so much, when those appealing and friendly people have so little; her striking out on her own on her voyages of self-discovery; and even her lust for the sweet, juicy cinnamon rolls that Peace Corps workers had taught Narayan's staff to bake.

In one of Marge's books I saw a sketch of Gora—the cook on her trek just after mine, who had also been the cook on my trek—wearing a tee shirt that said "Port Washington Thanksgiving Day Race." Marge had thought that the shirt was especially apropos, since Gora was holding the legs of the live chicken he was planning to cook for dinner. I had given that shirt to Gora the week before Marge had captured him with her paintbrush. I thought that the added synchronicity of her immortalizing that tee shirt on paper was a sign that she and I were meant to meet—and to affect each other's lives.

(*Synchronicity* was a new word for me, and a new concept; before I went to Nepal and became more accepting of phenomena I couldn't easily explain by rational means, I was aware of coincidence, but gave it scant weight in my life. Today I appreciate the fact that some of the most important events in my life are inexplicable.)

During the next nine months my friendship with Marge gestated in an intense correspondence, in which we learned how much we had in common. We were both at about the same stage in life—Marge just past 60, I only a couple of years short of it. We were both in sturdy long-term marriages (40 years for Marge, 36 for me); both involved with grown children (Marge's six, my three) and grandchildren (her eight, my three). We had both been active in the civil rights movement and were now committed to the goals of the women's movement. And we both filtered so many of our life experiences through our chosen callings—her art, my writing. In the two or three long, open, discursive letters that flew every month between New York and Illinois, we shared countless intimate feelings, thoughts, opinions, attitudes about life, death, love—all the important things.

And always, we wrote about Nepal. Both of us had fallen in love with this little Himalayan kingdom and her extraordinary people, a love that had brought us together in one of those serendipitous twists of fate that ended up changing both our lives and those of at least two children whom we would come to meet in the remote hill village of Badel (pronounced *BAH/dl*).

Both Marge and I had become entranced, not only by the incomparable beauty of the Himalayas, but by the remarkable sweetness and cheerfulness of the Nepali people. In view of the arrant poverty in which most of them struggle and the hard lives that are their lot, they do not show bitter, hostile or even resigned faces to the world, not even to those of us who in material ways are so much more fortunate than they—but exude a friendliness and a joy that neither of us had ever encountered anywhere else. What could these people, who wrest beauty from a harsh and primitive land, teach us, who live in one of the most technologically developed nations in the world? I had been especially curious about the women, few of whom I had met. Their lives were so very different from mine and so much more difficult; I wondered what their thoughts and feelings were, what dreams they harbored, what changes they could see in their future. And now Marge was proposing that we spend time in a Nepali village where we could seek answers to these questions.

What was so wild about this idea? What wasn't wild about it? We would be going to an isolated village in one of the poorest, most primitive Third World countries on earth. We could reach such a place only by flying halfway around the world to Kathmandu, and then boarding a small plane that would take us to a tiny airstrip, from which we would have to walk on narrow, twisting trails up and down mountains, through marshy rice paddies, over deep gorges and torrential rivers for several days, sleeping in tents along the way. We'd have to hire a staff consisting of guide, cook and several porters. For weeks we would be completely without telephones, mail service, electricity—totally out of touch with everyone we loved. No one would be able to reach us. We wouldn't be able to contact anyone in the outside world.

This kind of trip is usually taken by people at the threshold of adulthood, using what feels like unlimited time to explore strangers' lives in exotic places while they're wondering what they're going to do with their own lives. Or by anthropologists whose profession calls them to settle in unstudied communities for months or years so they can describe nuances of language and artifacts and culture for other scientists. We, of course, were neither: we were too old for the first and too unschooled for the second.

Furthermore, our lives were full; our time was limited. We would be taking a long break from work that was important to us and from family we loved (including our husbands, both of whom were definitely unenthusiastic about our plans), to be more than vacationing tourists, less than working explorers. We would be risking both health and safety in regions days away from any medical help. We wouldn't even be trekking to the most spectacular ranges of the Himalayan chain, which pull foreigners to them with the magnets of their magnificent views.

And finally, the idea of publishing a book was problematic. Although I was an established and often-published author, I had never written anything like the book Marge proposed. Although she had often exhibited her art and had won prizes for it, she had never published it commercially. Beautiful art like hers makes a book costly to produce. I got cold chills thinking about the folly of trying to produce a commercially viable book about our experience. Even though Marge and I had agreed that we would not judge this trip on whether a book came out of it, I knew myself. I knew how I transmute virtually everything I do into words on a page—sometimes in an article or book that gets published, sometimes in the pages of a journal that no one but myself will ever see.

In either case, writing is almost as much a part of my life as breathing. Sometimes I feel that I haven't fully experienced an event, haven't known a person, haven't really felt an emotion if I haven't filtered it through my head and then my fingers. Incised in my soul are the novelist John Cheever's words: "To write is to make sense of one's life, to aim to succeed in one's usefulness and one's loves, and to share this excitement with strangers." Writing is my way of living. Since this trip was inspired by both Marge's and my desire to share with strangers our excitement about, our admiration of and our affection for Nepal and her people, I cared terribly about how I would write about this particular experience. And of course the more I cared, the more anxious I felt. I knew that Marge had some of the same feelings about her art.

FROM MARGE'S JOURNAL:

My pencils, pens and brushes are my traveling companions. They are the foreign language that I never seem able to learn. They are my ears and eyes that record what passes before me. People ask how long it takes me to do one of my drawings. I have no idea. It could be an hour or only fifteen minutes. I don't know because when I draw I am in another time zone, one without watches, the one the Greeks call "kairos." We move into it whenever we are in love or totally absorbed in a task.

When I am in this world I am not aware of doing the drawing. It is as though some other power moves my hand and mixes my paints. In this altered state, the picture draws itself. The book is its own author. The dance owns the feet. The music flows without effort. When it works, the completed piece has soul. It has guts. When it fails, the work is tentative, clumsy, timid. I can't force it. I just have to have faith in what will come.

The more I thought about this idea, the wilder it seemed. And the more fiercely I wanted to do it. Both Marge and I managed to overcome our husbands' various objections to this journey of ours, and by November 25, 1992, four months before we were to leave for Nepal, I finally believed that this adventure would come to pass. At first it had been so remote, in such a distant future that I could talk about it easily, calmly. As our departure date crept closer, though, my excitement rose, along with heretofore unacknowledged fears and anxieties.

For months before we left, the two of us read nothing but books about Nepal. We recommended them to each other, burdened our mail carriers with them, shared our feelings about them afterwards. As enthralling as these books were, they were anything but reassuring. I read about visitors to Nepal itching all night because of bedbugs in the mattress. I read about the propensity of head lice to hop from the little heads of children to the big heads of the adults who spent time with them. I read about the packs of rabid dogs in the Kathmandu Valley and the villages, about the bandits who sometimes preyed on travelers on isolated paths, about broken bones shattered by sudden falls from steep ridges. Although we had both trekked in Nepal before, those trips had been under the care of a seasoned American trek leader, who provided clean tents, sanitary kitchen facilities, seasoned helpers, safe passage through the country. This time we would have a much slimmer buffer between us and Third World discomforts and dangers.

Then there were Marge's and my questions about each other. How would we get along? We were the closest of friends by post. But we had never spent any time together in person. Yes, we liked and admired each other's personality on the written page and in the occasional phone conversation. But how does that translate to being each other's only English-speaking companion for a month, to making joint decisions about meals, sleeping arrangements, day-to-day activities? I knew only the "disembodied" Marge, the one who wrote, the one who painted, the one who talked. Not the one who might take too long in the bathroom, the one who might be grumpy in the mornings, the one who might irritate with a thousand pesky habits. Nor did she know that Sally. Could that Marge and that Sally remain friends, while traveling and living together in close quarters and demanding conditions for a month, removed from familiar ground and from the comforts and conveniences we had always taken for granted? Further, both of us have powerful needs for private space, silent times, times to read and write and draw and paint. Could we respect those needs in each other, when we would be so far from home, practically yoked to one another, morning, noon and night?

So we previewed our togetherness. On a crisp November day in 1992 I flew to Chicago, Marge picked me up at O'Hare Airport, and the two of us immediately drove to the Roche family's cottage in the Michigan woods where she and I could be alone and free from any outside distractions. In the bright sunny mornings we sat together and filled legal-size yellow pads with lists of questions, items to buy, equipment, clothes, and gifts to pack. In the afternoons we breathed in the winey aroma of the carpet of autumn leaves underfoot as we walked through the woods behind the cottage, or felt the sand crunch under our steps on the deserted, driftwood-strewn beach along the lake. And always we shared thoughts and feelings, learning about each other and about ourselves. We talked and laughed and got along as if we had been childhood chums. It was glorious. We knew it would work.

But still there were nagging worries. For one, there was more than a possibility—in fact, a strong probability—of some kind of intestinal or respiratory illness, injury on the trail, and maybe worse. We would be courting new bacteria and new viruses in a milieu innocent of all the safeguards and protections we take for granted at home. And we would be miles away from medical diagnosis or care. We would be on our own. We would have to be up to date with tetanus and typhoid and polio inoculations. We would need gamma globulin against Hepatitis A. And maybe even Hepatitis B. And then there was rabies. Rabies?

In my entire life it had never occurred to me to receive a preventive shot against the eventuality that I might be bitten by a rabid animal. Rabies was funny-looking movie-cartoon dogs with mouths like soapsuds. I had never seen a rabid creature. But my guidebooks warned about the prevalence of rabies, especially in the villages. I remembered incessant all-night barking by packs of skinny, mangy mongrels—the kind that, in the absence of deliberate breeding, maintain generic canine features and shapes that characterize almost all dogs throughout the developing world. The ones I remembered were all loud, some mean. Still in my mind's eye was a dog I had kept my distance from during my last trip to Nepal—an especially ugly mastiff straining against a chain that I had prayed with all my might would hold. I remembered Marge's journal from a previous brief village visit.

FROM MARGE'S JOURNAL:

As we made our way through the village of Tekanpur to the house where I'd be staying the night, we were chased and surrounded by barking, snapping dogs—sometimes as many as a dozen in a pack. Prem, my porter, said they wanted to eat his little puppy, and he threw stones to keep them at bay. I just made sure I never got between the pack and Puppy. I wonder whether my scent is different from the Nepalis and it was me the dogs didn't like…. After dinner, Puppy and the fierce-looking house dog settle just in front of the wooden door. The old man of the house closes the door and places a bar across it. This is going to be a long night. I pray for dehydration so I won't have to get up in the middle of the night and try to pass the dogs. By morning I'm ready to burst—but I didn't go out all night!

I went to my doctor—and I got a short course in rabies. Flipping pages of *The Travel Medicine Advisor*, Dr. Gottridge looked up the incidence of human rabies, according to the World Health Organization and the Centers for Disease Control. From a low of 0.004 cases per million in the U.S., rates go up to 3.7 in Nepal. In developed countries like the U.S., the few cases that do occur are almost all from wild animals—raccoons, bats, skunks, foxes. But in the Third World, domestic animals are the ones to worry about.

Guidelines spelled out who should get the new series of three pre-exposure rabies prophylaxis: people who travel in a country with high rates; who are under 16; who will not be able to reach good medical care for a post-exposure shot within 24 hours; whose occupation involves contact with animals; who plan to spelunk, or to walk or bike in rural areas; and who will be staying more than one week in the area. I wouldn't be spelunking, and I could barely remember being 16—but I clearly fit the other four categories.

Since the most important one seems to be the 24-hour rule, and since rabies can be fatal if it's not stopped before it can reach the central nervous system, and since the village where I'd be staying is a three-day walk to the closest airport, from where I just *might* be able to get on a crowded flight to Kathmandu, I got the series. The shots were expensive—three, at $85 a pop. But after a minute's serious thought, I decided that my life was worth it. Feeling like a hypochondriac and a worry-wart, I rolled up my sleeve. Even though the preventive series is not 100 percent reliable, and I would need an immediate booster if some rabid cur got its saliva into me by biting or scratching me, or by licking a wound or any of my mucous membranes (eyes, inside of nose or mouth), I would still be better off with this than with nothing.

Marge decided against the rabies shots. "If we come across any mean-looking dogs, I'll just make you walk in front of me." At least one of us is protected. So I can check off one worry. What's left?

As Marge was putting a log in the fireplace during our weekend in Michigan, she said, "You have the hardest job—writing about our visit. I want to help you but I don't know how." When my artist friend Marianne was talking about how each of the paintings in her new show, based on places she had visited, developed differently because of what she wanted to say about each one, she said, "You know how it is—when you're creating something and you have to pull it out of yourself." And a bolt of lightning flashed through my body, lighting up the big question: What do I want to say about the Nepali way of life, what are my insights into them, into us? I wouldn't know until I was there.

Meanwhile, I pressed ahead with preparations. I phoned to make potentially valuable contacts with the United States Ambassador to Nepal and with the Nepal office of the organization Save the Children. Two weeks before my departure date, I started to train more seriously, adding more stair-climbing and more hiking to my regimen of a daily three-mile run and a weekly hike. I set aside the worn but usable clothes I'd be taking for our guides and porters and the village people. I took half a dozen lessons in Nepali, not enough to talk philosophy but enough to show the villagers that I was making an effort. I plunged ahead, seesawing wildly between euphoria and fear, my moods going up and down as steeply as those hills I would soon be traversing.

We made our reservations to leave from Los Angeles April 1. Every now and then I would think, "Suppose something happens to Mark or me while we're apart? Will I kick myself for not having spent this precious time with the person I love most of all in all the world?" But we can't live our lives under the shadow of the fear of disaster. As my youngest daughter always tells me, "Worry is like paying the interest on a debt you may never owe."

Late in February Marge and I did our final shopping. For our medicinal arsenal: over-the-counter remedies for diarrhea, joint pains and headaches; one kind of antibiotic for above the waist (respiratory infections—common in the hills, where every child has a runny nose), another for below the waist (intestinal illnesses caused by exotic bacteria lurking in the water), and still others for eye infections, cuts, whatever. Vitamins to make up for what promises to be a deficient diet. To enhance that diet: dried soups, trail mix, powdered milk, candies.

Clothes: skirts, blouses, tee shirts, jumper, sweater, hiking boots, socks, down vest, in various states of wear. Most of my wardrobe would be left in Nepal for the villagers. I didn't pack hiking pants since, in deference to Nepali modesty and dress standards, I would be traveling, trekking and visiting wearing calf-length skirts. Necessary supplies: notebooks and pens, tape recorder, lots of batteries, camera, lots of batteries, flashlight, reading light, lots of batteries, baby wipes for touch-up washing of strategic anatomical spots for those times when there's no shower within miles.

And then there were the gifts. We wanted to be good guests, and gracious guests come bearing welcome gifts. What kind should we bear?

FROM MARGE'S JOURNAL:

Oh, how I agonize over what gifts to bring to the village! The problem of deciding what to bring to a people who have nothing would seem, at first thought, a simple matter. Not so. Because they have so few material things, every new object that comes into the home gains an important status.

I think of the toys my grandchildren play with: Magic Markers, plastic cars, Barbie dolls, building blocks. I quickly disqualify all of them. They are either too heavy or bulky to take, or they would be inappropriate. I chuckle to think of little dark-skinned girls combing Barbie's long blonde tresses. They would probably love Barbie as all girls over the age of two seem to, but it won't be I who brings this serpent into the Garden of Eden. Certainly no plastics. They never go away, and ten years from now bright red and yellow bits of broken cars or dried-up marker will be surfacing on the dusty paths. What to bring for our hostesses was also a puzzlement. I could not think of a single household item that would blend into their uncluttered homes.

After much consultation, Marge and I pack picture books and flash cards and ballpoint pens to give to the school, beads and necklaces for the women, bandannas for the men, tee shirts and baby clothes for whomever they'd fit and a few small odds and ends for the children (coloring books, Silly Putty, origami papers, balls—and yes, a few plastic combs and bracelets; we hope they won't serve as an eternal reminder of our visit). We don't bring candy or pens to dispense to begging children, who along popular tourist routes come up to travelers, smile winsomely, look up at you with their big dark eyes and say "Bon-bons? Pens? Rupees?" Neither of us wants to be even partly responsible for encouraging these children of a proud and generous people to develop a beggar's mentality.

By the time March comes in, lamb-like, I'm feeling most unsettled. One month to go—and the excited nervous anxiety around my trip and all the mystery that surrounds it is with me constantly. The thrill of the unknown— and the fear of it. The uneasiness about being away from Mark for so long. The I-don't-know-what. Whatever it is, it's making me have anxiety dreams every night and making me feel like jumping out of my skin every day.

I phone Jungian analyst and author Clarissa Pinkola Estés for the magazine article I need to finish before I leave. As I wrap up my interview with her, I confide my anxiety about this trip. She has me wait on the phone while she looks up the original meaning of "anxious" in the 20-volume Oxford English Dictionary that she bought with the book advance for her best-seller, *Women Who Run with the Wolves*. I love the definition: "to be in suspense; to have a mystery cast about that which you do not understand; to stand at the threshold of mystery." In her soft, gentle voice, she points out to me: "The anxiety comes not from the actual thing that you're doing, but from the unknown elements surrounding it. And of course, this is what the excitement comes from too." I'm ready to embrace the anxiety, the mystery, the excitement!

The classic anxiety dream that keeps recurring, night after fitful night, has replaced the examination dreams of my university days. Now in my sleep I keep inviting people for dinner, wanting to take care of them—but not having enough food. How bourgeois, traditional, housewifey! Where is my "wild woman"? My woman who wants to run with wolves? Hiding in a kitchen, armed with a spatula. Aha! Maybe that's the point of this latest dream, in which a strange woman sits with company, while I serve her, along with everyone else. Maybe that other woman in my dream, that stranger sitting there with the company, not cooking or serving, is me too. The me that's taking care of me, not anyone else! My wild woman is doing just what I want to do—going to Nepal without my husband, without my children, without my obligations.

By the time Marge and I left, we had both independently reached the conclusion that the value of this trip would not hinge on whether or not a book would result from it: The real impetus behind our going was not a research project but a shared personal quest.

What, then, powered this pilgrimage? An ineffable spiritual longing. A need to make sense of the world we so lightly and so temporarily inhabit. A yearning for a purpose in life that—despite our joy in our families, our past achievements in our work, our comfortable circumstances, and our considerable good fortune—seemed to be eluding us. We wanted to reach across cultural boundaries to understand people in a vastly different place, almost of another time, so that we could better understand ourselves. We wanted to put our new friendship, born in such unexpected soil, to the service of exploring new ideas, different ways of being. As anthropologist Alma Gottlieb has put it, we wanted to examine "another set of propositions about how the world worked."

Our search, then, was for understanding, for universality, for values, for meaning—as well as for an adventure. If we could communicate the beauty of the people of Badel and their way of life to people on the other side of the globe, so much the better. If not, the two of us would still be lucky enough to know them ourselves. As Marge and I kept sharing our feelings, our beliefs, our outlooks, we realized how much we were enriching each other's life. This trip that we were planning would, we knew, be more than our discovery of Nepali women. It would be our discovery of each other—and, ultimately, of ourselves.

And so, of course, we did pursue it. After long conversations, longer letters and elaborate arrangements, we took the trip. Our expectations changed regularly; our plans remained fluid, shifting constantly like the surging rivers we eventually traversed to reach the remote hill village of Badel. And we came away vastly enriched by the experience, so enriched that we returned to Badel a year and a half later, and then again and yet again. We flew not only halfway around the world, but centuries into the past, as we lived in a village where the rhythms of life pulsate today to virtually the same beat that they have for hundreds of years—but a beat that has already begun to change and will undoubtedly undergo great transformations within the first few years of this new century.

In the little hill village of Badel, four days' walk from the nearest bus route and three days' walk from the closest airstrip, in one of the poorest, most primitive Third World countries to be found anywhere in the world, where the local populace scrabbles for elemental survival, we two—mature privileged women from affluent, sophisticated communities in the wealthiest country in the world—fulfilled the quest that had taken us to Nepal.

Here, then, is a glimpse into that other world, the one we were fortunate enough to share—not long—but long enough to learn who the people are, how they live, and what their lives can teach us.

Welcome to the village of Badel.

2

In Kathmandu: Letting Go

There will be shoes in plenty so long as you have feet.
—Nepali proverb

In the air, approaching the Kathmandu airport, my heart caught as I saw the now-familiar, still breathtaking snow-capped peaks ringing the city. As Marge and I stepped off the plane we had taken from Bangkok, we were plunged into the human maelstrom of Kathmandu, a city defined by its contradictions. After fighting off ragtag armies of persistent little boys who wanted to carry our bags, we found Dorje, the driver our hotel had sent to meet us. Dorje lived up to the meaning of his name ("Thunderbolt") as he swerved past sacred cows lying in the middle of busy thorough-fares, jeweled and painted temples on street corners, roaring motorcycles, fume-emitting taxis, and rickety bicycle-powered rickshaws, until we reached the crowded, colorful Thamel area.

Now I'm standing at my window at the Potala Guest House in Chhetrapati, Thamel, this low-rent, chaotic neighbor-hood of twisting, narrow streets, with its restaurants and guest houses that cater to young budget-minded trekkers, with its heady fragrances of incense and spices blending with the sweet smell of hashish. This noisy, crowded, colorful area overflows with little shops selling Tibetan, Indian and Nepalese goods; second-hand trekking and climbing gear; English-language books; and erotic note cards. Small, inexpensive restaurants offer foods of every ethnic stripe, from pizza to egg rolls to wiener schnitzel, as well as Tibetan *mo-mos* (dumplings) and Nepalese *dal bhat* (rice with lentil sauce). A walk through Thamel involves fending off the young men who sidle up offering hashish, Tibetan rugs, money changing and guide services; and trying to resist the pleas of ragged children begging for rupees or selling tiny containers of the all-purpose nostrum "Tiger Balm." No wonder practically every tee-shirt store displays one design that says, "No hashish. No rugs. No rupees. No problem."

In the courtyard below my room, an ever-changing performance plays out before me. First, children playing, shouting, laughing, squabbling. Later, a mother sitting behind her little girl picking lice from the child's head, a scene I'll see repeated in many variations over the next month. Now the dogs of Kathmandu—Third-World mongrels that run wild in packs and survive by foraging in the heaps of garbage on almost every corner—have set up their cacophonous howling, barking, whining concert, a staple street sound of this capital city, like none other in the world.

FROM MARGE'S JOURNAL:

I always get a room with windows on the street. It is very noisy, like sleeping right on the sidewalk. I like to wake up and know I am in Kathmandu; nowhere else has sounds like these. Before dawn I awake to the ever-present barking dogs. First there is just one faint barking, then another joins it, then another, and another, and soon there is a chorus of thousands working up to a shrieking, howling crescendo. Then suddenly all is quiet until the roosters start.

Now it is daylight and I can hear the swishing of the straw brooms as the shopkeepers and local residents move the dusty debris into piles in readiness for the garbage trucks that may, or may not, collect today. I think there is a garbage strike. Phew. Next comes the loud scraping, dragging of metal, clanging as the corrugated-iron overhead doors are raised to open the shops and guest houses to the street. Now come the mourners, wailing on their way to the "monkey temple" at Swayambunath to offer prayers and gifts for the spirits of the recently dead.

There is the hacking throat- and sinus-clearing as people clear their bodies of the Kathmandu Valley pollution. This morning I am right in there with the loudest of them as I try to clear my airways for another day of filthy air. The vendors are out now carrying their yokes weighted down almost to the ground with bright green scallions, beans, squash, eggplant, rosy tomatoes, oranges, bananas, exotic vegetables I have seen nowhere else. I lie and listen to the Nepalis chattering and laughing, children shouting, bicycle rickshaws and tempus grinding to a halt in front of the hotel in hopes of early morning customers. All this and so much more and it is only just past six in the morning. I leap out of bed and give a whoop of joy. Yes! Yes! I am back in Kathmandu!

Few people are neutral about Nepal—and especially about Kathmandu. Some fly into this noisy, chaotic, malodorous capital city and can't wait to get on the next plane out. Others are immediately captivated, can't seem to get enough of the country and her people, and keep returning, time after time, often to embark on projects that keep them here for years. Marge and I, on the fringes of the latter camp, know that Nepal holds answers for us, but so far even the questions are elusive. All we know for sure is that we have to pursue them. And we have to pursue them here.

Here at the Potala, Peter Owens, who led all the treks that both Marge and I have gone on in Nepal, keeps a small apartment which six months out of the year he calls home. During the other six months he teaches physics and chemistry at San Mateo Community College in California. Peter has been leading treks in Asia for some twenty years now, many of them for the Sierra Club, and over the years he's become knowledgeable about Nepal, fluent in Nepali and exquisitely sensitive to Nepalese customs and people. Peter's enthusiastic help with Marge's and my arrangements—this time not as a professional trek leader, but as a friend—has been invaluable.

Peter is back from his spring trek, with just a few days to go until he leaves with his next group. Marge and I walk up to the fourth floor of the Potala and, Nepali-style, take off our shoes before stepping into Peter's room, which is lush with vividly patterned Tibetan rugs, hand-painted *thangkas* (silk scrolls depicting events in the life of the Buddha), full-color photographs of Himalayan peaks, comfortable western-style couches and chairs. The American rock band Bon Jovi blares from the CD player, to the delight of the staffers present, as Peter holds court with them and with some of the trekkers from his last trip. Over the years Peter has built a loyal and able staff, promoting from within his ranks, treating his workers well, and from time to time bringing a few select guides over to the United States for months at a time to learn our language and customs.

"Namaste!" we greet everyone as, our palms together as if in prayer, we utter the universal "hello" and "goodbye," the Nepali word that means, "I salute the divine within you." The first person who returns our greeting is Jai Prasad Rai, the *sirdar* (Nepali leader) for both the treks that Mark and I had taken in Nepal and for several of Marge's treks.

When I first met Jai in 1987 he was a 21-year-old bundle of high spirits. A gifted mimic who picks up languages quickly and a joker who makes friends just as fast, Jai had a smooth rapport with both workers and trekkers. It wasn't hard to see why he had progressed quickly from porter to kitchen boy to cook to *sherpa* (guide), and then to sirdar. He said then that he was content to stay at this level. Still single, he was ready to marry and expected to marry a bride from his own ethnic group, the Rai, whom his parents would choose. Now, six years later, Jai is here in Peter's room with his wife, the lovely sloe-eyed Sita (whom, as it turned out, he chose himself), wearing a bright turquoise sari, and their three-year-old son, Kim, dressed as if he had just stepped out of The Gap. Like any little western boy, Kim is entranced by the box of 24 matchbox cars Marge brought him from Chicago. With his flat little face, high cheekbones, and slanted eyes, Kim is the image of his father.

Jai will help us make some of our preparations here in Kathmandu and will also accompany us to the village. He will not, however, be our chief guide. That role will fall to his wife's brother, Buddi Kumar Rai. Buddi, a handsome, slender, smooth-complexioned, fine-featured young man of 27, with the almond-shaped dark eyes and slightly golden skin like polished brass that are common among Rais, sits quietly in Peter's room as I burst in, hugging Peter, Jai and Kalu, a sherpa from my last trek. The wine flows and the conversation hums; a couple of other trekkers wander in; and in the confusion no one introduces Buddi. Then, after I finally introduce myself, Peter says, "He's your guide." I'm embarrassed for Buddi and hope he wasn't insulted by having been more or less overlooked in the general round of greetings, but he seems calm and untroubled. Marge and I will come to appreciate his serenity in many other settings during our four visits to Badel, the village where Buddi has lived his entire life except for his years at college in Kathmandu.

Peter had recommended Buddi highly to us as the ideal guide for our village visit. Besides speaking excellent English and knowing the area we'll be visiting as well as Jai does, Buddi has an intellectual interest in our project and wants to help us have a richly productive experience getting to know his culture. Unlike Jai, who never went beyond third grade, Buddi is a college graduate, the first in his village. He is now doing graduate work at Tribhuvan University for his master's degree in political science.

Now Jai, nicknamed "Motor Mouth" by trekkers, is talking a kilometer a minute to Marge and me about our plans: "First we fly Kathmandu to Lamidanda, then walk two, three days to my village, Badel, stay there few days, then go Bangdel, poorer place." Jai mentions two more villages before we return to Lamidanda, and then back to Kathmandu. Hearing this whirlwind tour, my head spins. I'm afraid that if we go to too many places, we'll be scattered and not get a feel for any of them. I'm also afraid we'll be so well taken care of that we won't have enough contact with village families. Between bringing our own food, having our own cook prepare it, sleeping in our own tents, relying on Buddi as our guide—it all feels too sanitized. We may have to fight to get more contact with local families.

The pressures are on the staff to take good care of us. Jai urges us to buy our own food and bring our own cook. I want to eat with the families from their usual fare, but Jai has other concerns: in some of the villages where we go, there might not be enough food to sell to us—even if we pay for it. He's also concerned that we might not like the monotonous Nepali fare—mostly *dal bhat* in two meals every day—or might get sick from it. And since he's assuming responsibility for us, we defer to his judgment in this.

FROM MARGE'S JOURNAL:

I am afraid Sally is beginning to question and doubt about the way our trek is being organized—or over-organized. She seems disappointed that we will have several porters, a cook and a guide. I think she feels, and I agree, that we are losing our hold on this thing and it is getting to be a big production. It is a bigger production than I first visualized it to be, but having been to a village I know we will need as much support as we can muster. There will be plenty of opportunities to mingle with the folk without having to struggle with cooking our rice and beans over our own cooking fire. I already know all I need to know about cooking, and if having a cook frees me up for more painting time, send in the cooks, porters and whoever else can make life easier.

Can I take the Buddhist attitude that whatever happens was meant to happen—and let go of my attachment to having things happen according to my blueprints? Marge and I exchange a look. I know we'll talk, but I wonder whether my vision is different from hers, even after all our letters and conversations about this trip. Or am I worrying for nothing? Am I not living in the moment? Once I get that thought, my anxiety leaves me and I decide to let events take their course. Which, as it turns out, was a good decision. Especially in light of one event.

One of the reasons Marge and I had decided to come to Kathmandu a week before we planned to leave for the village was to allow enough time to obtain any permits we might need to go into the hills. "Yes," Jai said adamantly when we asked him whether we would need trekking permits. "You want me to get?"

The times we had trekked before, our only involvement in getting our permits was to fill out a form and hand over a photo. Some anonymous staff member did the legwork. This time, Marge and I looked at each other, and as was so often true, we both wanted the same thing. "No, we'll do it ourselves."

Doubtful that we could handle Nepalese bureaucracy without him, Jai said, "Okay. But I meet you at Immigration Office. Tomorrow morning, about 9:30, when it opens. Bring photos and money."

Next morning, on Tuesday, the entrance to the immigration office is already almost totally obscured behind crowds of sturdy young foreign giants of both sexes wearing shorts and hiking boots and wiry young Nepali men asking foreigners, "You need guide?" At 9:30 precisely the doors open and Marge and I join one of the several long lines.

Jai suddenly appears in the throng. He has thought of something else we need: "You have money-change receipts for the money to pay for the permits?" he asks. Of course we don't. Jai knew as well as we did that when we changed money at our hotel, our dollars almost certainly went to the black market, which is not known for its attention to paperwork. We haven't seen a receipt. "You need, to get permit." He looks around, through the big dirty plate-glass window that faces onto the broad avenue in front. "There's a bank across street. You have traveler's cheques with you? Good. Go change a little at the bank."

The bank doesn't open until ten. This time we're first in line just outside the door as we wait for its opening, and then sit on a bench inside as we wait to be summoned to the window. Marge and I each change a fifty-dollar American Express traveler's cheque. I have one more left in the nifty little nylon travel purse I had bought back home, which has separate pockets for money, passport and credit cards and a belt-loop so that I can wear it safely inside my skirt. Today it's not in its usual place. I woke up this morning with my first ailment of the trip, complete with bloated, crampy stomach, and couldn't bear even the thought of anything tight around my waist. So I put on a loose jumper and put my purse in one of its deep front pockets, where it can't fall out, and where I can keep an eye on it.

Back to Immigration, where the lines are longer than ever. They're jolly, though. We talk to a middle-aged Canadian couple who've sold their house and most of their belongings, said goodbye to their three grown children and set out to travel around the world until they get homesick.

The bored-looking civil servant behind the enclosure asks for our passports, the form Marge and I filled out requesting trekking permits, and the rupee equivalent of $15 each, which I lay out for both of us. Noticeably absent, considering the trouble we've just gone to, is any interest in any proof of legitimate money-changing. "Come back this afternoon to get your passport and your permit," he says brusquely. "Next!"

Marge gives me her 750 rupees as soon as we turn from the window. We're both excruciatingly conscientious about keeping our finances straight with each other. We'd hate to see this beautiful, spiritual friendship riven by anything so crass as misunderstandings over money!

By now it's almost lunch time, and we head back toward the Potala. We walk for a couple of blocks with the Canadian couple, who are, on our recommendation, looking for the carpet dealer we visited yesterday. No one can remember his address—until I remember that I took his card. "Wait a minute, I have it in my purse." I reach into my comfortably deep pocket—but I don't find the card. In fact, I don't find anything. The pocket is empty. No purse. No $50.00 traveler's cheque. No 80-odd U.S. dollars worth of rupees. No American Express and Visa cards. Nothing but a little lint in the corners of the pocket.

My stomach does a few flips, and I retrace my steps the couple of blocks back to the Immigration office, eyes down, in the remote hope that the purse might have fallen out of my pocket, or that someone might have taken the cash and tossed away the rest. I look around the floor of the office. I see knots of young men clustered around the front door, who now look not like eager, friendly guides but like menacing predators waiting to pounce on the unwary. I speak to an official at another window. No one has seen anything. No one knows anything.

The afternoon is hot, busy, exhausting, as I chase bureaucrats all around Kathmandu. At the bank that serves as headquarters for Visa, I'm told I need a copy of an official police report to get a new Visa card. Over at the American

Express office, when I ask for a $300 advance in traveler's cheques, the clerk says, "Sure," then asks me, "Where's your American Express card?" It takes a few back-and-forths to get him to understand, "That's why I'm here!" The small local police station I go to doesn't know what to do, and, after some high-level conferrals among the officers, sends me to the central station a 30-minute ride away through frenetic traffic, as the bouncing *tempu* (a motorized tricycle-type vehicle with a semi-enclosed cab) I'm riding in detours around cows sleeping in the middle of the street, darts past buses, narrowly misses pedestrians.

"Do you have a photograph?" asks the nice young policeman who takes my report. "No, it was in the purse that was stolen." "The form is not official without the photograph. You need to come back tomorrow." I think it will be official enough for my purpose, to give to the Visa and American Express offices, so they can replace my cards and cheque. I have no illusions about catching the thief, who must have been a nimble opportunist who saw me take the money from Marge and put it in my temptingly accessible purse and who then deftly lifted the purse.

I take the filled-out form to one of the many photocopying shops that were not here in such abundance on my last visit only two years ago; Nepal is, little by little, acquiring the technological trappings of the western world. I make copies for the equivalent of two cents a copy, go back to the police station, back to the bank representing Visa, back to American Express. In between all these errands, I indulge in a spasm of self-blame, self-berating and "if-only's." Why did I slip up in my caution? Why couldn't I put up with a little discomfort to wear the purse the right way? Why hadn't I taken from home my around-the-neck purse that I could have worn under my jumper? Why weren't Marge and I more careful about transferring the money? Why did Jai insist that we change money at the bank, when the immigration clerk never even looked at the receipt? Why hadn't I let Jai handle the whole thing anyway, as he had offered to do? Why was I so stupid? Here I am wasting an entire precious day, for nothing.

FROM MARGE'S JOURNAL:

Damn! Just like the subway at home. One must be forever vigilant. We both felt foolish and angry, falling into the trap of blaming the victim, scolding ourselves: "We should have known better" We have not left it all behind, after all.

Back at the hotel, I collapse for a two-hour deep sleep, wake up forcing myself, despite my lack of appetite, to eat bananas and oranges, to drink water. I try to call my daughter in New York to ask her to call Visa for me, but the hotel phone is out of order and I don't have the energy to leave the room to search out another one. I'm grateful now that Marge had suggested we take separate rooms here. At the equivalent of $6.60 a night we can afford the luxury of privacy and solitude when we need it. I need it now. Aside from feeling tired, weak and nauseated, I feel stupid, which is probably the worst of all my ailments.

I write in my journal, count the money and traveler's cheques I have left. At 10:40 p.m. a dog barks constantly, and I mentally offer a *rani's* ransom of rupees to anyone who would shoot it. It is, as they say, getting on my last nerve—and I don't have many nerves left. And then one of the first of many benefits of this trip occurs. I let go.

Wednesday morning I wake up free of angst. First of all, I remember my fear before the trip that I wouldn't find anything worth writing about, and how, after reading the incident in Broughton Coburn's delightful book *Nepali Aama* in which the salty old woman who hosts the author while he teaches in the village school relates a tale of bandits who had come and tied up villagers, I had thought, "Oh, wouldn't that be exciting! Wouldn't that be something to write about!" And then realized I was crazy. Or just a writer. I heard a story about another writer who had been thrilled to have been held up at gunpoint—more grist for his literary mill. Now something untoward has happened, but it was not only undramatic, it was tediously typical both of tourists' mishaps in unfamiliar surroundings and in its brush with bureaucracy, which turns out to be the same the world over.

In any case, my malaise is gone, my energy is high, my spirits are joyous. As I run two-and-a-half miles along the streets of Kathmandu, I feel truly welcomed to Nepal as jogging platoons of soldiers show their good-natured amusement at seeing a middle-aged foreigner doing for fun what they have to do for duty and as a sari-garbed young woman who at first, I thought, looked disapprovingly at my immodest outfit of shorts and tee shirt, shyly smiles and returns my "Namaste." I come back and breakfast with Marge and Joan, a woman we had met on the flight from Bangkok to Kathmandu and brought to our hotel.

And I realize how unimportant my little loss is. Joan lost all her luggage for a three-month trip. The bright-eyed children who run up to us to hustle woolen carpets and wooden flutes and Tiger Balm salve never had anything tangible to lose. The old beggar who smiles so sweetly at us as he sits all day long on the tile floor in front of our hotel has lost fingers on both hands to leprosy. And I? Along with Iago, I can say, "Who steals my purse steals trash." I have my health, I have my loved ones, I have more money. I wasn't hurt, I wasn't even frightened. I only lost something that can easily be replaced. What happened to me was a minor inconvenience, not a disaster. I'm among those most highly blessed in this world. If I were a Buddhist, I'd know that I had done many good deeds in former lives.

"Look for the gift in your wounding," philosopher Jean Houston urges. Maybe my gift is an even deeper appreciation of all that I do have, all that I could never lose from a simple theft. This letting-go of attachments—to possessions, plans and people—is to mark the rest of my stay here in Nepal.

Our host
Jai Rai,
mother, father, guide
and good friend to
us.

3

Getting Ready:
Jati Rai, Uti Kuru

With the chance to eat, food goes in all at once. With the chance to speak, words come out all at once.
                                        —*Nepali proverb*

Marge and I sit on wooden benches in the old Kathmandu airport, waiting for our Lamidanda flight. The tiny two-story building, now used only for domestic flights since the construction of the bigger international terminal (still the smallest international airport I've ever flown in or out of), is thronged with tourists waiting to board early-morning sightseeing planes going over the Himalayas, trekkers headed for the airstrip at Lukla from where they'll hike up to Everest Base Camp, families of small children, old women, young adults laden with crates of eggs and vegetables. Two plastic bags full of rocks lean against a gate, and I wonder who's taking them where, and why. I'll never know.

As a phalanx of Japanese tourists disembarks from the flight from Lukla, I remember my own flight from that much smaller airport. On my last trek, to the Everest-Gokyo Lakes region, our group walked eight days, gaining about 1,000 feet of altitude a day, to reach Lukla, instead of taking the seductive 40-minute airplane service from Kathmandu. There is a steep price to pay for the airborne shortcut: telescoping the ascent brings the risk of altitude sickness, which regularly takes lives, by one estimate, of 1 in 1,000 Himalayan trekkers. It seems to strike the youngest and the fittest disproportionately, possibly because those are the trekkers with the most self-confidence and the least propensity for taking precautions. While we were on trek, a 30-year-old on a nearby mountaineering expedition succumbed; he went to sleep one night at 18,000 feet—and never awakened. We did fly back to Kathmandu, though, and I remember the anxiety looking at the rocky field that constitutes the Lukla airport, with its tiny downhill runway.

Marge and I won't have to worry about altitude sickness, since our destination, Badel, sits at only about 5,000 feet. I'm nervous enough about the flight itself. Since I was last in Nepal, two passenger planes crashed in the mountains just outside the Kathmandu airport, known as the most dangerous in the world. And if I thought the Lukla airstrip, where many tourists fly in and out of, was primitive, I hate to think what the one in Lamidanda, which carries mostly Nepalis, will be like. But back to my Buddhist-inspired philosophy: Be here now. Don't dwell on the past. Don't worry about the future.

FROM MARGE'S JOURNAL:

I sit here watching the Nepali women and marvel, as I have many times before, at how complete the Asian people look, how finished, relaxed and poised they seem. The women are so graceful the way they seem to sail along in their colorful saris, lunghis and Sherpa dresses. The heads of the men in their topis take on an almost perfect diamond shape, their prominent cheekbones forming the broadest point, the chin parallel with the flat top of the topi. In the crowd milling about in front of us I see the finely chiseled features of the Newaris and Indians, the flat broad brows and high prominent cheekbones of the Sherpas and Rais, whose ancestors came from Tibet. Before we are called for our plane I rush to sketch the old Tamang woman facing me, beautiful with her gold jewelry in her nose and ears.

Five minutes before seven o'clock this morning, Marge and I walked down the street from our hotel in Kathmandu, into Pizza Maya, a little restaurant that opens for breakfast at seven. We woke the waiter, who had apparently spent the night sleeping on a bench just inside the door. The handsome youth shook his thick black hair, arose with a smile and greeted us sleepily but warmly. We stepped outside to let him collect himself and came back to be greeted by an even brighter smile. You have to love a country whose people, roused from their dreams by insistent tourists, wake up smiling.

As soon as we returned to the Potala, Buddi picked us up, helped us get our duffels downstairs and taxied us to the airport to meet Jai, Saila (Jai's helper) and our food and supplies. We had prided ourselves on making this a simple trip; it's embarrassing to realize that it takes three people to take care of the two of us. Soon we'll need even more caretakers. Saila will stay in Kathmandu, but Jai and Buddi will fly with us to Lamidanda, where we'll pick up three new porters and a cook. This whole entourage will walk with us for three days to Badel, Jai and Buddi's home village in the Khotang district in Nepal's eastern hills. We'll meet their families and see their homes, and then, after a couple of days, we'll go on with Buddi to a more remote settlement—which one, we still don't know.

We yearn to be in a place where western women have not been before. We want the villagers we meet to be just as interested in us as we are in them. And we want to observe a society still unchanged by the outside world. Even though Nepal has been open to the west since 1951, there still are many such isolated pockets well off the tourist routes.

Tourists and trekkers cut wide swaths around the region where we'll be; the only westerners who have come through Badel in recent memory were a group of French high school students who trekked through and camped there one night about three or four years ago. But among the village population are men who work in trekking and mountaineering, Gurkha soldiers who have served in the British and Indian armies and sometimes taken their wives with them to distant posts, and university students matriculating in Kathmandu, all of whom have known westerners. We think it will be a much more sophisticated hamlet than we want to stay in. Jai has mentioned the names of some other nearby villages that he thinks would meet our qualifications, but even now, as we leave Kathmandu, we still have not made a firm plan.

Before we left the States, friends would ask, "Exactly where in Nepal will you be?" "I don't know," I would answer. "Will you be staying with families?" "I don't know." "Will you and Marge stay together or separately?" "I don't know." Not knowing is part of the adventure.

Today at the airport, Jai is, as usual, immaculately neat and looking as western as new American bluejeans, polo shirt and sweater can make him. With his round, wide, flat-featured face and his high cheekbones, Jai could pass for an ethnic Sherpa instead of the Rai he is—and he sometimes does pass, when he considers it politically expedient, as for example, in those Sherpa areas where some teahouse owners will not permit Rais or Tamangs to stay on their property—only trekkers and Sherpas.

The Sherpas are the best known of Nepal's numerous ethnic groups (which anthropologists estimate variously at somewhere between forty-five and sixty), who speak different languages, worship in different faiths, and observe different customs. The Sherpas' ancestors came down from Tibet many hundreds of years ago, and most Sherpas now live in northeast Nepal in the Khumbu and Solu Khumbu, near Mount Everest. So many have assumed the profession of guide to mountaineers and trekkers that their name has entered the English language; sherpa with a lower-case s means "guide."

Our destination, the village of Badel, lies nestled in the eastern hills of Nepal, due south of Everest and Sherpa country, a stronghold of the Rai people. The Rai, another of Nepal's ethnic groups, are thought to be descended from a people called the Kirati, who also came from Tibet sometime about 800 to 700 B.C. and ruled Nepal for 1,000 years. First mentioned in the ancient Hindu epic *The Mahabharata*, the Kirati are described as "fierce barbarians of the Mongoloid race." Although known chiefly as warriors, they also hunted and traded in tusks, yak-tails, shellac and cardamon. They were not known as Rais (a word that means "chief") until after 1786.

According to one story of how the Rais entered Nepal's eastern hills some 2,000 to 2,500 years ago, three brothers—Khambuho, Menho and Meratup—came through the Barahkshetra gorge of the Kosi Valley, the natural gateway into the region through the Mahabharat Range, which separates the inland hills from the plains. Once through the gorge the brothers separated, taking their followers with them, and all the Kirati branches claim ancestry to one of these three brothers. Separate groups settled in various areas, developed their own individual customs and social organizations. They also evolved different languages: at least fourteen separate Rai tongues have been identified. Still, the Rais do share a common cultural base and are more like each other than they are like members of other ethnic groups.

The saying *"jati Rai, uti kuru"* ("There are as many languages as there are Rais") expresses one reason why a Rai village is particularly promising from our point of view: Since they do not share a common language, most Rais speak Nepali so they can speak to fellow Rais from other communities. In many villages in Nepal, most people speak only their local dialect; the sole Nepali speakers in these hamlets are those who have gone to school, a select company that rarely includes adult women. And while our own Nepali is at the most rudimentary level (I've had only half a dozen lessons and Marge hasn't had any), we do want to make some attempts—limited though they may be—to communicate with the villagers in their own language.

In Nepal, a person's last name reveals his or her ethnic group; all Rais, therefore, are identified by their surnames. Like Jai Prasad Rai, Buddi Kumar Rai was born and grew up in Badel, is also married and the father of a child. In other ways, he is very unlike his brother-in-law. Whereas Jai left school in the third grade, Buddi is a college graduate now pursuing his master's degree. And while Jai left Badel and bought a house in Kathmandu, Buddi is still tied to his home village and plans eventually to make his permanent home here.

Jai will return to Kathmandu after a few days in Badel, and Buddi will remain with us during our entire village stay and will then take us back to

Kathmandu. We feel lucky to have Buddi as our guide. Quieter and less effervescent than Jai, Buddi also speaks excellent English and is knowledgeable both about Rai customs and local villages. What may be even more important is that he is friendly, caring, interested in preserving the Rai culture and enthusiastic about our project. He also has a whimsical sense of humor.

Buddi would like eventually to land a government job, but they're in painfully short supply even for scholars like him who are educated in government. They also tend to go to members of the "more elevated" Rana caste, whose members are better situated politically. Buddi would also be happy to teach at the college level after he gets his master's degree, but those jobs are scarce too. In present-day Nepal the old adage "It's not what you know—it's who you know" is responsible for the exodus of many educated young Nepalis. Buddi has a fierce love, though, for his country, his people and his family, and wants to stay in Nepal; if he can't find a job in government or university, he'll teach high school.

Buddi loved his two-year stint as a teacher in the Badel school, teaching English, math, geography, a little bit of everything to children in grades One through Six. What he didn't love was the pittance that teachers get paid here. Meanwhile, he is earning far more as a trekking and mountaineering guide than he will ever earn at even the best job in the profession he is being educated for. For now, he plans to earn as much as he can in the next few years, to save for his and his family's future.

Our flight was supposed to take off at 9:15 this morning, but at 9:00 Jai comes over to the bench where he ensconced us to tell us it will be late. "Maybe 10, take off." His eyes crinkle up and his teeth gleam as he smiles and shrugs. "Read, write. No problem." We read, write, look around—no problem—until we finally hear our flight being called.

Time to shoulder our heavy backpacks, loaded down by as many books and other weighty items we could fit into them, since passengers on these internal flights have a small weight allowance for checked baggage, but the only restrictions on what we can carry on our back or our person are muscular and skeletal.

In my pack I have books: *The Nepal Handbook, Anna Karenina,The Cult of Kumari, The Mountain Kingdom, Himalaya: Vanishing Cultures* (a beautiful picture book about a Sherpa family, which I'll give away), *The Yetis: A Sherpa Story for Kids* (which I'll also give away), and *Himalayan Flowers and Trees* (which, as it turns out, I'll hardly look at). We're wearing our heavy boots, but it's too hot to lighten our luggage by layering clothes, as Mark and I did when we flew from Lukla to Kathmandu two years ago. In the cursory security inspection, the pretty young officer who goes through my bag asks whether she can buy my one tube of lipstick. Feeling selfish at not giving it to her, I say no. I guess I'm not so successful at letting go, after all.

Finally, an hour and a half late taking off, we're on our twin-engine Royal Nepal Airlines 9N-ABI plane. The plane can take 19 Nepalis, but only 14 foreigners; we're bigger and we carry more luggage. On this flight all 19 seats are filled, and Marge and I are the only westerners. We cram our laden backpacks between our legs; the only other place for them would be our laps.

One of the two women in front of us wears fresh flowers in her glossy black hair, a red and yellow *tika* on her forehead, heavy dull-gold earrings hanging from the elongated openings in her pendulous earlobes, stretched into long slits after some sixty years of supporting heavy jewelry. Her seatmate wears a terrycloth towel wrapped around her head like a desert headdress, a common fashion among Nepali women. ("A new market for Martex!" Marge whispers in my ear.) The slim and pretty sari'd flight attendant passes out noxious-tasting hard candies and bits of absorbent cotton, which most of the passengers put in their ears to defend against the deafening buzz and roar of the engines.

After taxiing for twenty seconds and lifting up almost vertically to avoid the surrounding mountains, we fly low enough to get an extraordinary open view of the land below. It's lush and green, with ribbons of terraces, like stairs climbing up out of the big bowl of the Kathmandu Valley. But when we leave the fertile valley and enter the hills, we can see stark evidence of the need for conserving water, even in this river-rich country. Now the land is mostly brown, with little specks of green—crops and an occasional tree. Although we can spot some blue waters of swiftly flowing rivers, most of the riverbeds we fly over are dry. Land is terraced to virtually every cultivatable inch, hypnotic in its endless swirls that form intricately scrolled patterns on every hill as far as the eye can see.

The mountains rise steeply up and plunge just as steeply down. Nothing is level; everything is on a slope as hill after crenelated hill rises below us. There are no ridges on top of the hills. There are no roads through most of this convoluted, crumpled land. Only rivers can cut their way through the wrinkles. Every now and then we see a cluster of little houses, an isolated village buried in the folds of the hills.

FROM MARGE'S JOURNAL:

When I look down and see that every inch below me seems to be planted, I worry. There are so few trees. What will happen to the land and her people when all the trees are gone? Will it be barren desert like Africa? At the airport I overheard an American woman loudly telling her guide that Nepal should take advantage of wind and solar energy for power. She had just arrived in Nepal for the first time two days before. How can an American say how another country should save their environment when we are in such a terrible crisis of our own, with nowhere to put our spent fuel from our "very efficient" nuclear power plants? So many of us think we have the instant answers for everyone else's problems.

Thirty-five minutes after takeoff, the plane dips and slants, turns right, bumps the ground a couple of times and lands. We've arrived at Lamidanda. The ground is red clay; bordering the airfield is a green forest planted in neat rows. The airstrip is a stony field about the size of a football field; the airport is a minuscule stone structure; no other planes are in sight. The Lamidanda airfield is more primitive than Lukla's, but we're here and we're safe.

As we disembark we see a throng of young men standing expectantly, hopefully, behind a wire fence, most of them trying to pick up jobs as porters. Three are our own porters who walked here with our cook, Gora, from Badel, to meet us and go back with us to the village. It took them one day to make the trip that will take us the better part of three days. (Here in Nepal distances are reckoned not in miles, but in hours or days—which means that measures are very different for young Nepalis and for western grandmothers.)

There is 20-year-old Tara Mani, who left Kathmandu a few days before we did, took a bus and then walked two days to Badel, and has now walked here from the village. Small and wiry and prepubescent-looking with his bowl haircut, his sleeveless shirt and short shorts, he greets us with a merry smile. There's Mon Bahadur Bhujel, known as Mani, who looks to be about 40, is darker, taller, and paunchier than any other porter I've seen, and is dressed in traditional village costume of tunic over loose shorts. Our third porter is Kangsha Ram, a shy, sweet boy of 16, whose slightly tattered striped shirt will soon be replaced by a "Yale University" tee shirt we've brought with us; it will go well with his knee-length trousers. They have already been hired, but we have so much gear and so many supplies that Jai plucks one more young man from the crowd to help carry everything to Badel.

Barely minutes after all the passengers get off and all the bags are off-loaded, the impatient Nepalis waiting to board rush out to the waiting plane and climb the stairs; the plane closes up immediately and takes off. These domestic flights are almost always full, since there are so few scheduled between these remote areas and Kathmandu. Reservations for them have to be made far in advance; Jai had made ours months ago.

No matter what happens, we won't be able to fly back to Kathmandu for three weeks. We will be out of touch with the world, away from telephones, television, telegrams, faxes, all the telecommunications marvels of the modern world. We will be in a world where all discourse, all contact occurs face-to-face, person-to-person, with no wires or circuitry. In this land, where spirituality reigns the way technology does in ours, we are seeking ancient wisdom for contemporary lives.

Loxman Guts
making a doko. His fingers
moved very fast. He is
Being watched by a little
girl in very big blanket.

4

On the Trail: Don't Look Down, Don't Look Up

The feet will get wet if you cross the stream.
—*Nepali proverb*

A little teahouse survives by its proximity to the Lamidanda airstrip. Marge and the staff eat *dal bhat*, which Nepalis eat daily for both lunch and dinner, prepared by the young woman of the establishment, but since my stomach is still queasy from whatever ailed me last week in Kathmandu, I accept Gora's offer of plain noodles, which he himself cooks in the kitchen. I know that whatever he gives me will be as germ-free as he can make it; I have no confidence at all in the cleanliness of this establishment and feel safer eating our own food. Although I know that the strange dishes I'm eating the food from have received an uncertain handling, I resolve not to worry about anything that I can't control. Marge, just as suspicious as I am of the dishes, does manage to take a modicum of control. She doesn't tell me until later how the young woman of the establishment rinsed the plates with cold water, undoubtedly well-populated with hostile microbes, and wiped them with a dirty cloth. Knowing that the wash water for the dishes had not been boiled and would mix with her food, Marge calls Buddi over and asks him to take her bandanna and dry her plate with it. Those unfamiliar and threatening microbes that thrive in water cannot live on dry surfaces or in hot cooked food.

After we finish, we have to wait until our new porter eats his huge platter of dal bhat. Then the porters busy themselves reorganizing the loads of food and cooking utensils they are carrying in *dokos*, the cone-shaped woven bamboo baskets used in these hills to carry all sorts of loads, including firewood, trekking supplies and sick people en route to the hospital. The bearers support their dokos by a tumpline, a headband worn around the forehead and going under the base of the basket; the weight of the head helps to support the weight of the load, which is evenly distributed along the back.

Our small, slight porters carry more than their own body weight. They bend under their heavy doko-loads of Marge's and my duffel bags stuffed with our clothes, sleeping bags and all the personal items we knew we wouldn't be able to obtain in the village. They also carry food for all of us, kitchen supplies, tents and other paraphernalia. We peek into one especially heavy doko that no one wants to carry. I can see why: it holds one, two, three, four, five heads of cauliflower heaped among four heads of cabbage, about twenty pounds of potatoes, and more ginger root than both of our families would use at home in a year. All this for three weeks! All for us.

Finally the doko contents are equalized among the porter-loads and we set out down the wide dirt path that goes through the village of Lamidanda. About five minutes out from the airport, I'm startled to see a very young, very blonde woman with a diamond on the side of her nose. She wears American sport sandals and a beautiful purple and black *punjabi*, or *shalwar kameez*, an Indian ensemble consisting of a graceful loose-fitting dress over matching wide pants. She stops me with a smile.

"*Namaste*! Are you health workers?" she asks. After I tell her our mission, she nods pleasantly, says, "We don't see many *bedishis* [a polite word for foreign women] here," and wishes us luck. Kristi Sarosik from Ann Arbor, Michigan is a Peace Corps worker teaching English in the Lamidanda primary school. She is the only westerner we'll see for almost three weeks, until we return to Lamidanda, when we'll reconnect briefly with her and with her fellow Peace Corps worker, who is working with local people on a couple of water projects.

The path soon narrows down to a lane threaded between the fields, many of them just being planted. It's quintessential Nepali hiking—up and down, down and up, with only an occasional brief saunter along a level path. We watch the porters and try to remember to walk the way they do, taking tiny steps with knees bent, taking care not to skid on the slippery scree underfoot. When friends hear that there's no way to reach Badel and hundreds of other isolated villages other than on foot, many ask, "Can't you ride horses? Or mules?" It's hard for people who haven't been here to visualize these narrow, uneven, rocky paths, which are tricky enough for two-legged creatures to navigate and virtually impossible for pack animals. The only animals we ever see on trails are water buffaloes, which can occasionally be driven along some stretches of path, but even these slow-moving beasts cannot negotiate the 18-inch terraces running through the rice paddies.

The porters make frequent stops along the trail, to sit on a stone wall specially constructed around a thick banyan tree, so that travelers can rest their heavy loads against the tree without setting their dokos on the ground. Given the people-friendly shade and comfort fact that these trees offer to travelers, I at first thought that their Nepali name—*pipal*—was instead the English word "people." In the absence of a tree, with one hand the porters pull a T-shaped stick from the slot in the base of the doko, and set it on the ground with the doko resting on top of the T.

We walk over large rocks, through narrow terraces planted with millet, maize, barley, wheat or buckwheat (all are cultivated here, at different times of the year), along the edges of rice fields emerald with early shoots. We stop occasionally under the shade of one of these friendly pipal trees, dipping a bandanna in a pool of cold water to get some relief from the sweltering heat on this sunny day. I'm sweating so much that I'm dehydrated (I don't need to urinate all day), and I make a conscious effort to keep sipping from my water bottle.

By the time we reach our stop for the night—a teahouse in the village of Mongalabari, my legs are bone-weary, the neuroma (an inflamed nerve) on my left foot burns, my back and shoulders ache. I'm utterly exhausted. And I feel marvelous! It's the same kind of euphoria I felt on hard days on trek the last time I was here in Nepal. Making the effort, doing the work, knowing that I'm pushing my body to limits it usually doesn't approach is incredibly soul-satisfying.

As is the excruciating mindfulness that we need to exert with every step. There's no automatic walking here, while aimlessly looking around. I remember a story I heard about a young monk who saw his teacher in the dining room reading a book while eating his lunch. The novice stood quietly by the older monk until he raised his head from his book. "Yes?" "Excuse me, *roshi*," the young monk said. "But in your teaching this morning, did you not tell us, 'When you eat, eat. And when you read, read'?" "Yes, of course, I did." "But, roshi, here you are eating and reading!" "Yes, of course," the elder replied calmly. "When you eat and read, eat and read." And he went back to his soup and his book.

I smile, even as I realize that here in this place on this day I cannot walk and sightsee at the same time. As we cross slippery boulders over a river, negotiate a narrow swaying bridge, tread uneven rocky paths, paying attention is the price of survival. I am excruciatingly conscious of where I place my feet—I have to be. On the few occasions when I try to keep walking while looking at something else or when my mind wanders, my balance suffers. Several times I barely save myself from slipping into the watery ditches either side of the road.

As I walk, I realize why trekking in Nepal is an exercise in mindfulness. The narrow trail. The scree that unexpectedly slides under your feet. Ancient tree roots that snake across the road in odd, unpredictable patterns. Boulders tossed randomly to left or right, some ancient ones that look as if they were hurled from the bowels of the earth in thunderous upheavals over the centuries, some that landed here as recently as last month's landslide. Both kinds may shift disconcertingly when you step on them, and so steps have to be deliberately planted to be sure you have a firm footing. Huge moist mounds of slippery fresh water-buffalo dung scattered at crucial spots. Places where the only foothold is on the narrow top edge of upended rocks.

All this on a path that sometimes drops off sharply some twenty, forty, sixty feet or more, with the edge of the path often obscured by leaves or grass. Then, of course, there are the bridges over boulder-strewn roaring rivers, constructed of two or three timbers, with rotting places in the wood covered by rocks or nailed-on strips of fresh wood, either of which leave gaping holes. I am beginning to feel like President Gerald Ford who was ridiculed for "not being able to talk and chew gum at the same time," when I try to blow my nose as I continue walking. No can do. One thing at a time. An important lesson for me. One to take home to my multi-tasking life.

As demanding as this kind of walking is, it feeds the soul. There is a purity to doing one thing, and one thing only, at any one time. At home I spread myself thin. I telephone friends while I wash dishes. I read *The New York Times* while I eat breakfast. I sew buttons while I watch television. Focusing on saving time, I hardly ever focus completely on a single activity. This will change, I know.

At one point I hear a shout from Gora and turn to see Marge lying flat in a cornfield. A moment's distraction—and she fell off the path down onto the lower terrace. Unhurt but red-faced, she gets up with Gora's help and accepts with a grateful "Namaste" the walking stick he offers her. Still cheerful but more wary, we tramp along.

When I can't stand not drinking in the astonishing beauty of these endless hills, the completely different landscape from the one I live in, the country that has called me here yet again, I stop in my tracks, stand stock still and look around, like a sniffing animal sensing its surroundings. A young boy guides a wooden plow drawn by a pair of water buffalo. A little girl drops corn seeds as she walks six feet behind the plow blade that turns over the earth in front of her. I'm mindful now of what I'm seeing, where

I'm standing. And this ultra-mindfulness, this higher consciousness, this exquisite living in the moment, is exhilarating beyond belief.

Osta Maya, an ancient-looking, wrinkled, nut-brown 65-year-old woman from Badel, flew on our plane from Kathmandu, returning home after a visit to relatives. Buddi has taken her under his wing and included her in our party, so she has walked along with us, eaten with us. She indicated several times, with gestures and grimaces, that her stomach is upset, so we've given her Pepto-Bismol tablets and aspirin. Even not feeling well, even older than both Marge and me, Osta Maya keeps up a faster pace than either of us, moving surefootedly in her flat little treadless shoes, comfortably under her wool sweater and bright print *lunghi,* the ankle-length sarong-like skirt that the village women wear. When we rest too long, she harries us with "*Jaa! Jaa!*" ["Go! Go!"] In the village they've nicknamed her "Helicopter" because when she was young, she spoke in a loud, grating voice. She still does.

FROM MARGE'S JOURNAL:

I stumble even on the smooth ground; I never see Osta Maya slip. I drink two liters of water; she refuses any I offer. I sweat constantly; her flesh is dry. I work out all year round on a bike, stairs and weights; she plants and grinds corn. Am I of weaker stock? Or could it be that her simple diet of beans, rice and barley; no preservatives, pesticides or artificial flavorings, no sweets and little fat and hardly any meat have made her healthier and hardier? Or is the biggest difference between us familiarity? I grew up on the flat pavements of Chicago and the open Midwest cornfields; she has been scrambling over these jagged rocks all her life, barefoot most of the time. Whatever the reason, I salute you, Aama.

She sits so gracefully, squatting with her lunghi pulled between her legs, so that you never see an inch of flesh. She wears her long gray hair pulled back neatly by a band at the nape of her neck. There is an elegance about the Nepali women that makes both Marge and me, in our heavy boots and western clothes, feel super-klutzy. At several points along the trail, I realized how much merriment we were affording to children and adults alike as they watched us slipping and sliding, navigating rocks and mud and water on the path. But the laughter is always friendly, never ridiculing, so it's easy to join in and imagine what we must look like to them. I even add to the merriment as I elicit peals of laughter from my recitation of the folk saying I learned from my Nepal Handbook: "*Raato maato, chiplo baato.*" ("Red mud, slippery trail.")

We walk for about four and a half hours, from 12:45 to about 5:15, with frequent rest stops. Finally we have reached tonight's stop. We sit on a stone wall outside the teahouse in the crossroads of Mongelabari, where we have to wait thirty minutes for tea to be brewed. There's a big crowd here and only one woman in the dark kitchen inside. Sitting down and taking off my boots and socks is a treat. I enjoy the wait, relish being able to wiggle my toes, freed from my confining and heavy boots, thick wool socks, sweat-soaked sock liners.

We're the objects of curious stares from a ragtag group of porters, other transients and local residents, whose poverty is painfully obvious from their clothes. Shabby and skimpy shorts that look like swimming trunks, long pants torn at the knee (not bought that way—as in some expensive New York boutiques), faded and threadbare shirts ripped in front, in back or on the bottoms—or in all these places. Women pass through wearing well-worn blouses, cotton lunghis and the traditional three-yard-long cotton sash around the waist that serves as pocket, purse, padding for doko-loads and back support, as well as helping to keep their lunghis up. A small boy of about nine walks down the stone steps of the path, bent over under his heavily loaded doko.

Tonight's hotel is a hut with a dirt floor and a grass roof. We'll be sleeping in the upper story of the guest-house to the teahouse, especially maintained for overnight travelers. Osta Maya and our staff will stay here with us, all of us in the same loft-like space. We ascend to our sleeping quarters via a ladder slanted so widely that it's almost horizontal. Made of two long bamboo poles with five narrow, widely spaced rungs, it bends and creaks with every step. Marge declines tea with dinner, telling me: "I am certainly not going to negotiate this horror in the dark of night!" I pray that I'm still dehydrated enough so that I won't have to do it either.

We'll sleep in our sleeping bags, on our inflatable air mattresses, on straw mats laid on the dirt floor. From our rear "window" (the opening under the thatched roof), we look down upon a pair of water buffalo—one happily ensconced in a stable-like open-sided thatched-roof area, the other grazing free. We gaze out at overlapping hills (which would be called mountains anywhere else) beyond the winding Sunkosi River, the rice paddies, the fields of wheat, the terraces lushly green with growing millet. Marge says, "Do you realize what we'd have to pay for a hotel room with a view like this?"

The view is just as glorious after dark. In the blackness overhead the stars are brilliant, in numbers and a clarity that I haven't seen in years. Of course, I do have to leave our cozy little nest and make my way down the creaking ladder to see this splendid sky. The sequined magnificence above me elevates peeing in the rice fields to a scenic adventure. I try to burn my toilet paper, in the politically correct environmental procedure, but I can't get it to catch fire. Buddi assures us later that the monsoon rains will eventually dissolve it. "No problem." (Why does everyone who writes about Nepal include so much about toileting?) On my way back I manage not to step in the little brook coursing down over the rocks in the field.

Marge and I feel shamefully sybaritic as our staff ascends the ladder to bring us dinner—onion soup, cauliflower, green noodles, an orange. We feel colonial, getting this kind of treatment on our own private trek—when we had no idea what to expect. It's especially luxurious being able to stretch out so much more expansively than we could in a tent. After thinking this, I have to laugh at what this special friend and I consider luxury—what some of our friends would cry themselves to sleep over if forced to stay in these conditions! And once more I realize that in life it's the context more than the content. It's all in your point of view. It's what you bring to every experience, what you put into it, what you get out of it that determines what it's like for you.

Marge looks over from her corner, where she's changing for sleep in the privacy—despite a circle of half a dozen porters and Osta Maya only six feet away—afforded by turning off our flashlights. "Oh, isn't life wonderful!" Yes, it is. "What's the best trip you ever took?" "This one, of course!" A few minutes later she says sleepily, "This would be terrible if you were a different kind of person." I feel the same way. But we knew each other so well through our letters before we ever embarked on this adventure—we knew what kind of people we were.

I sleep better than I did in my hotel room in Kathmandu. I do wake up a few times during the night to the sounds of what I think at first is heavy rain, but which I eventually realize is the soothing sound of the river rushing below our paradise.

The next morning we set out, after breakfast, at 6:30, following the Rawa Khola (*khola* means "river"), then the Tap Khola, then back to the Rawa Khola, which, Buddi tells us, is a famous river. From strangers we encounter on the trail we keep hearing the usual greetings, "*Kahaa bata aaeko?*" (Where are you coming from?) and "*Kahaa jaane?*" (Where are you going?). Hardly anyone has heard of the tiny village of Badel, but everyone knows the Rawa Khola, and nods approvingly when they hear our route. Of course, I think they would nod approvingly whatever we said. Peter Owens had told us, "Never ask a Nepali a question that can be answered with 'yes,' because they're so polite that that's the answer you'll get, whether it's accurate or not."

We pass bamboo stands, banana trees, mango trees. Because of landslides along the way, our route is longer and even more up-and-down than it would have been a year ago. There had been a path that ran fairly level, along the river, but that was washed out last summer when the river flooded during the monsoons. We also see dramatic evidence of the uncertain life of the farmer—washed-out fields where rice and wheat once flourished.

What would have been a short hike before the flood and landslides becomes then a long journey fraught with danger. At one point we have to climb the steep mountainside and work our way along a very narrow ledge no wider than our feet. Marge gives me advice she learned from a rock climbing course she took eighteen years ago, which left her with no desire ever to pursue the sport again: "Don't look down. Don't look up. Don't ask how far or how long till we get there." She adds, "Be a good Buddhist. Live in the moment." As we climb over fallen boulders of every imaginable size and shape, lying at pre-carious angles, we worry that one might crash down on our heads. When Marge mentions her fear to Buddi, he answers, meaning to reassure her but falling somewhat short of that goal, "Yes, maybe, but not today, I think."

In the village where we stop for tea, Osta Maya visits briefly with her daughter and grandson. Later she runs into some younger cousins. They all put their palms together and briefly lower their heads as they raise their hands "Namaste-style." Then Osta Maya squats and touches her cousins' feet three times. She does it once to a young woman carrying her infant in a basket and once to a young man who seems to be the woman's husband. Jai tells us, "This is how Hindus greet each other. When my sister's husband comes to visit, my father greets him like this." The surprising thing to me is that it is the older person who touches the feet of the younger ones. I wonder whether my sons-in-law might like me to pay them my respects like this.

We won't reach tonight's campsite until about 3:30 this afternoon. With about two hours' worth of rest stops (tea, lunch, brief river swim, more lunch, various short rests), we keep walking up-and-down, down-and-up. When Jai and Buddi notice us flagging, they urge us to sit down for a little bit on one of the many benches under sheltering trees, constructed for just this purpose. "*Hotar chhaina*" they reassure us soothingly. ("No hurry!")

At many places, we skirt fields of rice, millet or wheat, walking on paths less than a foot wide at the edge of terraces with drops of eight feet or so. Jai had warned us that there would be a 25-minute steep climb. He had neglected to mention that for most of the way it was a hands-and-feet scramble. Marge says, "When I was in Outward Bound we were roped in for climbs like that!"

A mother brought us her baby. She had many sores. We had no medicine for her but we gave her clothes and soap. A medical worker from US will be here in two weeks. Perhaps there will be help for her.

Jana Rai

Mahadet .... wife and ..... baby

Misa Rai

At about 1:30 I think, "I am hotter and more exhausted than I have ever been in my life—even on the two treks when I walked longer and higher." My thighs have assumed personalities of their own, begging for mercy. The blisters on both my heels hurt with every uphill step (of which there are more than I care to remember) and the neuroma on my left foot burns on the downhill segments (also more numerous than comfort would dictate). My back aches between the shoulder blades from carrying my backpack, and my shoulders hurt from sunburn. My heart is beating double-time from better aerobic exercise than I could get in any gym. As an added bonus, my head is on fire from the relentless sun. I tell myself, "If I can keep going for another two hours, I can run the New York City Marathon this fall!" [In fact, I will do this.]

At the point of greatest exhaustion, we sit on rocks by the side of the path and look out at hill after overlapping hill, lavender in the distance, speaking of eternal truths, of a land that is here to change me, to offer its riches of generous, kind, humorous people living an elemental way of life that is almost lost from history.

Wherever we go, people stare. Marge and I are probably—almost certainly—the first western women many of these children and a fair number of these adults have ever seen. This is true for the people at the house where we're camping tonight, at a house in Rakha, just a couple of hours' walk from Badel. We just met the woman of the family on the trail a short time ago, and now we see her walking over here with a cackling white hen under her arm—tonight's dinner—provided along with the campsite for the modest payment that Jai negotiated with her. She, her three small daughters, a toothless old man, and two young neighbor girls watch our every move through the openings in our tents. Marge and I are tenting tonight in the yard, since there's not enough sleeping space in the house. The little girls, plus a few other children who materialized from nowhere, crowd the opening of our tents and gaze in fascination, occasionally bursting into giggle-fits.

They're greatly amused by all our doings—fascinated to watch us writing in our journals, opening the zippers of our tents, unfurling our sleeping bags, rummaging in our duffels. Brushing our teeth is an especially amusing performance.

After all, they've never seen a tent, a duffel, a flashlight or a toothbrush before—let alone a peculiar-looking western woman doing all sorts of strange actions with these items. They're interested in our clothing, too. In deference to the Nepali sense of modesty and local custom (as well as to uncertain toileting circumstances), we're both hiking in skirts rather than pants. This is the first time I've done this, and I find it more comfortable and convenient than I had ever imagined. Still, the amount of leg shown between our ankles and knees would ruin the reputation of any Nepali village woman.

"We are their television," Marge says. "And they are ours." Because we love to watch them, too. The most gratifying thing about their comfort in staring at us is that it gives us permission to stare back at them. I'm fascinated by the way they're dressed—their heads covered with cloths wrapped around desert-style; the women and older girls in their ankle-length lunghis; the thick bands of cloth wrapped around their waists; their simple blouses or tee shirts; their feet bare or in flip-flops. Our other company in the yard consists of a hen and her half dozen yellow-headed white chicks hopping about, and three black water buffalo in the open stable. We're relieved to see that the male is tied up, since, according to Jai, he's distinctly unfriendly. Even so, we both take to heart Jai's warning not to go near him on our way to pee in a corner of the field, and we make wide circles around the stable.

We eat dinner sitting on the clay front steps of our hostess's house, on little round straw mats she quickly pulled out for us. In the next couple of weeks we'll see that every house in these hill villages is well equipped with these mats, and that basic courtesy dictates whipping them out as soon as a guest makes the most preliminary motions to sit down.

Over the house's little front porch the family has hung family photos and a water-color portrait of the owner's son, who's studying at the university in Kathmandu. Sitting in the corner of the porch, the local shaman is counting out grains of rice and murmuring incantations, as the population around him grows. We realize that we are staying at the local clinic. With no medical facilities in these remote villages, anyone with any ailment comes to see the shaman. He treats a woman with a stomach-ache by praying over her, tossing some grains of rice in the air and sprinkling some on her stomach.

We climb into our tents at 7:15. It's too early to go to sleep, but we're both too exhausted to stay up. We talk a couple of minutes, read a couple more—and, for me, flashlight out at 7:40. Up intermittently during the night to the harsh rhythms of barking dogs, who sound uncomfortably close to the tent. Finally, at 4 a.m. my bladder wakes me and I want to sneak down to the fields to relieve myself before daybreak like the local women. My only reservation is the dogs. I hope that the Nepali proverb, "A barking dog does not bite," is reality-based. I take the chance—and, to my immense relief, don't hear a peep or see mangy hide nor bristly hair of any of the barkers. Of course, this is why I underwent the rabies prophylaxis before I left. Still, I'd rather not need it.

FROM MARGE'S JOURNAL:

It was a horrible night. There seemed to be dogs everywhere—whining, snarling, barking, growling, howling. When I crawled out of my tent to urinate I came face to face with one of them. My only thought was: "Oh, my God—and I was too cheap to get the anti-rabies vaccine!" But the animal showed no interest in me and just walked on by. This morning I asked Jai about the mangy mutt hanging around my tent. "He is very old and blind." "Pathetic animal," I cluck. "Why don't they kill it and put it out of its misery?" Jai's abrupt answer was: "Rai people don't kill."

Part II
In Badel: April 1993

A Carje Woman
she cannot come into
the house.

5

Arrival: You Walk a Day and It's Still Badel

Ask not the way to the village where you do not intend to go.
—Nepali proverb

We awake with excitement, since today we will leave the village of Rakha where we camped last night, and we'll finally reach Badel. Among the children who come to visit and view us in the yard very early this morning is Pansari Darje, who has the face of an angel, with radiant smile and dancing dark eyes. When we ask, she tells us that she's 15, but she looks only 12 or 13. Jai declares, "She don't know how old she is." When Marge asks her to pose for a drawing, Pansari runs away in embarrassment; after Jai talks her into coming back, she stands still, quiet and smiling, for about half an hour, until Marge puts down her pen and shows the model her sketch.

Pansari is a Darje, one of the occupational, or untouchable, castes, which include blacksmiths, tailors, potters, ferrymen, musicians and leather workers. Jai explains that she cannot go

65

into the home of anyone except for another Darje and cannot touch anyone. If she happens to touch someone while that person is collecting water, they have to throw out the water because it is considered polluted by her touch. A similar proscription applies to cooked food, which no Rai can accept from anyone from these castes. In the fourteenth century, when the caste system was first codified, those in the lowest castes were forbidden to wear shoes, caps or clothing with sleeves.

Today, even without these prohibitions, this caste system still exists. The Nepali government has passed laws against the system, in its efforts to bring Nepal into the modern world and to avoid making an accident of birth a sentence to a mean and restricted life. But in these remote regions the law in Kathmandu is impotent in the face of centuries of village customs.

Our hostess, whose name I never learn, has been watching us silently. Suddenly she gestures toward Pansari and her other two little daughters and asks with a smile, "Do you want to take any girls home with you?" I take her question as a joke, whether it was meant that way or not, laugh and say, "I have three daughters of my own." But I'm not feeling merry. The position of girls in Nepal—especially in rural Nepal—is troubling to me. This woman, with no husband in sight, cannot expect help from her daughters when they grow up, since by Nepali custom they will marry young men from other villages and will move to their homes, to live with their families, to do the bidding of their husbands' mothers. It's unlikely that they will learn to read, that they will have an independent income, that they will own any property other than their clothing and jewelry.

Our hostess asks whether we have medicine, since all three of her daughters have diarrhea. Jai adds, "This is the season for it." Because of the planting, people are out in the fields more, where they pick up bacteria on their hands and bare feet; the organisms then enter the system and cause intestinal havoc. When I first came to Nepal in 1987, Peter Owens took our small group of trekkers to visit the United Nepal Mission hospital at Amp Pipal, where we met with its remarkable director, Dr. Helen Huston, a regal-looking Canadian then in her seventies. Tall, with long steel-gray hair braided and coiled neatly in back of her head, she was clearly a woman of strength, dedication and great spiritual, as well as physical, beauty. Most of the ills brought to the hospital are, she told us, preventable. "We could eliminate the debilitating—and for small children, often fatal—problems of dysentery and parasites in a year's time if we had a clean water supply and if the Nepalis would use latrines instead of defecating in the fields, the streets and other public places." But habits laid down over generations are hard to kill.

I protest that whatever medicine we would give would be too little to do any good, but Buddi presses us to give something: "It will make them feel better." I come up with six Pepto-Bismol tablets, hope that the placebo effect works—and then decide not to keep doing this. Not because I begrudge these little pink pills, but because of my concern that giving nostrums that do no good will take away people's faith in western medicine, so that when something more serious comes up, they won't trust the western health workers.

Besides, this kind of chronic diarrhea is resistant to practically anything we have—unlike the situation last night, when our hostess burned herself on a lighted cigarette that had been tossed down onto the ground. Marge put her experience as nurse and as mother to good use; she applied antibiotic ointment to the wound, bandaged it, gave the woman a small bar of soap and told her to keep it clean, to avoid infection. That treatment would work and was well worth giving. This seems to be the line we need to draw.

Probably the soap is more important than either the antibiotic salve or the bandage. I remember the O. Henry story of a "snake-oil" salesman early in the twentieth century, who was asked how his conscience could let him sell poor people "magic sand" to keep their lamps from exploding, when he knew there was nothing magic about it. "Listen," he said, "I instruct her to keep her lamp clean and well filled. If she does that it can't burst. And with the sand in it she knows it can't and she don't worry." So in the same way, if the burnt woman keeps her wound clean with simple soap, she will probably be exercising the best self-care she can manage.

We've had all this activity—plus packing up our duffels, having our tents struck by our staff and eating breakfast—by 6:45 a.m. The day begins and ends early in a village with no electricity. We set out and almost immediately begin walking uphill—often steep, steep, steep uphill. The trail is similar to yesterday's, except for a much sharper elevation that continues for almost all four hours of this last day of our trek to Badel. The vegetation changes quickly here because of the abrupt ascents and descents. Early in the morning we pass agave and cholla cactus, and I think of the desert in the American southwest. Then, descending to exuberant greenery surrounding little ponds and creeks, I look into a lush gorge typical of a tropical rain forest. Now the erect spindles of bamboo, the blushing pink rhododendrons, the fruit trees in bloom emerge.

Thanks to our ever-cheerful and ever-helpful guides, we keep going on this last, hardest leg of our journey. They take our hands to lead us down slippery sandy slopes, up scrambly rocky climbs, over jumbles of boulders as we cross swiftly flowing rivers—today the Liding Khola ("Leading Cola"—good name for a soft drink—is how I remember it). When our steps slow, Jai reassures us: "*Hotar chhaina*" (no hurry) and Buddi adds, "*piccar chhaina*" (no problem). They both often urge us, "Grandma, take rest here." "Here, Grandma, eat orange." I, who will at home carry waste paper in my pocket for hours instead of throwing it down, quickly adjust to the prevalent practice here of tossing anything organic on the ground, after I'm assured: "No problem, Grandma. Buffalo will have lunch too!"

After climbing up an almost vertical hillside, we sit down to rest for a few minutes and look at the broad green fields around us, the rushing river below, no sign of habitation anywhere. And suddenly a slim young woman walks toward us apparently out of nowhere, barefoot, her floral-print lunghi grazing her ankles, gracefully balancing a tray with five tall metal cups of six-ingredient tea (tea, milk, sugar, salt, pepper and water). We thank her for her hospitality and drink the tea, hoping for the best while wondering: How clean are the cups? How pure the water? How safe the fresh, unpasteurized milk? A bigger source of wonderment are our other questions: How did she know we were here? How did she know how many cups to bring? How was the message communicated? Nepali hill villagers manage to get the word through without phones or faxes or email.

Our guides amuse us to keep up our flagging spirits. When I told Buddi yesterday that I wanted to help the women of Badel with their work, he thought that was the funniest idea he'd heard in weeks. Now he won't let me forget it. He keeps telling me, "You'll have lots of work, Grandma, from morning till night. When we get to Badel, staff play volleyball—grandmas go out to work in the fields!" When we come to a fork in the road and ask, "Which path?" Jai says, "Down for Nepalis, up for grandmas!"

They tell us stories. Buddi tells of the time, about five years ago, when his father asked him to take care of the water buffalo for the afternoon. "That mean buffalo came at me before I knew it. His big head knocked me down!" He points to his ribs, his elbow, his knee. "I had cuts, sores everywhere." He explains why he doesn't go swimming: "When I was maybe eight years old, I thought I go into the river." He shakes his head and smiles ruefully. "I did go in, I went all the way in. All the way down too. Lucky for me, the river pushed me up again. But I never go swimming again."

Gora, our gentle cook (who was immortalized in Marge's journal, wearing the Port Washington Thanksgiving Run tee shirt), walks with me, helping me negotiate some of the roughest spots on this trail, which alternates between slippery mud and daunting boulders. He tells me a little bit of his life history, which, in the previous two treks on which he cooked for our group, I had never heard. The cooks on trek, although among the most important staff members, have the least amount of contact with the trekkers. So I never knew Gora's story. Like Jai, he came up the ranks from porter to kitchen boy. But instead of becoming a guide, he left trekking and took a job as cook in a restaurant. But since he found indoor work too confining, he became a cook on Peter Owens's treks. "I like walking up and down, getting exercise, talking and laughing with staff, meeting members [i.e., trekkers], being outside," Gora tells me as he holds out his hand to help me over an immense rock, slippery with its green moss blanket. "Every day different. In restaurant every day the same."

Just after we cross the Liding Khola river, at about 10:30, the air is suddenly perfumed by orange and lemon blossoms. And then we reach the bottom slopes of Badel. We hear their shouts before we see a dozen or so children rushing out to get a first look at these big, funny-looking people from so far away. Our welcoming committee lines up along the ridge above us, gazing intently. Then the older children run down laughing, barefoot or in flip-flops, their thin brown legs sticking out from shorts or short dresses. Like lithe little mountain goats, they make what look like death-defying leaps among the jagged rocks and boulders. The children clamber up the rocks with us—circling around ahead and then stopping to wait while we catch up—up, up, up to Jai's family's home in Badel. We see a few houses scattered here and there on the side of the hill. They're reached from narrow, *bango-tingo* (crooked, winding) footpaths, rocky lanes, and crude but helpful staircases made from boulders, which meander back and forth, up and down, for a distance of several kilometers.

We can't see most of Badel's houses from here, though, because of the topography. The hills scroll around the village, hiding the houses. Those dwellings we do see are arrayed among the folds of the hills in no noticeable pattern, as if they had been dropped from the sky like a giant fistful of grains and left to sprout wherever they landed. They are small two-story structures built of stone covered with a smooth plaster made from the local ochre clay, partly painted white and partly left its natural reddish brown color. Each one has a thatched roof and more straw thatching on the overhang above a little porch area and is unadorned except for the wood framing around doors and windows. In some of the grander homes, this framing is carved in simple geometric patterns; but even these houses carry a minimum of decoration.

This pretty village, bathed in sunshine, consists of somewhere between 1,500 and 3,000 people living in from 200 to 500 households (depending on who our census informant is). "How big is Badel?" we ask Buddi as we huff and puff up the hill. "To go from one end of village to the other, one hour," he tells us. But then he waves his arm expansively and says, "You walk a day and it's still Badel." That's because, even beyond the area where the houses sit and the people live, Badel continues into the wooded area known here as the "jungle," which consists of a few bamboo stands among increasingly defoliated, debranched conifers and oaks, stripped by the villagers' constant needs for firewood. The woods are also dense with forty-feet-high rhododendron trees, which we're lucky enough to see festooned in brilliant pink and red and white blooms.

Jai, who has not been back to his village for three years, seems to be about to explode as he leaps over boulders and streams to reach his family's house. About ten minutes from when we hit the bottom slopes, he guides us down rocks set into the hill at crazy angles onto a courtyard between what looks at first like two identical buildings. Jai points to one and says, "This is my father's new house. You'll stay in that one." Most of the families in Badel build a second house as soon as they can afford to, across a courtyard and just a few feet away from the family's primary house. One of the two structures may then be used to accommodate the overflow of a large family, possibly put up a married son and his wife and children, provide storage space for grains and vegetables, and house out-of-town relatives who come *en masse* to celebrate weddings, funerals and seasonal festivals.

Jai's entry into Badel is jubilant, as he is welcomed by family, friends and neighbors. He is coming back to his village as the "local boy who made good." Even given his high working status as a well-paid sirdar, Jai married unusually high above his social status by wedding Sita, a daughter of the richest man in the village and a high school graduate (a considerable achievement in Nepal, especially for a woman). But Sita married well, too. Jai, a hard worker and a good manager, has saved enough money to buy land and build a house in Kathmandu and to send his son, Kim, to private school, where the three-year-old is already learning English. What's more, every indication shows that Jai will continue to do well. With his ability, his intelligence and his saucy personality, he seems marked for more and more success. Marge and I are confident that he'll start his own trekking agency someday.

"This is my family!" he grins as he introduces us to his mother, his father, two of his three sisters and two younger brothers, all of whom show a strong family resemblance. They all grin widely too and nod their heads as they shyly look at their son and brother and at us. There are no hugs, kisses and tears of joy as we westerners might expect after such a long absence. That is not their way.

Marge asks Jai to tell his family, "We are very happy to be in Badel. Tomorrow is Easter, a very important day in my religion, and God has given me a fine gift in bringing me to Badel and in getting such a good welcome. We thank you." I chime in, asking Jai to express my thanks also. It is an important time in my tradition too, since this year Easter Sunday falls during the eight-day holiday of Passover.

Jai's relatives smile and nod, as do about a dozen women, young children and babies who are arrayed on the ground, watching our every move with great interest. The women, wearing gracefully wrapped lunghis and tee shirts or blouses, catch their lovely long black hair in clasps at the back of the neck or in single braids down their backs. The children wear few clothes; what they do have on is the color of the red-brown earth. A few wear flip-flops on their dusty feet; a few have on torn canvas shoes; most are barefoot. Despite their ragged appearance, though, none look malnourished, a testament to the fertility of the land in this country where ninety-five percent of the population are farmers and their families.

A fleecy lamb stands in a pen, a red-combed rooster in an upturned basket. I look around and note happily that the family has no dog. Buddi lives two minutes away, up the hill, but instead of rushing home to his parents, wife and little daughter, all of whom he has not seen for a couple of months, he stays for a couple of friendly hands of cards. As important as family ties are here, they are honored differently from our ways back home.

Jai's family consists of his mother, Dilkumari, and father, Gokana, and their children: Indra Maya, 30 (who has done the family and herself proud by bearing three sons: Bikas, 7; Santos, 3; and Monos, 11 months); Jai Prasad, 27 (who has also, of course, done the family proud by his financial success and his high-status marriage, as well as by the son Sita has borne); and the four youngest children, all still single: the girls, Kali Maya, 25, and Mithu Maya, 20; and the boys, Prem Kumar, 14; and Kul Bahadur, 12. The Nepali language recognizes the fact that practically everyone in Nepal marries: you describe single people by saying they are "not yet married."

No one here calls anyone by their actual names. Like Native Americans, Nepalis believe that if you say someone's name out loud, the evil spirits can hear and get power over them, and be able to harm the person. So people call children the words for "firstborn" (*Jethi* for a girl, *Jetha* for a boy), "second-born" (*Maili*), "third-born" (*Saili*), and so on down to the sixteenth level—Nepalis have big families. ("*Kaanchi*" is the "youngest.") Among adults, you use other relationship terms; there are about fifty in Nepali, showing both the importance of family and the inclusive attitude that treats everyone as a relative. Addressing a woman older than you—even if she's a stranger you have never set eyes on before—you say, "*Didi*" ("older sister"). Unless she's old enough to be your mother, in which case she's "*Aama*" ("mother"). Then there's "younger sister," "younger and older brother," "older brother's wife," "father" and so on.

But no one seems to mind when Marge and I use people's names; Nepalis accept the fact that foreigners' ways are very different from theirs, and they realize how much of an effort we're making just to remember the names, let alone the relationship terms! Jai's family are a warm, friendly group, full of wide, toothy smiles, who immediately make us feel welcome.

After an early lunch of cheese, bread, peanut butter, marmalade, tea and canned pineapple, Jai shows Marge and me up to the room we'll be sharing for the next few days, in his father's second house, which will receive its formal dedication tomorrow from the village shaman. Our accommodations are far grander than we had expected, after our one night on the ground in a tent in a yard and the other night above a stable, in the open-air loft that we shared with Osta Maya and our staff.

Now Jai takes us up a narrow flight of a dozen short, steep, banister-less earthen steps climbing up the outside of the house. On the ground floor, just behind the staircase, is a small dark room where our staff cooks by day and sleeps by night. At the top of the stairs Jai has spread his sleeping bag on a small terrace-like space, covered by the roof but otherwise open. From this terrace a door opens to our quarters. The cozy room about twelve feet square has a clay floor that holds two wooden beds covered with straw mats, separated by a wooden table covered with papers and schoolbooks. We know we're in a prosperous, western-influenced home, since furniture, except for the ever-present small bamboo stools, is a rarity in Rai houses, where most inhabitants sit and sleep on the floor, on bamboo mats.

The ceiling, made of numerous narrow strips of wood, is supported by a single horizontal beam across the width of the room and seven crosswise beams. Propped in a corner, a doko full of corn kernels leans next to a notched wooden ladder, which leads up to a storage loft just under the thatched roof. I climb up the ladder. Scattered about up in the loft are more dokos, a metal trunk, a few straw mats and a pile of corncobs being saved to use as fuel for the fire; in this village nothing is wasted.

From time to time, Mithu, Jai's 20-year-old sister, slips into our room and, smiling to us, quietly pads up the ladder to fetch some item from the attic. She never knocks. In Nepal, no one does. Privacy has a far different construct in Asia from our western notion. In a society in which family members often sleep in the same room, frequently in the same bed, people have neither secrets nor solitude, and don't seem to want them. There's no sense of intrusion when someone comes in; the welcome mat always seems to be out. I don't ask the obvious question, but imagine that parents take advantage of those times when they can count on their children's sleeping soundly.

Marge and I are both discomfited to see by the personal items and pictures on the walls that we are displacing Mithu and one of her younger brothers from their beds. But our embarrassment is tempered partly by the gracious welcome we have received, and even more by the knowledge that the modest board we'll pay ($20.00 for the week for the two of us) will be of significant help to the family. The level of the English-lesson pages on the wall over Marge's bed and the school books on the shelf just above by the bed, signal that her bed is ordinarily slept in by one of Jai's younger brothers, but there's no name to tell us which one.

My bed is usually occupied by Mithu, a senior in high school; since village children often don't start school until age seven or eight, they are older than western youths when they finish. With differences in specifics, her decorating is not so different from what I remember of my own three daughters' rooms when they were in high school. The wall next to the bed is covered by pages from newspapers and magazines, some written in the Devanagri script used for the Nepali language, some in English. There are articles about traffic woes in Beijing and markets on the Burma-China border; travel brochures from the Empire State Building in New York, St. Joseph's School in Japan and Tiffany's ("The Original Transvestite Cabaret") in Pattaya, Thailand. Most of these printed materials came from Jai, who's sent them home from his journeys over the years. Mithu has also placed on display photos of Indian film stars and some of her own drawings—of young lovers, a peacock, and a surrealistic picture containing an eye, a table with a vase of flowers, a pointing finger and "Mithu Maya Rai" in three-dimensional block letters.

Since these comfortable digs, showing the prosperity of our host family, are more secluded than we had expected, we feel free to leave the door open for ventilation. But just as the two of us curl into our sleeping bags for a nap, an old neighbor woman walks in and begins to make conversation. We want to talk to the villagers; we've come here just to do this. But at this particular moment, these two tired travelers are both just as happy to see Jai materialize and politely usher her out. He continues to take good care of us grandmas.

I sleep for about an hour and come downstairs to chat with the family, or rather, sit among them and smile, in view of the fact that they speak no English and my Nepali is most rudimentary. Marge is still in bed. She is coughing now and feverish. She took aspirin and one of the above-the-waist antibiotics we brought with us "just in case," trying to shake whatever it is she has.

I look over at the assemblage of family, neighbors and staff, and see that much of the clothing we brought from the States has already found takers. Buddi and Gora, both scrubbed clean, are wearing new tee shirts. My husband's jacket from his velour warm-up suit fits Buddi perfectly; until he gives the suit to his father, it will keep him warm. Our kitchen helper, Kangsha, sports a bright green tee shirt from Yale University; Marge's red turtleneck shirt compliments Tara Mani's bronze skin and black hair. Then I see an adorable round-faced, almond-eyed baby; Buddi has gone home and returned with his two-and-a-half-year-old daughter, Kusum. I give him a 12-month-size floral-print dress that my granddaughter wore as an infant; it looks as if it will fit Kusum perfectly. The next time I see her she's wearing it; it does.

Jai looks around to be sure that everyone in his family has received some small gift from the simple stores of bandannas and rubber balls and tee shirts and the like that we brought over to give away, and when he sees someone who has not received any largesse, he asks what we have left. This is how his seven-year-old nephew Bikas comes to receive a pink wool scarf. For the rest of the time we're in Badel that scarf is wrapped around Bikas's neck, although by the time we leave it's impossible to see that it once was a bright pink. I appreciate Jai's help in this operation, since in this sea of unfamiliar faces I can't keep track of who received what. I would have liked to wait for Marge to do the distribution, but the pressure is on to do it now and do it fast.

Children just hanging out

For the hour or so that I'm down in the little courtyard, a ring of village boys eye me intently. I can't remember the last time I've been such an object of undisguised interest—probably the first time I came to Nepal, when we trekked through villages rarely visited by westerners. I'm becoming more comfortable about gazing back—at the people and at their surroundings. Last night I peeked into the kitchen of the home where we camped and admired the shelves full of gleaming metal plates and cups. I continue to be impressed by the Nepalis' brave attempts at cleanliness in the face of an aggressively dusty environment, limited supplies of cold water and major efforts needed to fetch it and then heat it.

Marge wakes up refreshed from her nap and comes downstairs to join the company.

FROM MARGE'S JOURNAL:

I am struck by the contrast between Jai and the other men. Jai in his blue jeans, red tee shirt and cap that we bought for him in the Los Angeles airport shop, and new lightweight imported hiking boots is the small-town boy who has made it in the big city and returned proudly home to show it all off. I suppose that bringing these two visitors from outer space makes him even more of the village hero. Jai has been to the United States twice, where he studied English and visited the homes of trekkers from New York to California. He has picked up many western ways and seems comfortable with one foot in each culture. But today belongs to Jai; he is in his glory. His grin doesn't ever stop. Nor does the one on his father's face.

I see the strong family resemblance, the crinkles around both men's eyes and the easy, friendly smiles. Gokana seems a proud, happy father. I ask myself, is pride a universal concept? Maybe pride—for good or ill—is unknown in the Rai culture. When I think of pride I think of competitiveness. From what I have seen of the Nepalis, competition is not a part of their lives.

At 2:30 the heavens open up to a sudden downpour, our first rain of the trip. Huge drops splatter down—and stop in less than five minutes. Fifteen minutes later, everything happens at once—crashing thunder, flashing lightning, egg-sized pellets of hail, sheets of rain that turn the yard between the two houses into a muddy swamp, white with hailstones. This is a typical springtime harbinger of the wet monsoon season, which will come in June and last through September. Until then we can expect frequent rainstorms, heralding the transition from spring to summer. If the villagers are lucky, the strong winds and battering hail will not damage the crops.

Jai's father rushes to rescue the lamb and bring it into the house. Our audience scatters, some taking shelter in the house, some running home. It looks like an all-day, all-night storm; I hope it's not an all-week one. Marge and I head up to our sanctuary, where we share intimate feelings and talk about our lives. We're still getting to know each other, and with each confidence we become closer.

Soon we receive our second visitor, a curious hen, who lives, with her five cheeping chicks, in a pile of straw on the tiny balcony just outside our room. Besides being the hen house, the balcony also serves as the drying room, a function made apparent by the laundry looped over its railing. Every now and then a family or staff member comes through our room (without knocking, of course), wet laundry over an arm, to hang out more wash. The sublime view from the balcony—of the houses and barns below, the green hills across the river and the cloudy sky above—frees the spirit and refreshes the eyes.

Tara Mani brings our dinner up to us—cream-of-mushroom soup, dal bhat and vegetable curry, followed by an apple and tea. We've been eating well—and healthily—except for the junk that we brought and share, to everyone's delight—melted, misshapen mini-Snickers and melted, hardened sheets of M&Ms. I don't feel too guilty offering these tooth-destroyers to the villagers, since they won't be a regular part of their virtually fat-free, sugar-free diets and so are not likely to wreak much dental damage.

We stay upstairs after dinner. Marge is still feeling very sick, and either because of the morning's hard trek or the excitement of arrival or whatever, I'm weary. I feel cowardly not spending more time downstairs with the family. But Jai and Buddi, our interpreters, are both away, Jai visiting other relatives,

Buddi enjoying his family—and I am shy about going down myself. With my bare handful of Nepali words, I am not equipped for social conversation. I tell myself how much easier it will be to communicate when one of our guides is on hand to translate.

Marge and I still don't know how long we'll stay here in Badel. We're content to take each day as it comes. We don't know what will happen beyond tomorrow. For tonight, that is enough.

6

Women of Badel: "I Don't Know English"

What takes a year for a man to do takes but a moment for a woman.

—Nepali proverb

I look up from the journal I've been writing in, startled to see Dilkumari Rai, Jai's mother, and his three round-faced, cheerful sisters standing in our now open doorway. They have come to our room this afternoon, our second day here in Badel, to look at photos of our families, which they heard about from Jai. Both Marge and I are happy that we were not in the process of dressing or undressing. We forgot that no one knocks on a door in Nepal. You are always assumed to be ready to greet visitors.

To everyone's disappointment, Marge forgot her family photos in Kathmandu. It's especially frustrating since Marge, with her six children and eight grandchildren, holds high status here, where large families are greatly admired. Quite a change from the States, where Marge often finds herself apologizing for her fecundity!

83

However, my motherhood of only three children is acceptable, for a *bideshi*, and everyone is keenly interested in looking at the photos of my family and my home.

Dilkumari has a broad face with the high cheekbones and almond-shaped eyes that reveal the Mongol ancestry of the Rai, and a sweet, shy smile. She is wearing all her personal wealth in gold—earrings, a stud in the side of her nose, a ring dangling between her nostrils, a narrow necklace and a wide bracelet. Her traditional village garb includes dark-printed *chola* (blouse), lunghi, a three-yard-long green sash around her waist, and a cotton scarf around her head, wrapped desert-style. Indra Maya, the only married sister, is the only one of the young women to wear the gold ring through her septum. Otherwise, all three sisters—Indra, 30, Kali Maya, 25, and Mithu Maya, 20—are dressed similarly, with western tee shirts (from trekkers, via Jai) over lunghis, studs in the side of the nose, bead necklaces. All the women are barefoot.

"*Bhitra aunos*," I say, thankful for that phrase in my Nepali lessons. "Come in."

"*Basnos*." ("Sit down.")

They all admire the photos, one by one, of my children ("Like Nepali," they exclaim, pointing to my daughters' dark eyes and long straight dark hair), my grandchildren (especially my grandson with his green eyes and blond curls), my husband (since he looks fit and healthy, they are surprised that I have come to Nepal without him; so are quite a few of my friends and family at home, who mistrust a marriage in which husband and wife pursue different interests), my house (in two seasons—showing flowers in one, snow in the other), my neighborhood by Manhasset Bay, off Long Island Sound. "*Ramro!*" ("Beautiful!") they keep exclaiming.

Kali points to a picture of my husband and asks me how old both he and I are. Her mother looks embarrassed and tries to hush her, but I answer the question. I'm surprised at Dilkumari's reaction, since this question is a common—and a polite—one here. Nepalis do not regard age as a confidential matter, because they revere it. When meeting people whose age you are unsure of, you will be observing the highest level of courtesy if you address them by the term suitable for an older person. Unlike the United States, where everybody wants to be young—or at least look young, where experience and wisdom are discounted and where the supreme compliment is: "I never dreamed you could really be as old as you are!"

On my first trek, our young porters called me "*Didi*" (older sister); four years later I had become "*Aama*" (mother); and this time, on the walk to Badel from Lamidanda, the staff has been referring to Marge and me as "Grandma." From now on we answer to "Grandma Marge" or "Grandma Sally." When we asked Shiva, Jai's mother-in-law and Buddi's mother, whether we should adopt Buddi's suggestion to call her "*Bauju*" ("older brother's wife," in deference to her husband's 70 years), this 55-year-old woman, only four years younger than I but an elder in her land where the average life expectancy for women is only 53 years, shook her head and told us "*Bahini.*" This word literally means "younger sister," but in everyday parlance, it is the term used for addressing little girls. Shiva was offering Marge and me the magnanimous tribute of respect for our seniority. "*Piccar chhaina*," I assure Dilkumari ("No problem"), and tell Kali that I am 59, my husband 72.

As we talk, Indra, sitting on the bed, nurses her fat good-natured 10-month-old son, Monos, at her ample breast. The room quickly fills up with Jai's elderly aunt, our porter Tara Mani's little brother, Indra's son Bikas, and briefly, before he feels outnumbered by the women, Jai's father.

After everyone has seen the photos and only the women and children remain, Marge cries out with a broad smile, "Time for show-and-tell!" To the rapt fascination of her audience, she pulls out the contents of her duffel, item by intriguing item. From her bottle of hand lotion, she squeezes some onto everyone's hands—except Tara Mani's little brother who yanks his away and says in no uncertain terms, "No!" Holding up a bottle of shampoo, she mimes washing her hair, to much laughter. She demonstrates her dental floss. She invites everyone to dip a finger in her gooey sunblock and then puts some on her lips. She files her nails, then cuts them with her clipper. She combs and brushes her hair. She could not have a more attentive audience if she were doing a solo star turn on Broadway. She gives away a jar of bath gel from

Bangkok's Airport Hotel, and "Auntie," thinking it's more lotion, puts it on her hands and then exclaims at their stickiness. Marge pulls out blouses, pants, rain-pants with full-length zippers—which elicit choruses of "oohs" and "ahhhs."

The hilarity reaches a new high when Marge takes out her towel and pantomimes washing and drying herself, when she fetches our lace-trimmed nylon panties from the railing outside (Nepali women don't wear underpants), when I pull out my running shorts and mime jogging, when I hold my bathing suit up in front of me (they don't wear these, either), and when we both hold up our bras (including my lacy black one) in front of our chests (another item absent from Nepali wardrobes).

I polish Mithu's, Indra's and Kali's fingernails with the scarlet nail enamel I threw into my duffel at the last minute before I left home. Marge makes necklaces for everyone, each with one blue bead on a string. As soon as "Auntie" gets hers, she jumps up, twirls around and does an impromptu dance, so when I get my bead, I do too. Both our efforts are greeted by howls of laughter. I pass around miniature Snickers. Indra gives hers to her baby, and "Auntie"—to whom I gave three, thinking she'd pass the extras to the two people behind her—reveals no such intention. Apparently in Badel, what you get is what you keep.

When Marge starts to pull out picture books she's brought for the schools, a crowd of children suddenly materializes, including Buddi's eleven-year-old brother, Kiran, who sounds out the English words phonetically and clearly. Since children's books are less interesting to the women than lotions and lingerie, they slip away one by one, and only the children remain with us. But both Marge and I feel that we have begun to build bridges linking western women to eastern ones.

Jai's sisters seem to become more and more comfortable with us over the next couple of days. Mithu smiles radiantly whenever she sees us, which she does often, as she passes through our room to reach the stores in the attic above us. She lets me try my hand at winnowing the rice and popping the corn over the open fire and giggles in a friendly fashion at my colossal ineptitude at both chores. Indra readily answers my questions about her children, her husband, her home in Rakha, a two-hour walk away.

But then my epiphany comes. After having besieged Indra with my questions and getting her answers as translated by Jai, I ask him to ask her if she has anything she wants to ask me. He translates her reply: "I would like to talk to you, but I don't know English."

"Tell her she can tell you her questions," I urge Jai, "and you'll translate for us." But Indra tosses her head up and sideways in the Nepali gesture that means "no," smiles to both Jai and me to take away the sting of a refusal and says, "I don't want to have to go through him." She doesn't want to interpose her brother between us. She wants to talk directly to me, woman-to-woman. Of course, this is what I would love, too—and what I have been finding one of the most frustrating aspects of this trip. It's like reading sub-titles in a foreign-language movie when you know the actors are saying much more than the few words at the bottom of the screen. Not only do Jai and Buddi translate only a fraction of what their friends and family say to us, and we to them, but the very fact of its having to be translated inevitably changes the message.

And I realize that my earlier thoughts of writing about the women of Badel will not be viable. When I first thought about the book I wanted to write about our village visit, I thought immediately about the women. I longed to find out how they felt, what they thought about their lives in this land that, like so many Asian nations, is such a formidable bastion of male supremacy. What is it like to be a little girl and know that your birth is responsible for your father's freedom to take on a second wife because you were not a boy? To be a girl old enough to go to school but not sent because your brothers need the education and your family needs your labor at home? To be a young bride forced to leave your family, your friends and the village where you have lived all your life, to go and live far from home in your husband's family's house where you will in effect be his mother's servant?

Are there compensations for such treatment, which to the mind of a western woman seems such a harsh derogation to an inferior status? And how do girls and women feel today, now that life is changing—infinitesimally slowly, but changing nevertheless? But there's no way I can get answers to these questions. Not only am I a foreigner with my own ethnocentric viewpoint, but every bit of spoken information I'm getting comes filtered through the minds of men. They're the only proficient English-speakers around here. So the only writing about these women that I'll be able to do will have to emerge from our own quick impressions—like the fast-brushstroke water-color paintings filling Marge's pad.

As I think about this change in my expectations, I have to let go of my original ambition—to write about the women in rural, isolated pockets of Nepal, like this village. Whatever results will be different from what I had originally envisioned. One of the most powerful effects of being here is a new-found ability to adopt the eastern attitude of acceptance of life as it comes, giving up attachments to my blueprints of how life should be structured. I conclude that I was not meant to focus primarily on the lives of the women, an understanding that allows me to cast a wider gaze on the lives of all the villagers—female and male, young and old. Maybe, in fact, I'll learn more about the women's lives that way.

We do, of course, learn a great deal about the women's lives just by being among them. Like the times when we take our meals with the families, and we are embarrassed to see that the women of the house wait on us and don't eat themselves until all of us—the men, the children and the visitors—have finished. Like hearing about Shiva's twenty pregnancies and the babies she delivered herself on the road, on her way home from working in the fields.

Like our recognition that in the system under which Nepali villages operate, almost all property belongs to the male head of household. No one ever refers to a house as belonging to So-and-so's parents; it's always the father's home, the father's farm, the father's water buffalo. The mother's property usually consists only of her clothing and her gold or silver jewelry. These adornments constitute her only wealth, generally having come in the form of gifts from her father or husband. Any land or other property coming from father to child goes to the male child, not the female, who will go, property-less except for clothes and jewelry, to her husband's home in his village.

Laxmi Dorje.   Mahadeb Guri

Like our awareness when we visit the school of how the girl students are outnumbered by the boys: many youngsters do not get sent to school because they're "only" girls. Like the revelations from the village midwife about the women who die in childbirth because there's no doctor or hospital available to help in a complicated birth. This is one reason why Nepal, like other Asian countries, has an imbalance in the population of males over females.

Both Marge and I wonder what kind of life lies in store for Laxmi Darje. One day, as I sat on a rock by a river, waiting for Buddi, this beautiful and sweet thirteen-year-old set down her doko of firewood and came over to sit by me. She let loose a torrent of rapid Nepali, fixed her hazel-eyed gaze on me and beamed her breathtakingly radiant smile. I smiled back, shrugged helplessly and said "*Maile bujhina.*" ["I don't understand."] She said something about "*timro saathi*" ["your friend"], which was probably a question about the whereabouts of Marge, my almost-constant companion in Badel. I gave Laxmi my one-bead necklace that Marge had given me and told her "blue." Laxmi pointed to my wedding band and asked, "*Suun?*" ["gold?"] When I nodded, she smiled again, and kept smiling and nodding and saying "*aachh,*" apparently to agree with whatever I was saying.

What will happen to this lovely child? The daughter of a mute, widowed mother of five children, Laxmi has never gone to school. Her mother cannot spare her, because Laxmi helps to support the family. She works all day, babysitting either for her own younger siblings or for other people's children or fetching wood.

FROM MARGE'S JOURNAL:

I know I have to do something more for the young girls in Nepal. I don't know yet just what form it will take, but for starters I probably will arrange to have a sale of Nepali handicrafts for the organization Educate the Children. I want to send Laxmi to school, but she may be too old—and how to arrange it? I suppose it is best not to interfere with "their way." But it was very disturbing when Buddi told us matter-of-factly that the boys don't work in the fields as the girls do, because school is the boys' work.

What makes Laxmi's situation even more troubling to Marge and me is her status as a Darje, a member of the untouchable caste. She cannot even enter the home of a higher-caste family, and she can only marry another Darje.

What kind of future will the child have? I can't bear the awful thought that a trafficker in human flesh will spot Laxmi's beauty and her family's poverty, offer a sum the mother can't refuse to "employ" the girl—perhaps telling the family that he would find her work as a housemaid—and then sell her for $1,000 to a brothel in Bombay, India, where so many innocent young Nepali village girls, like the sixteen-year-old virgin depicted in the Indian movie *Salaam, Bombay!*, have begun lives never dreamed of in their families' worst nightmares. [A copy of *Time* Magazine that I pick up after I return home to New York reports that some 7,000 young girls from Nepal's hill villages are sold each year into prostitution.] If those parents who sell their daughters for a handful of rupees had any idea what was in store for them—debasement, servitude, beatings, AIDS—they would surely find a way to keep these enchanting girls at home. I see parents cuddling and kissing their little daughters and beaming at their older ones, and I know with a crystalline certainty that those kind people who welcome us so graciously to their homes surely value the treasures in their own families. But then I think of the mother in Rakha who asked us, only half in jest, if we wanted to take her little girls.

To me the plight of girls and women is one of the most troubling aspects of life in Nepal, and I have a hard time adopting my new attitude of eastern acceptance toward what we find here. Despite my resolution not to judge a culture I don't know well enough to understand, I can't help being heartened to see that some of this is changing, albeit ever so slowly. At least the awareness of inequality and suffering is there, as evidenced by the outrage shown by the eight Nepali authors of articles in the sad little book, *Red Light Traffic: The Trade in Nepali Girls*, which I came across in Pilgrim's Book Shop in Kathmandu. And by the locally written articles about the problems of Nepali women and children in the local magazine *Quarterly Development Review*.

thyme

Laxmi's mother

A Damai woman, I saw a sadness in her eyes. Buddhi tells me she cannot speak. She helps with outside work. She cannot enter the house of a Rai because she is a low caste Hindu.

A number of NGO's (non-governmental organizations) are working actively to reverse the patterns of centuries, to help the girls and women of Nepal create new lives for themselves. Back in Kathmandu after our village visit, we'll get the chance to meet with Keith Leslie, director of Save the Children in Nepal. He tells us about his agency's programs for more than 100 groups of women of child-bearing age (most of them, in this land of early and frequent fecundity, from ages 14 to 30). Nepali staff members teach about "family planning" (the international institutionalese euphemism for birth control); health, sanitation and nutrition; income generation; and early childhood education.

Then there's Educate the Children, the organization founded by an American businesswoman, Pamela Carson, who came to Nepal as a trekker and came back again and again as an activist. Besides sending street children to school, ETC also sponsors women's groups in communities throughout Nepal, under the premise that for children's lives to be better, their mothers must become more in control of their own lives. The women in these groups freely express feelings to each other and to their leaders that none of the women of Badel either feel, or want to show to us: feelings of being exploited by the men in their communities. They eagerly welcome the training and the loans of money they get to help them pursue such income-producing activities as raising goats, pigeons, pigs, and chickens; peanut and vegetable farming; and broom making. With these skills, which will eventually enable them to support themselves and to own their own property—and with the education they seek about their legal rights, these few lucky ones may well be on the road to independence. Will this mean a better life for them? I wish I knew.

7

A Shaman's Blessing: "Chabu-Bu-Bu-Bu"

A layman's distress is a fortune for the priest.
                                        —*Nepali proverb*

Today is Easter Sunday. It is also one of the eight days of Passover. Although I am here at a religious observance, I am in neither church nor synagogue. (Nor am I in my kitchen on Long Island making matzo balls for my family seder.)

Instead, I'm here in Badel, watching the officiant in the center of the room. Gadja Bahadur Rai is neither priest, minister nor rabbi, but a shaman in the Mudhum religion, an animistic belief that clings to the ancient gods of nature, while incorporating some of the rituals of Hinduism and Buddhism, the two most prominent faiths of Nepal. In full regalia for the shamanic ceremony he is conducting today, Gadja Bahadur wears a white cloth wrapped turban-style around his head and hanging down in back. Long light-colored, light-weight cotton trousers covered by a full gathered skirt reach almost down to his broad bare feet; a

95

garland of dried golden marigolds criss-crosses his muscular chest and back; and, around his waist, a belt jangles bells and cymbals.

Gadja Bahadur squats on his haunches before an elaborate array of ceremonial items on the floor in front of him—four pairs of animal horns, two from deer and two from the goat-like Himalayan tahr; a metal trident about the size of my salad server back home in my suburban kitchen; a pint-size cup fashioned of leaves and holding a small flickering fire; little urns overflowing with greenery; several different-sized bowls and baskets holding rice, millet, and corn; bamboo baskets containing ginger root and chunks of wood; and a bottle of *rakshi* (the ubiquitous homemade "moonshine" liquor that accompanies every Rai ceremony and social occasion).

As the shaman chants, he rhythmically strikes a metal plate with a single tahr horn, in cadence to the constant drumming behind him, a drumming that echoes rhythms that have resounded through centuries as links to the spirit world and paths to altered states of consciousness. The shaman's voice goes up and down, in a tuneless every-religion *ur*-chant, to the dozen or so people ringing the room, including Marge and me.

This sturdily built, strong-featured man of 61—just two years older than I am—reminds me of the French matinée idol Yves Montand. His good looks and his contemporaneity of age make me see him as a man, not just a representative of an exotic culture. When Marge and I met Gadja Bahadur yesterday, after we first walked into Badel, he was dressed in typical Nepalese village garb: loose cotton jodphurs, a knit sweater-vest over a long-sleeved cotton shirt, a cotton *topi* (traditional brimless hat shaped like an upside-down pail that sits on the head at a jaunty angle) and Chinese sneakers, all in the same shade of a drab grayish-beige, topped by a dark brown cotton vest. Then he did not look like the shaman (also known here as a *jhankri*, or witch-doctor) that he's been since the age of 13, but like the farmer that he is when he is not serving his neighbors spiritually. His broad, eye-crinkling smile has been consistently benign and all-inclusive. Although he is often called in cases of illness or death, today he is here on a happy occasion for the village of Badel.

Serendipitously for Marge and me, Gadja Bahadur has come today to bless the house where Marge and I are in temporary residence. And now we're ready to take part in the ceremony ourselves. It seems like a good omen that this quest, so important to both Marge and me, should coincide with important holidays in both our traditions—and should begin with a blessing. The benediction to be bestowed on both structure and occupants is typically offered two or three years after the completion of a dwelling, thus giving it the opportunity of showing that it has stood the initial test of time and is not in imminent danger of capricious collapse. The house being blessed today was built three years ago by Gokana Rai, largely with the help of his son Jai's earnings.

Both Jai and Buddi now live in Kathmandu, Nepal's capital; both speak excellent English; both have adopted many western ways. It's a revelation to see them here among the people they grew up with, as they help us bridge the gap between our culture and theirs. About a dozen friends and relatives of Gokana Rai and his wife have come early on this afternoon to join the family for the ceremonial blessing, which will protect the house from evil spirits. Although this benefit is being conferred on Gokana Rai's second house, the ceremony is taking place in Gokana's main house.

Earlier, when we first came in from the bright sunshine, I found myself squinting as my eyes adjusted to the darkness inside. Everything in this small, cramped room is dark: the ceiling, posts and walls all black from the soot of countless fires; the room itself, with barely any light coming in from the two small squares cut out of the wall that serve as windows; the people with their brown skin, their clothes in dusty, dull shades of gray, blue, brown. And as hard as I try, I can't help coughing as clouds of acrid smoke—from the fire in the pit in the center of the room and also from the hand-rolled cigarettes that every adult here keeps puffing on—invade my throat and lungs. I wouldn't stay for a minute in a New York restaurant that was half this smoky. But I'm not in New York now; I have come halfway around the world to this tiny village in the foothills of the Himalayas, seeking answers to only half-formed questions.

As Gadja Bahadur chants, one of the women in the room serves him rakshi in a hand-carved wooden cup; he murmurs some prayers, she replies. Then there's some general conversation, punctuated by laughter, among the group sitting in a semicircle on straw mats on the floor, facing the altar. A couple of the women and men direct some comments to Marge and me, and while neither of us understands the words, we absorb, and smile to, the welcoming tone, feeling honored to be included in this important occasion. But then a glimmer of doubt about this quest of Marge's and mine intrudes on my pleasure in being here: If we don't understand what these people are saying, how can we enter into their minds, as we have hoped to do, looking for a wisdom we feel sure they can impart? But I dismiss my trepidation, calling upon our passion about this journey and our confidence in our young guides and translators. Somehow we'll overcome this obstacle as we have the others we've faced down to make this trip.

We remember to sit cross-legged on the floor, twisting our ankles rather than putting our feet straight out in front of us, so that we won't offend anyone by pointing the soles of our feet toward them. Here in Nepal, the feet are considered unclean; it is a great insult to be faced with the bottoms of anyone else's feet. When my knees can't take it one more bent minute, I put both my legs together and tuck them under me sidewise as long as I can; then I shift to a kneeling position. By constantly contorting myself from one position to another, I manage. The straight-backed old woman sitting next to me keeps smiling beatifically, putting her arm around me, drawing me close to her, making me feel especially welcome here. (Earlier today she came up to our room to welcome Marge and me to her village, took each of our faces into her small, careworn hands and showered warm, smiling kisses and hugs on us both. Our nonverbal communication seemed to work.)

During the ceremony, Jai's two younger brothers, his three sisters and his two small nephews run in and out of the room, with no interruption in the proceedings. His wrinkled grandmother rolls her cigarette in a leaf from a pipal tree. As the shaman chants, he sways rhythmically forward and back— and the prayers he intones (in Nachheri, the language of the Badel Rais) carry

the same rhythmic cadence as those I have heard from Orthodox Jewish rab-
bis, Catholic prelates, Native American priests.

As he prays, Gadja Bahadur puts small amounts of millet in one hand of
each of us sitting around him. After chanting a few lines, at his signal all the
worshippers drop their fistfuls of grain into one of the bowls, as an offering to
the gods. Each bowl is set aside for a different god—the gods of the river, the
trees, the hills, the household fire. In Mudhum and other animistic religions
practiced here in the hills, there are no formal temples, no daily pujas to be
made or prayers to be spoken. As Buddi tells us, "In Mudhum we don't worship every day. We are free about religion. We just call shaman when somebody gets married, baby is born, somebody sick, or somebody gets
dead—times like these. Then we need shaman to speak to gods."

Like other shamans in other cultures, Gadja Bahadur "journeys" in an altered
state of consciousness to help the people of his community. He diagnoses and
treats illnesses, he foretells the future, he communicates with the spirits of the
dead and with other spiritual advisers to guide his own actions and those of his
fellow villagers. Buddi tells us, "The shaman must to know everything. He must
have to know how to do everything for culture, for religion."

Today, Gadja Bahadur amiably takes time out from the ritual to pose, ceremonial objects in hand, for the photo-opportunities that Jai, Marge and I
request. Then he puts on his spectacles—the only ones we'll see in this entire
village of some 1500 people—to peer at Marge's sketches in her drawing pad.
As she begins to draw him, he goes back to his own work. At one point in the
ceremony, he asks the assemblage for money, which has to be in the form of
coins, Jai tells us. In an aside to Jai, he jokes, "Two hundred rupees wouldn't
hurt!" (Even this amount—only about four U.S. dollars—would represent an
Everest of metal, since Nepalese coins are issued only in one-rupee or smaller
denominations; all other currency is issued in paper notes.)

As Jai explains the ritual to Marge and me, he can't help saying, with a
shrug and an embarrassed smile, "I don't believe this. Not any of it. But the
people here—they don't have doctors. So they come to the shaman to make
them well, to bless them, their families, their houses, the whole village." In the

midst of his explanation, Jai tells us that the shaman's 75-year-old wife (whom he married when she was a widow of 35 and he was only 21—a not uncommon arrangement in these parts) is gravely ill with kidney disease.

So when, at a certain point in Gadja Bahadur's prayers, he breaks down into loud, wrenching sobs, I whisper to Jai, "Is he worried about his wife?" Jai laughs: "No, he's talking about God—about how God left him and how he wants God to come back, so he cries. In our culture we cry a lot!" Jai—westernized, sophisticated Jai—again seems disconcerted by the beliefs he is describing to us. "I have a house in Kathmandu," he says, his white teeth gleaming. "I don't ask him to bless my house!" He shrugs and laughs. And I see the future, when fewer young people will believe in the ways of their ancestors, when the way of life in this village will be altered forever. Although the advent of modern medicine will be a gain, I fear that abandoning some of the ancient beliefs will create a void that modern culture has not figured out how to fill. Although not an observant believer myself, I always find myself stirred by ritual, in other religions as well as Judaism, and I feel a tingle of embarrassment at Jai's mocking of his people's beliefs. Especially since I've crossed continents to be here with these people.

After about an hour, Marge and I are surprised to see the shaman get up and walk out of the house, followed by the others in the room. "Where is he going?" I ask Jai. It turns out that Gadja Bahadur is heading for the jungle to look for herbs and other items to use in the ceremony; after a few hours, he'll come back to resume the blessing. The prayers will start again at about 8 p.m., along with music, drumming, singing and dancing that will go on all night. Marge and I welcome the break. After walking for three hard, hot days and sleeping fitfully in our makeshift campsites, we've both been having trouble staying awake this afternoon. We go back to our room in the other house, just a few feet away from the primary house, where the blessing will take place. We clamber up the narrow flight of a dozen short, steep, banister-less earthen steps climbing up the outside of the house, to the room we may continue to occupy for the next week, if we stay in Badel.

Before I give into the need to nap, I squash something crawling in my hair just behind my ear. "Can't be bedbugs, could it?" I ask Marge. She laughs. "Could be. Could be lice. Could be anything." On top of the straw mat is my inflated air mattress. On top of that, my sleeping bag, my previously bug-free sleeping bag.

"Oh, please," whispers this devout agnostic, remembering all the books about Nepal that I have read, many of which tell tales of travelers who attract a wide range of exotic wildlife in strange beds in far-off lands. Although I have trekked in Nepal twice before, on both trips I was well sheltered and protected by being in a group with a guide who supplied all of us trekkers with our own certified clean tents. This time there's less oversight, more uncertainty. "Oh, please, God—Jewish, Christian, Hindu, Buddhist, or Mudhum—please don't bring lice into my life!" Someone may have heard me because I never do feel any more creepy-crawlies. I fall into a deep dreamless sleep until 7:30, when Jai comes up to fetch us for the rest of the ceremony.

Marge is now coughing and feverish. She has felt sick, off and on, ever since we left Kathmandu, and over the past few days her condition has worsened, with brief moments of well-being. Now she urges me to go down to the continuation of the ceremony without her. "Take notes," she manages to croak out before falling back into a deep sleep.

One of my biggest anxieties before setting out on this trip was that one or both of us would fall ill, as travelers to this part of the world so often do. I knew the strong probability of serious intestinal or respiratory illness, or injury, and maybe worse. Days away from any medical diagnosis or care, we're on our own—except for any ministrations we might get from the shaman. I hope my worst fears are not starting to come true. Before I go down below for the ceremony, I fetch Marge's aspirin for her, along with one of the above-the-waist antibiotics we brought with us "just in case" of respiratory infection. So far we haven't touched our trove of below-the-waist nostrums against intestinal onslaughts. She again urges me to go down, and I leave her, hoping she'll shake whatever it is she has—and hoping I won't catch it.

I follow Jai down to the little courtyard, to find it packed with about fifty people—a gaggle of lively youngsters, a dozen or so teenagers, and a sprinkling of adults and babies. The teens sing and dance; old and young watch and listen. Strains of Nepalese melodies familiar from my earlier treks fill the air, as the young people sing of *"laligourans"* (rhododendrons), *"mero ghar"* ("my home"), of sweethearts and love and sadness. The dancers are mostly male, except for Jai's 20-year-old sister Mithu and their cousin, Chamana, a chunky teenager with pigtails who could easily pass for a Native American maiden. Inside Gadja Bahadur Rai continues the blessing of the house.

Seeing Mithu's open smile, I see in memory the merry faces of the three young women just about her age whom I met during my first trek, in 1987. I had first glimpsed them climbing up a grassy slope with headbands around their foreheads connected to the empty dokos on their backs. The next time I saw them they were on their way down bent under the weight of those cone-shaped baskets, now full of wood, each doko holding about 75 pounds. These fresh-faced, almond-eyed young beauties stopped, set down their burdens and sat on a large rock at the edge of the site where our group was picnicking, so that they could chat and watch us as they took out their knitting.

This lively trio of unmarried sisters joked and flirted with our staff, most of whom wandered over, attracted by the easy peals of feminine laughter. I wandered over too, and pulled out my family photos, which I had found a good vehicle for rudimentary communication in foreign lands. The sisters' gaiety, their open delight in the photo of my little blond grandson, the fun they had on this break from their day's labor stayed with me as I witnessed how hard these slight women had to work for the basic necessities of daily life—and how lightly they seemed to bear what looked like back-breaking loads. During the weeks of that first trek these three sisters came to exemplify qualities that Marge and I had found awe-inspiring, that had inspired this quest of ours.

Whenever I would see two or more Nepalis in conversation, I saw smiles and heard laughter. I thought about the lives that I and most of the people I know lead—how privileged we are, and yet how much we find to complain about. I yearned to know more about these people's outlook on life, the way they think, their inner resources. And then I met Marge, who also harbored this longing. And so here we were.

I stay with the group until about 10:30, alternating between watching the dancing outside and the ceremony inside. I'm not that sleepy anymore, but sharp pains are shooting up my back and my bent knees are aching. These aging muscles are not used to sitting for hours without back support, with feet politely tucked away on a hard floor. I can't get comfortable, and I respond to another glimmer of doubt by asking myself: "You just arrived yesterday and you're aching already—how will you do this for the next few weeks?" These villagers can squat for hours at a time, whereas my "civilized" shortened leg muscles cry out if I don't have a chair. Their backs are straight and strong, despite—or maybe because of—the doko loads they carry on their backs from early childhood on. Their teeth, by and large, hold up well in the absence of a sugary diet. Maybe I'm just too civilized.

FROM MARGE'S JOURNAL:

This afternoon, when I tossed to the children the small rubber ball I brought with me, I was surprised by how fast they caught onto the game and how well they threw and caught. Here, if you are not well coordinated, you don't last beyond your second birthday. This culture is truly an example of the survival of the fittest. The children's compact little bodies turn and twist on a dime and their tough little bare feet grip the slimy stones like suction cups. Their coordination even filters down to the fine motor skills, shown by so much of the precise work they do.

I leave the drumming and the dancing, the prayers and the people, and make my way back up to our room. Marge is sleeping heavily, and I am out as soon as I hit the bed. At 2:00 a.m. I wake to a soft, steady beat of drums from down below, and I muster up the energy to get out of bed and head down again for more of the all-night ceremony. Marge burrows deeper into her sleeping bag, so I go down alone, walking carefully down the open outdoor staircase. I make my way across the courtyard by the bright light of the full moon, and as I walk into the crowded house below and go to sit on a ledge next to a young boy, he leaps up to fetch me a round straw mat to sit on. On our trek here this courtesy has been unfailingly extended toward us—and other visitors—in every single home we have visited, no matter how humble.

As Gadja Bahadur conducts the service, a baby naps under a pile of roughly woven brown-and-white-striped blankets in a corner, and sleeping bodies of adults and children fill every niche, oblivious to the chanting and the drumming. Behind the shaman two men sit cross-legged on either side of the large drum, which is vertically suspended between two bamboo poles. Each drummer holds two long sticks in each hand and thrums two-handed constantly, rhythmically, hypnotically—ta-dum, ta-dum, ta-dum. Gadja Bahadur rises to his feet, lifts one bare foot, then the other in a half-dance, to the tinkling sounds of his bells, the soft clanging of his cymbals and the deeper thumps of the constant drumming. Ever so slowly he turns away from his altar until he faces the drum. On the top of the longer pole holding it, next to the wall, a bunch of greenery contains a few white blossoms. Continuing to intone in barely audible syllables, apparently in a trance, the shaman extends a hand to the greenery and explodes in a short, loud exclamation, "*Chabu-bu-bu-bu!*" (Jai tells me this is shamanic shorthand for: "God give me the power to cut the leaves!")

He pulls a single white flower from the top of the pole, bends over and places it in the hair of one of the drumming men. He repeats the procedure for the other drummer, but this man's flower drops, and as the drummer picks it up and puts it behind his ear, his long sticks point toward me, uncomfortably close. I instinctively move away from them, feeling as I do on crowded New York streets dodging people holding their umbrellas horizontally under their arms. (Even here on the other side of the world I realize how tied I am to my home as I keep relating my experiences here to my other life.)

The shaman keeps chanting and keeps plucking flowers and leaves to the same ritual words, "*Chabu-bu-bu-bu!*" He then tosses the blossoms and leaves to the assemblage until everyone—including me—has something, before he turns and sits again. Through all of this there's as much activity as if this were high noon instead of the middle of the night. Mithu pads out, barefoot, and returns several times in the couple of hours I'm down here. Jai loudly calls to me in English from across the room. People hold spirited side conversations among themselves. Jai's mother brings him and his father bowls of *chang* (the homemade beer made of millet that's even more omnipresent a drink than rakshi), then borrows Jai's big red flashlight to go up the dark staircase to the second floor, where she pours a cup of rakshi to bring to the shaman. In between Gadja Bahadur's solemnly intoned prayers and trances, he joins in the various conversations. Judging from the periodic bursts of deep, belly-rich laughter, he makes many lively jokes, a number of them bawdy. ("Dirty words," Jai whispers to me with a grin—and with no offer to translate—after one raucous outburst.)

This religion is not a solemn one. Maybe when religion is so much a part of people's lives that they take it for granted, they can feel at home in it, as in the nest of a loving family. They don't need formal, sober "church manners." As I ponder this, I can't help thinking that maybe this helps to explain much about another religious ceremony that's fresh in my mind: the Passover seder I attended the week before I came here, on the grounds of the Israeli Embassy in Kathmandu. A recently established annual tradition in Kathmandu, that event attracted some one thousand Jewish travelers, mostly young Israelis. I took the clamor of that audience in stride, as those energetic and raucous young cele- brants took their observance away from its ostensible leader. Video cameras whirred, flashbulbs popped, young people greeted friends they hadn't seen since the year before. A dozen colorfully garbed dancers linked arms and burst into a merry refrain. Was I romanticizing, I wondered afterward, seeing their gaiety as the joyful expression by those tough young sabras (whose very toughness is a major factor in the survival of their little nation), celebrating their common traditions, not caring about proving their Jewishness, not needing to?

No, I decide, as this very different religious observation brings that other one to mind. Those Israelis are not Jewish only on holidays, only in temple. They live their Jewishness every day of their lives, fight for it in the military, know that it is a deep part of them, at the core of their identity. And part of the activity that so embarrassed and angered the young Israeli woman who shared a taxi with Marge and me the day after the seder—the passing of marijuana back and forth during the seder service—may also be seen as incorporating intoxicants into formal rites, as Jews and Catholics ceremonially do with wine, Hindus with marijuana and Rais with chang and rakshi.

After a while, the shaman stops his chanting, sits and chats and drinks and jokes. "He is taking a rest," Jai explains. Gadja Bahadur has taken two or three such rests since 8 o'clock, which will allow him to continue the ceremony until daybreak. During his break, he stands up, walks over to a corner of the room, lifts out a standing partition and blows his nose behind it, Nepali style, covering one nostril with his hand and letting loose exuberantly with the other, in effect using the floor as his handkerchief. I've been having great trouble keeping my eyes open, and this seems like a propitious moment to leave. As I carefully climb the stairs to the bedroom my friend and I are sharing, I am overwhelmed by an intensity of conflicting emotions.

This celebration falls on the eve of the Nepali New Year—2050. To my question whether this ceremony was in observance of the New Year, Jai gave that upward, sideways shake of the head that here in Nepal means "no." Nor is it, as I'd first thought, in tribute to Marge's and my first night in Badel, nor even in honor of Jai's homecoming, his first in three years. It is purely to bless the house, and only coincidental with regard to all these other occasions.

This inconsequential misunderstanding brings home to me how much of an alien I am in this world. Still, this is what I have come for—to step into another world, a way of life so different from mine at home, a way of life that is sure to vanish within the next century, but a way of life that can teach me lessons I could never learn on Long Island.

I can't help thinking that it is more than coincidence that this holiday so closely overlaps with the major Christian and Jewish holy days of Easter and Passover, the one that Marge observes, the other that I do. This confluence seems like a fruitful omen to the quest my friend and I have embarked upon— to try to absorb the wisdom of these people who impressed us so much when we met them so superficially as tourists trekking in their beautiful land. Can we delve below those smiles and that courtesy and that friendliness to discover the core of beliefs that will help us live our own lives more fruitfully? Or will such deep knowledge elude us? Are we deluding ourselves over what we can learn in just a few weeks' time, when we and our would-be teachers don't even share a common language? Are we guilty of hubris? Or just naivete? Only time will tell. Here in this house that has been so amply blessed I drift off into a deep sleep to the soothing pulse, pulse, pulse of the drums.

8

Changing Expectations: Grandma Boy and Grandma Yeti

When you raise a cow, she provides food. But when you raise your brother, he provides brotherhood.

—Nepali proverb

We are having a relaxed afternoon at Jai's house. The lamb is asleep in its basket. The rooster is strutting around the yard. Half a dozen tiny fluffy chicks are hopping about. A couple of mangy ducks waddle around. They have white breasts, red beaks, black-and-white speckled heads and iridescent green feathers on their wings. These young Chinese ducks will grow into their clownishly big webbed feet, will grow fat—and will become dinner. Although they belong to fourteen-year-old Prem now, they are not his pets. Like farm children everywhere, village youngsters neither name nor become sentimentally attached to their animals. They know

109

and accept the animals' purpose in life, which is to help sustain the lives of the human beings who own them.

Bikas, Indra's seven-year-old son, and Ghaum Bahadur Darje, 10, a neighbor boy, have been standing around in the yard, shifting from one foot to the other, silently watching us with dark saucer eyes, and occasionally whispering and giggling to each other. Although Darje children cannot enter the homes of non-Darje villagers, they play freely with the other children, and in the schoolyard, children from different castes casually stroll with their arms around each other. In Badel, "untouchable" does not really mean untouchable. Neither of these boys goes to school, although Bikas will go in a year or two. Ghaum has made it over to the school on two occasions but cannot go regularly because he has to help his mother take care of several younger siblings.

Marge has just given the boys crayons and paper to draw pictures. Bikas makes a few tentative purple lines; Ghaum makes a single scribble and then shyly stops. Neither boy has ever held a pencil, pen or crayon before. Bikas is supposed to be watching his baby brother, Monos, who, like other 11-month-olds, is more interested in exploring the Crayola box than the crayons in it.

I get up from the steps where we have been sitting and go into the kitchen to investigate the rattling noise and elusively familiar aroma wafting out to the porch. Indra, sitting cross-legged on the floor in front of the open fire, her legs drawn up under her lunghi, is vigorously shaking a long flat pan back and forth, making popcorn. When I come in, she smiles widely up at me and lets me have a go at the pan, but I don't shake it fast enough to suit her, so with a jolly laugh, she takes it back. I'm humbled by the number of simple tasks that I don't know how to do, at which every adult here is competent. What better lesson could I learn about cultural priorities?

Hanging from a rack over the fire are the legs and side of ribs cut from the pig that Tara Mani slaughtered this morning. At 5:45 this morning I saw Jai's family's pig for the first time. At 7 o'clock this morning I saw it alive for the last time. Tara Mani, with help from Kangsha, plunged a sharp bamboo stick into the animal, just below what would, in a human, be the armpit. It hit a main artery, blood spurted and the end came instantly. We had heard the porker squealing loudly as they were catching it, obviously in a clear presentiment of its coming doom. But the actual killing was so fast that only a quick couple of squeals emerged before the deed was done. This was Tara Mani's first pig-sticking; he did it like a pro. (Something else I wouldn't have the faintest idea how to do. But this skill I wouldn't be expected to know; here in Badel killing a pig is a job reserved strictly for men. This is not a gender-blind society.)

The next step involved covering the pig's carcass with straw and setting that on fire to burn off the bristles. The children formed a silent ring around the pen watching the singeing and skinning. "Killing pig," Jai tells us, "we only do for important times." Today he is the cause of the important time: Tonight will be Jai's last dinner home for who knows how long—maybe another three years? Tomorrow, after the meat has smoked for a full day, Jai will carry some back to Kathmandu in the bamboo doko we saw Gora's brother weave today. Every village has its own distinct pattern that is woven into the doko, so hill people can, with one look, almost always tell where a basket came from.

Part of the relaxation here is not knowing the language, not having to make conversation, being able just to sit and let the unknown syllables wash over me. It's the same kind of peaceful feeling I have known when I have been in the woods and heard nothing but the soughing of the wind in the trees. I noticed this even in the tumult of the Kathmandu airport when we were waiting for our flight to Lamidanda. When all I heard was Nepali, it was like music playing softly in the background. I could write, think, be solitary. But as soon as that very large, very loud American woman and her guide sat down next to me and spoke English, I was jolted out of my solitude, forced against myself to pay attention to their conversation. I have not yet mastered the Buddhist ability to be alone in a crowd—at least, a crowd of English speakers.

An old neighbor woman comes into the courtyard, sits on her haunches for a while, intently observing me. Then, absolutely overcome with curiosity, she asks Tara Mani a burning question. He looks over at me, answers her and they both laugh. By this time, I'm curious.

"What did she ask you?" I ask Tara Mani.

"Aama wants to know if you're a boy or a girl. I tell her, 'girl.'" He laughs merrily again.

Sure, here I am. Under my long baggy sweater, my breasts are not obvious. My plain unpatterned navy blue skirt is unlike the brightly printed lunghis of the women, more like the one the village shaman wears when he conducts ceremonies. My hair is cut very short, shorter even than that of most of the men and boys, and I wear no ribbons in it. I have small gold rings in my ears, but then so do many young men these days. I have a small ring on one toe; no one of either sex in Badel (or at home in Port Washington either, so far as I know) wears one of these. And my nose is naked, with no gold or gems either on the side or through the septum. How is anyone to know that I'm a woman? All the signs that in my culture point so clearly to my femaleness are as meaningless here as the words in this language I'm ignorant of are to me.

Marge bursts out laughing: "If they think you're a man, they must think I'm a yeti!"

FROM MARGE'S JOURNAL:

In any ordinary place there would be no question of Sally's gender. But this is no ordinary place. That is why we are here. At five feet, eight inches, I am tall, taller than anybody in the village, male or female. Buddi is the tallest man, and I am at least an inch taller than he is. Today I am wearing purple flowered pants and a loose black shirt. On other days I wear my alternate outfit, a purple tee shirt and a denim skirt with a large red dragon on its front, embroidered by a Kathmandu tailor. I am weighed down with jewelry. Gold penetrates my ears, four bracelets encircle my wrists, two pendants hang from chains that tangle with the amber and turquoise chokers that decorate my neck.

It is not vanity alone that causes me to adorn myself with all this metal and beads. Several years ago while walking alone in the Rolwaling valley, I was chased by some curious young girls on their way home from working in the fields. They tried to lift my skirt, and I was only able to free it from their strong hands because they were encumbered by their dokos. When I told Peter, he guffawed and said, "Why didn't you just show them you're a woman?" Now I leave nothing to guesswork in Nepal. I decorate my body as I see the local women do. I have everything they have except a nose ring, and I'm thinking of getting one of those.

So from now on it is "Grandma Boy" and "Grandma Yeti," who throughout these three weeks in these hills continue to learn that our way is not their way, that so many of the customs and signs that we take for granted at home do not apply here.

As we have become used to being aware that anyone can feel free at any time to walk into our room without knocking, to relieving ourselves by squatting in the fields or in the outdoor *charpi* (latrine), to emphasizing how old we are rather than how young we can act or look, and to countless other different but equally valid ways of looking at the universe, we have been able to let go of our attachments to one preconception after another.

Every other trip I have ever taken—even to other Third World countries, even my previous treks in Nepal—have paid strong obeisance to my standards of convenience and comfort as an upper-middle-class American. Even in the simplest of tourist accommodations or the most casual group camp, I have been insulated much more from local customs than I realized at the time.

Even here, of course, Marge and I are protected and coddled and treated largely in terms of our backgrounds. But by being in this village where we are the only foreigners (for that matter, the only non-villagers) and where we are living with local families, we are privileged to open a much wider window into other ways of doing things. In some ways we are like Alice, stepping through the Looking Glass into a world in which little is the same as it was on the other side. Badel is our Looking Glass. We still, of course, see this Wonderland with our American eyes and process it through our American brains. But now that we have stepped through the mirror, we realize that our perceptions of the world, on both sides, will never again be as they were.

OM RAI   6 YEARS OLD
two years ago he had
a cleft lip repaired.
now he has a beautiful
smile.

M Roche

9

Medical Miracles: New Smiles

The fragrance of a flower spreads in the neighborhood; the essence of a man reaches beyond the hills.

—*Nepali proverb*

Besides the small gifts we have brought for individual villagers, Jai and Buddi suggested the perfect present for the entire village. Before we left Kathmandu they asked us whether we would like to contribute toward the cost of a volleyball and net. In concert, Marge and I said we would reimburse them for the total cost—all of twenty dollars. Within an hour of our arrival, the net is in place in the school yard, and an hour or so later, after leaving his card game to greet his family, Buddi asks us, "You need me? No? Okay, I go play volleyball with my friends. See you later."

Since Buddi helped to build the court in the school yard some years ago, volleyball, the only sport in Badel, became wildly popular with the village boys and young men. After so much punishment, the first ball is now patched and threadbare, and the net is

115

too full of rips and holes for even these resourceful Nepalis to fix. Still, the old ball is kept in play. Jai's young brothers bat it over a length of bamboo set on stakes in their side yard.

There is another, much more important gift that Marge and I plan to leave here. After everyone in Jai's family has received some little thing, we hold court in the front yard. Relatives, neighbors, old friends of Jai's keep coming around to get a look at us. We're delighted, since the more villagers we see and meet, the happier we are.

We're especially happy when our porter Mon Bahadur Bhujel comes around, proudly showing off his family—his wife, two daughters and two sons. Mani, as he is known, is quieter than the other staff members, possibly because he is older, or maybe because he either speaks no English or is bashful about doing so. He communicates goodwill through smiles and nods. And through today's visit.

His real name is Mon Bahadur Darje, but Jai "rechristened" him "Bhujel" instead of Darje so that when Mani goes on trek, no one will know that he belongs to the untouchable Darje caste. I would think that Mani's dark complexion would give him away, but apparently there are other swarthy ethnic groups here that don't fall into the lowest caste. If Mani's true status were known, he would not be able to stay in anyone's house, and often on trek the staff takes shelter in private homes. Jai tells us, "In Kathmandu and on trek, we don't go by those customs. But in village we honor them." Here in Badel neither Mani nor his wife and children can enter the homes of any villagers other than fellow Darjes.

Mani's twelve-year-old daughter is named for the Hindu goddess Kumari, the beautiful virgin incarnation of Parvati, bride of the great and all-powerful Shiva. Kumari has been worshipped for centuries, since at least as early as the sixth century A.D. In Kathmandu when I visited the Temple of Kumari, I saw the pretty little "Living Goddess," heavily made up and dressed in gorgeous gold and crimson robes, as she appeared briefly at her upper-story window.

According to this cult of virgin worship, a little girl is chosen at the age of five to be the Kumari, or the Living Goddess. After being taken from her family to live in the temple, she is waited upon in every aspect of her daily life—until puberty when she begins to menstruate and is sent back to her family. A new Kumari is then chosen. It is considered bad luck for a man to marry a former Kumari. No wonder: How can a former goddess metamorphose into a properly submissive Nepali wife? I can't help wondering what kind of life the Living Goddess can have as an adult. What a novel could be written about her when she rejoins the world!

The child who will be the Living Goddess has to meet strict criteria of eligibility. These include perfect health, no loss of teeth or other cause of bleeding, black hair and eyes, a well-proportioned body and a face free of blemish. Mani's daughter Kumari has beautiful dancing eyes—large and dark and deeply set—and glossy black hair. Both features could have put her in the running for the Kumari—if only she were not an untouchable! And then we see that being an untouchable is the least of Kumari's problems.

Like the other girls and women of Badel, Kumari wears a scarf around her head and shoulders; unlike them, she keeps it drawn over the lower part of her face. We understand why when, after a few minutes, the scarf drops to reveal a cleft lip. Kumari seems to want to smile, but her split lip is drawn up into a snarl, as if a thread had been sewn from the nostril to the lip and then gathered up. Several teeth and the gums on the left side of her mouth are exposed by the deformity. Reality hits us hard. This is no Utopia when a pretty little girl with an easily treatable defect goes untreated. Kumari is the third Nepali child I've seen with this condition. The condition is more prevalent here and in other Asian countries; furthermore, it's seen less often in the States since it is repaired so routinely in infancy.

Marge and I have an experience that is amazingly frequent during our month together: we both have the same thought at the same time. I still don't remember which of us utters the first word on the subject, but I do know that the other one picks it up immediately. We agree, with virtually no discussion, to arrange and pay for an operation to repair Kumari's lip. But will Kumari's parents permit our intervention or will they consider it interference? We ask Jai and Buddi to find out. In their usual matter-of-fact tone, they say, "Maybe. We will see." Their reaction shows no more surprise than if we had asked whether it will rain today. It is not easy to read the Rais by what they say; while they are open and generous with laughter and smiles, they are not spendthrifts with words.

We also ask Buddi what would be involved, and we learn that we would be paying for Kumari and one of her parents to go to Kathmandu by plane or bus, for the costs of both of them staying there for as long as she needs to remain in or near the hospital and for the surgery itself. Buddi thinks, "Maybe one hundred dollars for everything." For the price of a New York dinner for two at a moderately upscale restaurant this girl's life can be transformed.

We hope that Kumari is still young enough to get a good result. We know that surgeons can do amazing things for infants with this condition, and that volunteer foreign doctors come regularly to Nepal to perform such operations. We don't know the prognosis for patients who have reached the teen years. We'll need to find out.

Since Mani also works as a porter for Peter Owens, some money might be able to come from Peter's trekker alumni, who often contribute money to help his staff with medical and other emergencies, to send their children—especially their daughters—to school, and to help in countless other situations. Probably, however, Marge and I will pay it all ourselves. After all, how many opportunities do any of us get in a lifetime to transform the life of another human being?

Buddi speaks to Mani in rapid-fire Nepali. He turns to us to tell us that Mani happily agrees to the surgery. Without it, Kumari has no chance for marriage. She would be an impoverished outcast all her adult life. Mani tells Buddi that he would have had it done a long time ago, but he did not have the money. Then Mani says something else to Buddi. "He says his brother's son, three-year-old Om, has the same thing," Buddi tells Marge and me. We look at each other and say, "We'll do him, too." We'll have to wait to make the arrangements until after our stay in the village, when we'll get the information we need in Kathmandu.

We're relieved that no one—not Mani, nor Buddi, nor anyone else—thanks us extravagantly for our proposal. It's less embarrassing for us, since we don't want to feel like Ladies Bountiful. We're not surprised at the lack of expressed gratitude. There was no word for thank you in the Nepali language until westerners began to come, and even now the word *dhanyabad* is used sparingly. This fits in with the view that those who do a good deed are helping themselves even more than they help the recipient of the favor, since they are thus ensuring themselves a better life in their next reincarnation. So by taking care of little Om too, we're doubling our chances for reward in the next go-around! (This philosophy echoes that in Judaism, in which anonymous charity is considered the highest form and in which doers of good deeds should not be thanked because by doing them, the donors are ensuring that their names will be written in the Book of Life, which God will see when it comes time to determine whether they should go to Heaven.)

The next day we take photos of Kumari and Om, in case the doctor in Kathmandu will want an advance look. The surgery will have to wait until the summer monsoon season, when the children's fathers will be able to take the time from their work—Mani from his portering and his brother from his farming—to take the children to Kathmandu and stay there with them for the week or so needed.

Two weeks later, Marge and I are back in Kathmandu. A couple of days before we are to leave Nepal, Buddi fetches us from the Hotel Potala, and we all take a tempu to the Kanti Children's Hospital, where we'll make inquiries about the cleft-lip repairs for Kumari and Om.

What a satisfying end to our trip—this hospital visit! A tall Newari man in a white coat turns out to be an administrator; he suggests to Buddi that we speak to a Dr. Babu Ram Marasain on the surgical ward. But the doctor is out. We get a clue to where he might be: A sign on the wall invites all doctors to come to a noon celebration of the hospital's thirtieth anniversary, followed by a seminar on rehydration, an important health measure in this country where diarrhea is a big baby-killer. It's now 11:45 a.m.

I look up to see a sign that I can't imagine finding in a large public hospital in the United States:

"HOSPITAL IS A TEMPLE.
PATIENTS ARE GODS.
MEDICINE THE RELIGION.
NURSING A WORSHIP."

Another sign speaks eloquently of the importance of children and the need for their dedicated care. Marge exclaims over the sense of caring communicated here: "Someone is really working here to see that children come first. In the States, you so often get the sense from doctors, nurses and hospital staff that patients are a nuisance. But where would all these health professionals be without patients? Without a job!"

The three of us climb the broad staircase to the upper floors, still looking for information about the lip operations. No one looks at us with any special interest; no one stops us; no one asks where we're going. Clearly, patient security is not an issue in Nepal. We wander the halls until we come to the door leading to the operating theater.

FROM MARGE'S JOURNAL:

First I am shaken to tears for the poverty and the dinginess of the old gray cement buildings, but everywhere I look, I see signs and illustrations explaining the care given and the importance of children to the world. This is unlike any hospital I have ever seen. But what I do see is caring and love and lots of cleaning going on. In Kathmandu it is impossible to keep the dust down so everything gets filthy an hour after it's washed. But everywhere we go we see washing, washing, washing. I begin to notice that there is an orderliness amidst what I first thought was a very haphazard casual operation.

I stop and read the categories of surgery and their prices listed outside the operating room. Some of the operations are very sophisticated, although no heart surgery is done here. I introduce myself as a former nurse to a woman I assume to be the charge nurse (she is) and ask if we can have a tour of the "operating theater." She brings us gowns, slippers, masks and caps to wear, and then shows us around the three rooms—emergency surgery, minor surgery and major surgery. No throw-away instruments here. They do use disposable IV tubing and needles and that's about it. They autoclave and reuse rubber gloves. It all reminds me of Wesly Hospital back in 1950. We reused everything then.

We finally find a doctor, who explains the procedures for Kumari and Om. The children will have to stay a week, and their hospital care and operations will cost well under $100 per child. Buddi again says that $200 will more than cover the bus transport of both children and their fathers from Badel, the operations, and any other expenses. He offers to put the two men up in his apartment in Kathmandu, so they will not have to pay rent. This evening we take Peter Owens to dinner and discuss the plans with him. He agrees to help Buddi in any way needed. We all feel happy that this summer both Kumari and Om will have beautiful new smiles.

Six months later, in October, Marge and I are both back home. We receive a fax from Peter:

"Namaste, Both operations have been done. Buddi is on trek so I have not seen him, but Jai has given me details. The boy went perfectly. The girl had one stitch open up during post-operative care. She may need a "touch-up" in the future. Jai said both much better than before and $200 covered everything."

Both Marge and I write immediately to Buddi, asking him to get an advance from Peter for Kumari's second operation if she needs one, and telling him we will pay all expenses for the second surgery, too. A week later Buddi's letter to us crosses ours in the mail:

"Namaste! I am fine here and I hope that you are also fine and in good health over there. Kumari and Om Bhugel's lip operation was success. They came Kathmandu in starting of September with their fathers Mon Bahadur and Bharunei Bhugel. The doctor advice them, if the patient get some problem, they must come back in Kathmandu. I have enough money which you left. I bought them some clothes, too. They seem very happy. They already gone home in September. I will send you a picture of them later."

Four months after we received this letter, the photo comes of Kumari and Om, post-surgery. I have to smile myself when I see the picture of Om, a sweet, normal looking little boy with a shy expression. But then my heart sinks as I see the bad news the camera reveals about Kumari. The photo is not a clear one. Kumari's face is so obscured by the long shadows falling across the yard that it is hard to see what she looks like. What we can make out, though, is discouraging. Her appearance does not seem much improved. It looks as if modern medicine, the efforts of her family, her neighbor, the doctors and two foreign women failed this young girl, doomed her to the prison of her defect.

Both Marge and I are mystified then by Buddi's upbeat letters to each of us:

"I checked Kumari and Om this time with my doctor friend. His house is next village, called Bakachol. He advice us better to not do another operation. It looks not bad."

So we don't know whether Kumari will ever get the beautiful new smile we wanted to give her. We don't know whether Mani and Buddi are putting a good face on the situation because they don't want to pursue the matter further. Or whether Kumari's age worked against her and no better result is possible. Or whether the slipped stitch sabotaged the surgery. Or whether something else went wrong. Or whether the child is still willing to undergo more pain and discomfort in the pursuit of that new smile. Or whether another operation can even give her that precious gift.

In any case, it is at this moment, in the shock of seeing this grimly disappointing picture, that both Marge and I begin to set our dates for a return to Badel. We have given this child hope. We cannot abandon her now without doing everything within our power to fulfill the promise we made. No, this Kumari will never be the Living Goddess. But if this lovely child can, after all, lead a normal life among her people, that simple, splendid result may well be the most important consequence of the visit to Badel of two grandmothers from the other side of the world.

[Afterword: Since this chapter was written, Marge and I have returned to Badel three times, and she came back again by herself, most recently in 2000. We have seen Kumari and Om on each visit. Today no one would ever know that Om ever had any defect; he is a good-looking little boy who loves to dance and almost always flashes a smile. Kumari too smiles easily and often, even though her surgery was not the overwhelming success that Om's was. Upon the last visit, we were disappointed to learn that she has not yet married, but there is still hope that she will find a good husband and have a good life.]

We all played hop scotch — On the line is out!! The children and adults learn the rules quickly.

10

Lessons:
The Lesson Learned Is Not
Always the Lesson Sought

To find a god while looking for a stone.

—Nepali proverb

On Tuesday morning, two days after our arrival in Badel, Buddi's brother-in-law, Dhan Bahadur Rai, 48 years old, stops by Jai's house one morning to meet the American visitors, and incidentally to practice conversational English. Dhan married Buddi's older sister, Gita, eighteen years ago, and for these same eighteen years Dhan has been an English teacher in the village school. He admits to us with a wry smile and an embarrassed shrug, however, "I don't speak it well because I do not practice. I can read it. I can write a good letter. But education here is not good. Nepal is a small country, very poor."

What can I say to him? Yes, Nepal is very, very poor by any economic measure. In fact, the paradox of Nepal is that many of the country's charms, the very qualities that endear it so to travelers, stem precisely from its poverty: its isolation, its remoteness, its vast differences from the industrialized world.

But what will happen when and if this nation's economy improves and it achieves the kind of progress that those of us who love it would want for its people? Will we still love it? What's more to the point, how will progress that comes in the form of better roads, better communication and a higher standard of living change its people? Will the change be for the better? As a believer in education, I'm convinced that better education would help Nepalis deal with the changes in their society that are sure to come. As a realist, I have to concede that Nepal has a long way to go before its school system comes up to what we in the western world would consider the most minimal level.

Marge and I know about the high illiteracy rate in Nepal, especially among the women. We have visited schools in poor villages during our previous treks and lamented their lack of what we consider the most basic appurtenances. Some don't even have buildings; I remember stopping on trek to spend a little time with a class of barefoot children whose bodies were barely covered with rags being taught in a "school" that had a thatched roof but no walls, no structure of any kind other than the poles holding up the roof.

We arrived in Badel three days ago, and still don't know where we're heading from here. Although we've wanted to explore Badel as much as possible before we set out for another, more remote hamlet, because of the heavy rains over the past two days we have not strayed far from Jai's house, not even to the little village school that we have been so eager to visit. Finally, on this sunny Wednesday afternoon, we walk up the hill with Buddi, our backpacks loaded with pens, crayons, paper, flash cards and a few picture books with simple English text that we have brought from home.

When we reach the cleared piece of level land a ten-minute hike up from Jai's house, we realize why Buddi discouraged us from visiting in the rain or its immediate aftermath: What is now the volleyball court would, after rain, be viscous mud flats. And then there are those steep outside stairs that would be like a slick ice slide when wet. And that incredibly narrow balcony leading into classrooms for the older children. I'm glad we waited. But I wonder what it was like for the children, who had to come to school in spite of the rains?

FROM MARGE'S JOURNAL:

The school is a two-story stone structure with four classrooms on the first floor. A flight of narrow plastered stairs outside the building leads to a treacherous catwalk 18 inches wide. There is no protective banister or railing on either the stairs or the catwalk. There are only the uprights that support the roof. Absolutely nothing would stop a fall of 12 feet to the cement-hard clay below.

The older children have to walk this dangerous thoroughfare to reach the three upper-grade classrooms and the office, all on the second floor. Knowing all too well how children push and roughhouse, it is a wonder to me that the graveyard down by the river is not full to capacity with dead boys and girls with broken heads. I ask Buddi, "Do children ever fall off here?" His answer, "Sometimes," with the rising intonation that in "their way" tells me little except not to pursue the subject. I take many pictures. My daughter, a lawyer who represents school boards in liability cases, will never believe my description without documentation.

We walk along the catwalk, pressing our shoulders to the cement wall so we won't slip off the edge, and enter the sixth graders' room. Like the five other classrooms, it is lit only by the open doorway and one small window on the opposite side. Also like the other classrooms, its walls are bare of any decoration and it has no furniture except for a few rough-hewn wooden benches and long narrow tables in front that serve as desks. The twenty-one students—fifteen boys and six girls—sitting on these benches rise as we enter the dim room.

FROM MARGE'S JOURNAL:

I introduce myself and say, "I am from America." I also say proudly, using my limited Nepali, "Nepali naramro"" A look of shock crosses the staring young faces.

Jai, who has followed us into the classroom, saves me from further disgrace. "No, you mean your Nepal language not good, not Nepal people not good." I had started out my acquaintance with these children with my big sandaled western foot right in my mouth! Jai makes the correction, along with my apologies, to the children. My acculturation leads me to expect rowdiness, rudeness or at least a few giggles. No. They forgive my blooper and are all attentiveness and eagerness to please and even to hear what we have to tell them.

At 11, Buddi's brother Kiran is the youngest and the smallest child in the sixth class; the oldest are a handsome seventeen-year-old young man with a deep voice and a bosomy sixteen-year-old young woman in pigtails. Marge and I ask each pupil in turn: "What is your name?" Each stands and answers slowly and precisely, "My name is…" To our "How old are you?" each carefully replies, "I am…years old." For the most part, their conversational skills do not go much beyond this.

We show them pictures in the books we brought, and they show us their books. Unlike American school books, theirs (which they have to buy themselves, along with their pens, pencils and notebooks) seem pretty dull, with no story lines, no lively characters, no brightly colored illustrations, nothing to entice a reluctant learner. These children learn mostly by rote. Most of their answers to us are halting; there's some shyness, some nervousness, and a general lack of ease with English, which they began studying two years ago, in the fourth grade.

Marge and I have been so impressed by the facility in reading and speaking English shown by Kiran that we wonder how the Badel school overcame its limitations to turn out such an accomplished young scholar. Kiran's accomplishments look even more impressive here in class than they did before when he visited us at Jai's house. As young as he is, he is the most proficient speaker of English here. Bright-eyed, alert, eager to learn—and to practice what he's learned, he stands out. Maybe this is less a tribute to the school than it is to his family, his upbringing, his native intelligence and the role model he has in "Buddi-Dai" (Kiran's affectionate term for his older brother). There may well be a strong connection between the fact that Buddi was the first person in Badel to graduate from university and that Kiran shows strong signs of following in his brother's accomplished footsteps.

Marge, a natural teacher, moves over to the blackboard, which is just that—a slab of wood painted black. She has learned a few pointers from her husband, Dwyer, who for eight years has been a volunteer teacher of English as a foreign language. He has taught children and adults in the United States, and also in Poland and Indonesia. Dwyer has told Marge: "Speak slowly. Use few words. Use body language." She draws a boot and writes the word, which the class knows. She goes on to more of the wardrobe: skirt, shirt, pants. They know them all. But when she gets to "blouse," the only one who gets it is Kiran, who sounds it out phonetically.

FROM MARGE'S JOURNAL:

I ask one of the older boys to read from his English textbook. He reads the paragraph slowly but correctly. I cannot ask him to tell me if he knows what he has just read because I cannot speak his language. I am lost. The children, though, have not lost interest. They wait quietly and patiently to hear what other gems of knowledge this big person from America in the purple flowered pants and big boots has to drop on them. I sing "Eensy weensy spider" and bow out to the sound of their laughter and mine.

Jai takes us into the office to meet the teachers, who congregate there between classes—and more than occasionally, during classes. This is the only room in the building with decorations on the walls. We see a map of Nepal; a couple of posters showing the English alphabet, but none of the Nepali alphabet; one encouraging family planning ("Two children are enough"); one encouraging parents to send their daughters, as well as their sons, to school; and one promoting immunizations for children. The Shree Jalpa Lawor Secondary School of Badel has six teachers, who instruct their 250 students from first through sixth grades in Nepali, English, Sanskrit, mathematics, sociology, history, science, health and agriculture.

The first teacher we meet is the only woman on the faculty; in Nepal teaching is almost entirely a male profession. This attractive young sari-clad woman barely says a word in either English or Nepali; we don't understand what she does say, and she doesn't seem to understand most of what we say. It comes as a surprise, then, to learn that she is the school's other English teacher. After we learn that she walks two hours from her home village to get here each school day, we understand that her near-silence may stem more from fatigue than from ignorance of English.

We also meet a couple of the male teachers, and I wonder who's in the classroom with all the children. After our visits to this school and the one in Rakha, I'm not surprised when two weeks later, back in Lamidanda for our return flight to Kathmandu, Kristi, the Peace Corps worker teaching in the Lamidanda school, answers our question, "What do you think the schools need most?" with "For the teachers to go to class!" Of course, if teachers were better paid and better educated, if they didn't have such grueling daily commutes, if they had the great stores of supplies and teaching aids that we in America take for granted, they would undoubtedly be more highly motivated to teach.

As it is, these children are so well behaved most of the time that even during all those unsupervised hours, they do their work and stay out of trouble. Throughout our days in the village, we don't see children being scolded, spanked or even isolated, either at home or in school. Neither do we see children acting mean, aggressive or disobedient. These children do what adults ask them to do, and although they horse around with one another, their boisterousness rarely gets out of hand.

Why, I wonder? Because the children here get more attention when they're younger than ours do, as American parents rush around, pressured by multiple demands on their time? But the parents in Badel cannot afford to focus solely on their children: they work hard all day, and the little ones are often minded by an older sibling or a neighbor, right from infancy. So that's not it. Because their life is simple? Because they don't have roomfuls of toys and clothes and gadgets and an onslaught of visual and aural noise to distract them? Because their society expects respect and decent behavior—and gets it? We don't know the reason, but we love the result.

These children are not namby-pamby goody-goodies, though. They're high-spirited and lively, fun to be with, quick to laugh, able to find amusement and delight in the simplest aspects of daily life. And there's not the same worry about their safety. After all, any kid who can survive the catwalk at the school every day isn't going to fall off a mere mountain.

Comes recess time, and all the children rush out onto the second floor balcony. They tear down its length and clop down the steps in the flip-flops most of them wear. They dash over to the hillside where we've been sitting and watching the volleyball game being played by Jai, Buddi, Gora, Tara Mani and a passel of village boys and men we don't know.

The children quickly surround us, and, our view of the game completely obliterated, we switch our attention to make the most of their eager presence. Marge holds up her sketchbook to show them the pictures she has drawn, and we're grateful for the respectful three-foot envelope of air they leave around us. And for the fact that they don't push or fight for a better position. Marge then draws from her bag one of the most inspired items she brought with her, brightly colored squares of origami paper, which she folds into animals and birds that she then gives to the children.

FROM MARGE'S JOURNAL:

I make six swans and give them to the smallest children. I thought I was careful to spread these gifts around, but somehow, of these six foldings one little boy ends up with two and about 20 get none. I cannot make him understand that he should share and give up one of his papers. To my surprise the other children seem to accept this unfair distribution, and they don't try to grab anything away from him. This is almost too good to be true.

I put on my own show for another throng of children who either can't get close to Marge or don't have the patience to watch her making paper animals.

As I sing and act out songs like "Old McDonald" and "Hokey-pokey," I try to get my gang of onlookers to participate, but only a few join in. Mostly they just love watching me, and they swarm in until I can't see anything but rapt little runny-nosed faces under thick dark heads of hair. They crowd around so closely—leaving no envelope of air this time—that I feel oxygen deprivation.

This culture holds a very different sense of personal space than ours does, possibly because most of these people live, sleep and eat so close to one another. Space is a luxury they not only don't have; they don't even seem to think about it. I'm not used to all these bodies all this close, but I'm enjoying it—until I suddenly get visions of head lice, viruses and bacteria jumping from their adorable little heads to my big one. In self-defense, feeling like Gulliver, I jump up. I also get some fresh air as I loom above the Lilliputians.

It's hard for me to accept the Nepalis' laissez-faire attitude toward school. Although official starting time is 10:00 a.m., so many kids and teachers come late that actual starting time is not until after 11:00. The second week we're in Badel, Tuesday is a holiday, Thursday is an all-day field trip with a long hike, Friday is a half day and school is never in session on Saturday. Sunday morning, a regular work and school day in Nepal, we walk over to the school to give away more supplies and to talk to the health worker who is supposed to be there but isn't. We wonder whether the buzz we heard about her presence in the village was no more than an unfounded rumor. Or maybe she's already been here and left. Life here in Badel seems to hold many more uncertainties than life at home, and the only way to be comfortable with them seems to be an easygoing acceptance of whatever transpires. Which, of course, would be a useful way to deal with the uncertainties back home also.

When we arrive for our second visit to the school, a little after 11 on Sunday, half of the student body is milling about outside on the field, the headmaster is nowhere on the premises and only three teachers are present. None of them is with the pupils; they're all in the office, talking to each other. Amazing that any of the children learn anything! This is when Buddi tells us that the English teacher is tired, after having walked two hours to get here.

Marge says, "We should all volunteer to take a class!" and Buddi takes her seriously. So Marge takes the sixth class, I nervously take the fifth and Buddi keeps order downstairs.

FROM MARGE'S JOURNAL:

Not having the slightest idea what I'm going to teach, I pick the sixth class because they are the oldest and know the most English words. Now to remember some of the things Dwyer told me. I draw pictures on the boards and say the names of different items of clothing and some action words. We talk about the sounds the letters make, and before I know it, the thirty minutes are up. I don't know how much they will retain, or if they learned anything, but they are attentive and seem to enjoy the lesson. Imagine a Nepali walking into a sixth grade classroom in America and holding the children's attention while speaking only Nepali—and without a teacher there to maintain discipline!

As for me, I find teaching hard work! Although I have no idea what to do, I plunge in. First, I take the picture book we brought with us today, and emphasize saying the numbers in English. The children know their numbers already, and I make a game of having the class call the numbers out to me. Then I sing "This Old Man" very slowly, with motions to teach numbers and body parts. I don't know how much the children learn, but I've never had such an absorbed audience, not even with my own children. (But then I wasn't an exotic stranger to my own children.) I go around the room asking names and ages; I ask them questions from their English book; I go through the months, and with twelve children in the class, I have each one in turn say the name of a month. I run out of things to say, look at my watch and realize, with relief, that our agreed-upon period of thirty minutes has passed.

I feel terribly inadequate as a teacher, and I'm thankful that I never took my mother's advice to get my degree in education. ("If anything happens and your husband won't be able to support you, you'll always have a job, no matter how bad times get. And you'll have the same schedule as your children. Teaching is a good job for a woman.") I have even more respect for my buddy

Marge when I pop into the sixth grade class and see her making pictures on the blackboard, and then, amid shouts and giggles, acting out "falling down" and "crying." The kids are clearly having a good time. And so is Marge.

Later we talk a little bit about what each of us did, and I draw enough inspiration from her to attempt another class tomorrow. But Buddi's schedule for us interferes, and we don't make it tomorrow.

Tomorrow evening Kiran doesn't come home from school until 5:00 p.m. The school day in Badel generally runs from 10 a.m. till 4 p.m., with an hour's break for play, but today as Kiran trudges into the house exhausted, he tells us where he's been: "My class, we went up on mountain." Kiran and 100 of his schoolmates went on a school field trip—a walk that began at 6 a.m. and took them climbing up mountainous terrain for about 3,000 feet to an altitude of some 8,000 feet. For all those hours only one teacher was in charge of all 100 children—an unheard-of ratio in the States, where there would be at least one adult for every ten children. Why weren't any of the other teachers there? One was doing political work, one was building a new house, and one didn't want to walk so far. What U.S. school district would let them off the hook so easily? Of course, in what U.S. school district could one teacher handle all these children?

After eating a healthy portion of *dal bhat*, Kiran gets enough energy to come up to visit us on our balcony. Not enough energy, though, to play cards. This is the first time since we've been in Badel, that Kiran hasn't begged us to play "Fish" and "War" and "Concentration." Instead, as we all sprawl over Marge's bed, Marge suggests, "Let's teach Kiran to play, 'I'm going to my grandmother's house and I'm taking…'" This old memory game (in which each player in turn adds one item to the previous ones and each player has to recite the entire list, from the beginning) was always popular with our own children.

Kiran starts out strong, but once the string of items reaches about half a dozen, he runs into trouble remembering them. So we change the rules to simplify the game. First, we reorder the objects, naming them in alphabetical order. When we realize that that little maneuver has simplified the game for us but not for Kiran, we decide to simplify it for him by using the Nepali words for the objects we "take to grandmother's house": apple, banana, cat, dog, elephant, fox, goat, etc. We ask Kiran to teach us the Nepali words, a reversal of roles he adopts enthusiastically.

Marge and I mouth the unfamiliar syllables, trying hard—and usually failing—to get them right. Throughout our efforts, Kiran never once laughs at our difficulties with pronunciation. Nor, despite the renewed flood of energy that an eleven-year-old can feel even after an exhausting day, does he get impatient and ask to go back to playing cards. Nor is he ready to give up on these slow learning grandmas. Instead, with seemingly infinite patience, he corrects us, over and over again, enunciating the words slowly and precisely to give us the exact intonations for us to reproduce faithfully. Still, the results leave something to be desired as we wrap the words around our tongues, think they are echoes of Kiran's model and are corrected with a smile, time and time again.

We had set out to teach Kiran an American game, then tried to expand the game into an English lesson, and finally tried to learn some Nepali ourselves. We didn't get far with any of these goals—but, as we later come to realize, sometimes the best lessons are learned when we have gone in search of something else.

After Kiran finally clatters down the stairs in response to a call from his mother, Marge turns to me: "What did we learn—the words for apple, banana, cat and dog? Or did we learn a bigger lesson?" Like how hard it is to function in a foreign language. We knew that, of course. I knew how hard I had worked to learn the few Nepali words and phrases I had been able to master, and both of us knew how little success Marge, with her visually oriented mind, has in learning any foreign language.

But still, our epiphany from this game made us realize that we hadn't empathized nearly enough with the difficulties experienced by some of the adults here—especially the teachers—to master rudimentary English. Despite our generally nonjudgmental natures and our determination not to come here and criticize a different way of life, we were, despite ourselves, surprised at—and secretly critical of—the lack of facility with the English language shown by the young woman who teaches English at the Badel school.

Yet we know that these villagers—including the teachers—are learning a foreign language in a milieu completely devoid of any reason for speaking it, of any feedback on accuracy, of any practice outside of school. When I put their efforts into perspective, I'm astonished that they do as well as they do. How can we judge them for not doing any better when we, here in their country, with the benefits of a university education behind each of us and with a universe of potential conversational partners around us, still have so much trouble forming the sounds that any child can make? Yes, we have learned a valuable lesson. In humility.

Sometimes what we learn isn't what we think we're learning. The lesson learned is not always the lesson sought.

This lesson reminds me of another one. I think back to my first meeting with Mr. Baikuntha Prasad Arjyal a couple of months before I left New York. I had been trying to find someone who would teach me rudimentary Nepali so that I would be able to show the villagers that I was at least trying to communicate with them in their tongue. I called several adult education centers, including Berlitz, but my efforts to find Nepali lessons had been in vain. Until I called the Nepal Mission to the United Nations and asked the soft-voiced man who answered the phone whether he knew anyone who could give me a few lessons. "I will be happy to do that, Madam," my informant said in mellifluous tones.

The following week I made my way up to the second floor of 820 Second Avenue in Manhattan, to the modest offices of the Nepal Mission. On the wall of the small waiting room were posters of Everest and Kathmandu, along with a map of Nepal. A round-faced, smiling man who emerged from behind the glass window to greet me turned out to be my teacher. It's unusual to see a chubby Nepali; Mr. Arjyal had clearly been enjoying American food for the year he had been in New York.

We shook hands, and Mr. Arjyal graciously offered me tea or coffee. Fresh from lunch, I shook my head. "No, thank you." But he persisted. "No, Madam, you must take one or the other." After another attempt to decline, I realized I was up against a stronger force than a full stomach, and I asked for coffee, which Mr. Arjyal went into the back office to make. He brought it out to the waiting room, motioned a chair for me to sit on and we talked about what I wanted to learn (a few words that would help me carry on a simple conversation), what he wanted to teach (the ability to read and write the Nepali alphabet!), and where and when the lessons would take place. (We managed to get together half a dozen times, and I did learn my few words and phrases. And I finally gave in to his desire to write out and sound out the Nepali alphabet, even though—aside from the fact that few of the people in Badel could read or write Nepali themselves—I knew that I had a better chance of translating the Rosetta stone in my lifetime than of learning these Devanagri characters.)

I had thought that this first meeting at the Mission would be my first lesson in Nepali, and I was disappointed that it was only a get-acquainted session. I rode down the elevator, frustrated that I had learned nothing from the encounter. By the time I reached the street, I realized that I had indeed received my first lesson from Mr. Arjyal. It was one of hospitality: One must always offer and one must always accept. Yes, the lesson sought is not always the lesson learned.

Marge and I do go back to the school one last time, the day before we leave Badel, so we can say goodbye to the children. As we start up the hill, we see a few children heading down. Buddi turns to us and says, "School's over." "What?" we ask. "It's only 2:15. Doesn't school end at 4?" "Because of rain." It's true, there are dark storm clouds looming over the schoolyard, but it looks as if at least half the children are still at the school, so we proceed toward them.

All those who haven't already left the school grounds stop in their tracks when they see us celebrity visitors arriving, and they pay no heed to the advancing storm. We take group photos of all the children and Buddi. He translates speeches from Marge and me to the children: "We want to say goodbye to you, to tell you how much we enjoyed meeting you and being in your village. We will show your photos to the children in America and tell them about you. Especially about how well you read and how hard you study. You keep studying hard, and when we come back, you will be able to speak English with us!"

Then we perform our silly, out-of-tune song, "Side by Side." (Marge and I discovered the other day that we both know the same camp and Girl Scout songs—and we both sing them all off-key! But our audience doesn't care a bit.) Then many smiling, tearful "Namaste's" from us and trilling "Bye-bye's" from the children, until the rain begins to pelt us, and we all scatter to rush for shelter. Rain falls suddenly and hard here in the hills. But we do get home a little before three, before the storm unleashes its full fury.

I go up to the balcony and listen to Marge, downstairs stringing beads and once again teaching "Eensy Weensy Spider" to half a dozen of our faithful little followers. I can see why she had six children and I had only three. And I have another epiphany. As much as I love children, I have a much more limited capacity for being with them than I thought I had. As appealing as these kids are, I think I'll scream if I have to do "Eensy Weensy Spider" one more time! Finally this morning I wrote out the words for Rahanta, in hopes that she'd sound them out, or take them to school and get help from one of the teachers in learning them.

From what we've seen of these children, I feel confident that Rahanta can learn these words if she wants to. I guess it's not too grandiose to think that our little legacy here in Badel may add up to a handful of happy memories and the words to a children's rhyme, which these children may someday teach their own children. Their legacy to us is far richer, a belief in the indomitability of the human spirit, of the ingenuity and resourcefulness of children in humble circumstances, of the ability to find joyousness in the simplest offerings of every day. And realizing this, we know that Nepal is, in the important things in life, the things that really count, wealthy beyond earthly measure.

11

Moving Day: Chickens in the Charpi

A pipal tree may grow out of a crow's droppings.
—*Nepali proverb*

For the next two weeks Marge and I will be completely in Buddi's slender, capable hands. Today, our sixth day in Badel, Jai will head back to Kathmandu with Gora, the cook, and Mani Bhujel, the porter. There they will meet Peter and go on trek with him, so we have to make our goodbyes to these three now. We have stayed in Badel longer than we originally planned to.

Last night, in one of the many instances in which Marge and I independently get the same thought or arrive at the same conclusion, each of us decided that we don't want to move. We are finding here so much of what we sought in Nepal that we can't believe our good fortune. Neither of our original concerns about Badel turned out to be valid. Not the first, that there would be too much familiarity with westerners and their ways and so the villagers would not find our visit interesting. While there probably are somewhere

141

between fifty and a hundred men who have had contact with foreigners through trekking or military service, few of the men, hardly any of the women and none of the children have ever spoken to a non-Nepali. And everyone in the village seems eager to meet us, talk with us and offer us hospitality.

And not the second, either, that western culture would have infiltrated the village, seeping into its ancient traditions, contaminating it with technology and plastics and alien values. Neither the presence of a few portable radios blaring pop music and news broadcasts nor a smattering of western tee shirts and jeans has sent ripples through the venerable ponds of ancient ways. The rhythms of Badel are still basically the same ones that have governed life here for hundreds of years.

After Jai leaves today, Marge and I will move up the hill to Buddi's house. This morning we paid Jai for seven days—for the one day in Kathmandu when he helped us organize and shop for our trip, and then for the six days of getting us to Badel and staying with us here. In Kathmandu we had asked Jai what he would want to be paid. To our dismay, he said only, "If you want to give me something, it's okay." We answered, "Of course we'll pay you—we don't expect you to do this for nothing." But he wouldn't tell us how much he wanted; nor did Peter give us any guidance. We had to do our own research.

I had left my copy of the newest edition of Dr. Stephen Bezruchka's bible for trekkers, *Trekking in Nepal*, in New York. So Marge and I walked over to Pilgrim's Bookstore, Kathmandu's treasure trove of English-language books on all manner of subjects Nepali and Asian. From the Potala Guest House in Chhetrapati to the bookstore in Thamel, we made our way through rutted narrow streets thronged with tourists, packs of scavenging dogs digging in the piles of garbage at almost every corner, rickshaws, bicycles, vendors hawking goods ranging from the all-purpose nostrum Tiger Balm to wooden flutes displayed on poles like branches on trees. Redolent with the aromas of frying oil, eastern spices, cow manure, sweat, garlic, hashish, decaying garbage and gasoline fumes from the cars inching their way through the crush of foot traffic and from the screeching motor scooters weaving in and out and sometimes grazing our sides, this neighborhood was as frenetic as Badel is peaceful.

Once inside the haven of the book store, we found the paragraph in Bezruchka that advised that since guides' and porters' salaries keep changing, it's best to check with trekking stores for the most current going fees. Back in the streets, we looked closely at the little stores, found one selling trekking supplies and walked in. Inside the dimly lit shop, we posed our question to a knot of young men sitting around on stools and counters. With the high rates of unemployment in Nepal, there are knots of young men everywhere in Kathmandu, sitting, standing, chatting, passing the time. When we mentioned a figure—modest by United States standards—and asked whether they thought that would be fair, they all widened their eyes, nodded vigorously and clearly expressed their opinion that that would be very good pay, pay any one of them would do practically anything to get.

Now, in Badel, Jai says (a trifle disingenuously, I think), "I didn't expect a salary." He smiles broadly, flashing those beautiful white teeth that his exposure to western diets still hasn't ruined. "Money good to have. I give 200 rupees to my father, lend money to someone in village, get it back in few months."

I head up to our room and wonder why the door is closed. I start to go in without knocking, Nepali-style, but back off when I realize that Jai and his father are having a private talk. Despite the less open demonstrations of affection in Nepal, these two clearly have deep bonds of attachment. I realize that the parameters I've always relied upon to judge affection and intimacy are not reliable measures for other cultures. As are so many parameters for judging a world of other qualities.

FROM MARGE'S JOURNAL:

Sally and I hug and kiss Jai, and along with his pay we wish him safe journey and give him many thanks for sharing his home and family with us. A few years ago I never would have shown such bad manners as to hug a male Nepali in public. This western habit of public embrace is certainly not their way. I have never seen a Nepali man show any public sign of affection to his wife. I don't think I have even seen husband and wife speak to each other in public. But we have taught the porters and staff the kissing game, and now it is an accepted and, with the regulars like Jai, expected practice to hug and squeeze. It is certainly not the usual practice in this village, and I hope in our exuberance we did not offend. But I have a hunch that Jai enjoyed every kiss and hug, and even here it might be fun to shock the neighbors. Especially when you are the young man who comes home after making it big out in the world.

Today is moving day. We pack our duffels and ask Mithu for a broom to sweep our room. As good guests, we want to leave it as clean as we found it. But Mithu says, "No, porters will clean." We readily agree. We are paying Tara Mani and Kangsha for the days they are in the village, and they have had very little to do other than our laundry. The pay is embarrassingly minimal—three dollars a day—but in this poor country, it is a much sought after salary.

Our next formation is our move up to Buddi's house. When Jai told us we would be staying with Buddi's family for our second week in Badel, he said, "Buddi's house much bigger than mine." He was speaking the truth. Buddi's father, Dhojuman Rai, 70, is a former Gurkha soldier whose first wife died without bearing him any children. He met his present wife, Shiva, now 55, when he served in Darjeeling, a city in northeastern India that sits in the foothills of the Himalayas and borders southern Nepal. From the twenty pregnancies she underwent, Shiva now has three sons and five daughters. Gita, 35, is married to Dhan Bahadur Rai, the English teacher at the Badel school who visited us at Jai's house. He is also the proprietor of the only store in Badel. Their seventeen-year-old daughter lives in Kathmandu with Gita's sister, Rita, near their other sister, Sita. Dhan and Gita's sons, Ishwor, 14, and Uttam, 15, both attend the Badel elementary school.

— Bahadi's parents Shiba and Dajuman Rai.
Dajuman is 72 years old and a gurka soldier. He fought
in Italy, Austria, Germany, Yugoslavia and India in World War II

Next in age is Bina, 33, who married a man from the Terai, the flat, hot, dusty plains country in southern Nepal, best known to foreigners as the home of Royal Chitwan National Park and Tiger Tops Lodge. She lives down there with her husband and their two or three children and has not seen the rest of her family in many years. Sita Devi, 28, married to Jai, is the mother of three-and-a-half-year-old Kim. Our guide, Buddi Kumar, 27, is Shiva's eldest son. Married to Dhana, 21, Buddi is the father of a two-and-a-half-year-old daughter, Kusum. Rita, 25, lives in Kathmandu with her husband and their small sons, and Susila, 20, is currently living with Jai and Sita in Kathmandu while she looks for a job there. Dilip, 17, a high school student, is currently off on trek, working as a porter with Peter Owens. And the youngest son, Kiran Kumar, 11, is the bright, lively, adorable boy who quickly won both Marge's and my hearts.

The house where Dhojuman and Shiva live with their three sons and Buddi's wife and daughter is one of the three grandest, biggest, most elaborate dwellings in Badel. All white with blue trim, all three belong to family members; Dhojuman's brother, currently a Gurkha soldier, owns one, Gita and Dhan the other. Dhojuman's money has come from his salary and then his pension as a Gurkha soldier, as well as from Buddi's contributions from his earnings as a trekking and mountaineering guide. Still, the family lives simply, and Dhojuman continues to farm. Their wealth is apparent, however, in many small ways besides the size of their house—their more extensive wardrobes; the presence of a hired farmhand, Bhomi, a young man Buddi's age who can neither hear nor speak; the educational achievements of their children—both sons and daughters; and Shiva's generosity toward her less affluent neighbors. She regularly feeds anyone in want, and I am reminded of the grandmother I never knew who, my mother used to tell me, never turned away anyone who came to her back door asking for food. We are to see Shiva similarly sharing her own good fortune.

Our move up the hill from Jai's house to Buddi's looks like something out of a nineteenth-century print of explorers in Africa or a scene exposing the excesses of imperialism from a grainy old British movie. Marge and I carried our backpacks up here, but not much else. Now, as I look down from the second-floor balcony that will be our *al fresco* bedroom, dining room, library and living room for the next week, I see the procession winding up through the rocky hillside.

On her back Mithu carries a doko holding both Marge's and my sleeping bags. On her back, twelve-year-old Kumari, the porter Mani Bhujel's daughter, carries her five-year-old sister, while slung over her shoulder is a large, lumpy sack filled with our stuff. One of Kumari's little brothers strides up on his sturdy little legs bearing a tent; another one brings up the rear with a cooking pot. Buddi brings a duffel, and Mani Bhujel totes our kitchen equipment. Tara Mani and Kangsha haul the rest—pots, pans, dishes, food and personal gear.

All in all, the two of us required twelve carriers for a trip of 200 yards. What *is* all this stuff? And we thought we were traveling light! Here where many people have only one change of clothes and can fit all their possessions into a single doko, we realize how we are ruled by our surfeit of belongings. In a surfeit of embarrassment, I resolve to go home and get rid of things.

Buddi asks us whether we want to sleep in his bedroom or outside on the balcony. "Outside," Marge and I exclaim at once. We wouldn't dream of letting him, Dhana and Kusum give up their double bed for us. Besides, one glimpse of the incredible view of the mountains across the river gives us the answer. Sleeping outside will be no sacrifice at all. Another meeting of our minds. As Marge says, "Here is a view a developer in America would beg, borrow or steal for, and it will be all ours for the rest of our stay in Badel!" (And another twenty dollars for the week.)

We'll be sleeping in luxury on this long balcony—on nice wide wooden beds. When we first arrived, the balcony held only one bed. Since the other one wouldn't fit up the narrow indoor stairway, it had to be hoisted up from the ground, over the balcony railing. Buddi and Tara leaned way over the balcony working the ropes, while Kangsha and Mani Bhujel manipulated the bed—and Marge and I held our breath. After our solicitous workers put just the right-sized rocks under the legs to stabilize the beds, they brought out foam mattresses. And then Shiva brought in the final touches for our elegant accommodations—flower-printed sheets and pillows in hand-embroidered soft cotton cases bought long ago when she was with her soldier husband in Singapore.

The best part is the view we have of the glorious hills on the other side of the Liding Khola. We sit on our beds and look off to the southeast at the spectacular green mountains climbing lushly up the opposite side of the river. The hills are terraced and planted with corn and vegetables half way up, and the rest of the mountain is emerald forest. The houses of the neighboring villages of Bangdel and Mudi are sparsely scattered specks on the hillside. They blend so well into the landscape that they seem to be growing there. No gleaming metal roofs detract from the natural environment.

It's 6:10 in the morning after our first night on the balcony. I have been lying here on my wooden bed for the past hour and a half. I watched the tiny crescent moon appear, then vanish behind the early-morning mist. Then I looked at the sky lightening. The rounded bumps of the hills emerged, first in silhouette, then in forested green at the top and brown terraced cones farther down, dotted with houses and trees. Long streaks of white and pale blue (a true "sky blue") replaced the foggy gray that had been above me. As the sky lightens, the conical thatched roof of the storage barn below comes into view. Little birds and big insects—both unidentified—fly in and out, around the balcony's railing posts. The sparrows twitter overhead; the cocks crow and hens cluck below. I feel I'm in a bubble of time when nothing exists but what is happening in this moment, in this place.

Now the household is waking. Kusum is crying, and Shiva, in the time-honored tradition of grandmothering, is comforting her. I know I'll be a better grandmother for this time spent here, seeing Shiva with her granddaughter, seeing Marge, watching her reaching out to—and connecting with—these village youngsters, her surrogate grandchildren.

FROM MARGE'S JOURNAL:

So many words left unwritten, so many stories left untold, so many pictures left unpainted. But they are all there written in my head, my being, my soul. And each one changes me. I must be careful of what I say and do because I do not want to change the people of Badel. As I sit here and watch a hen brood with her chicks, time has stopped moving for me. Vocal interaction becomes harder and harder. I just want to fade into the background and watch and draw and—oh yes—play with the children. Even writing in this journal takes me out of the moment.

As I get up to meet the day, I hear a single flute piping, the laughter and voices of the family below, the shouts of children farther down the valley, faint sounds of Nepali music from a distant radio, an occasional crowing of a rooster, the chirping of baby chicks, the cawing of crows. An immense wave of peace rises up and washes over me. (Later I will learn that at almost this very moment, Marge was writing in her journal, "Contentment and harmony define this moment.")

The rhythms of life are so different here from the ones at home. At home, I am always on the move. I am always doing. I don't take the time to be. Time at home feels like such a precious commodity that I am parsimonious of it by doing two or three things at once. I don't go anywhere without something to read or do, so that I won't waste time. Now I realize that by my dread of wasting time, I don't savor it. When I get home, I can see myself just sitting and listening and looking, oblivious of deadlines and correspondence and social life and obligations of any sort. What a revolutionary thought!

FROM MARGE'S JOURNAL:

Down in the courtyard the children are waiting for us. I give Rahanta a big pink comb. She runs over to the little stoop undoing the braids in her sister's hair as she runs. She combs and yanks at the poor child's hair so that it hurts me to watch. Muna, the little sister, sits like a stone statue, never flinching. I take the comb from

Rahanta and gently comb through the braids. Muna's hair is fine, so it is not a tedious task to part it and get it ready for new braids.

While Rahanta braids, I run upstairs to get the torn piece of fabric Sally used to bundle the gifts we brought. We tie the frayed ribbons on the ends of the neat braids. Now Rahanta goes to work on her own hair, yanking and pulling with no more mercy than she showed little Muna. I pour a few drops of sweet-smelling lotion into the outstretched hands of the growing crowd of grinning children. The manicurist arrives, and Sally paints the fingernails of all the little girls and one index fingernail of one brave little boy. The children's clothes are so ragged I wish I had thought to bring clothing for them. Sally brought a few baby things that her grandchildren had outgrown but neither of us thought to bring clothes for these older children.

Kusum has been crying all morning. She does not feel well; she was coughing last night, has fever this morning and is inconsolable, even when held in the arms of her parents or grandmother. After some minutes, I realize that I haven't heard her sad little cries for some time. I look down and see Dhana walking back and forth along the path below the house, Kusum cradled in her arms, resting her small dark head on her mother's shoulder. Yes, this culture is different from ours in so many ways, but some things—like mother love—are universal.

I give Kiran the beautiful picture book about a Sherpa family that I bought a year ago when I came across it in my local book store. He can read some of *Himalaya: Vanishing Cultures* now and will be able to read all of it soon, I'm sure. I feel good about his having it because it's about his country, even if not about his ethnic group. A crowd gathers, and both children and adults (including Dhana and Shiva) look with great interest at the photos. A good trip for this book, from the Dolphin Book Shop in Port Washington to a Rai home in the village of Badel. I inscribe it "To my friend, Kiran Kumar Rai, with affection and admiration. I'm happy I know you! Sally Olds—Badel—16 April 1993."

Our morning's project is a visit to Gita, Buddi's eldest sister. She lives five minutes up the hill in the blue-and-white house that looks very like her father's. Kusum, much livelier now, comes with us, making the journey in Buddi's arms. Nepali children spend much more time being carried than do most American children. This is probably one reason why it is so rare to hear a child crying.

Next to Gita and Dhan's house is their little store. Its walls are covered with pages from Nepali newspapers; its shelves (made by Dhan) hold a meager stock of batteries and copy books, a few boxes of soap. They plan to get more stock—mainly cookies—but goods are hard to come by here. No wonder—everything has to come from the market at Aiselakharka or Katari, each one a three days' walk from here. Dhan's a good—well, an adequate—carpenter, who also made the small chairs, sized for compact Nepali derrières, that he invites us to sit on. (Marge complains that every time she sits on one of these, her backside goes to sleep!) But from the looks of the shop, it seems that his talents do not run to retail business.

We arrived at about 9:00 a.m., and when we leave at about 10:30, he still has not gone to teach his classes at school. "He has work to do in his fields," Buddi explains. Marge and I show an amused surprise at the casual attitude toward school on the part of both students and teachers. Buddi shrugs and says, "Nobody checks."

Turn right
at the Bhaisi
and climb over
the rocks to*
the CHARPI. It's
behind the
Yellow Flowers.

M Pyche
10/94

Charpi is outhouse in Nepal!

Gita does not speak English, so again our only conversationalists are the men. As we sit around the fire in the middle of the kitchen floor, Gita brings us rakshi and black tea, made with black pepper, cinnamon and sugar. A delicious concoction—but with liquids being offered every time we turn around, and with our guestly manners insisting that we accept the gracious hospitality—I'm giving the *charpi* (latrine) good use. By 10:30 this morning I have already consumed full cups each of wake-up tea, hot Tang, coffee, and now the pepper tea. When we get home at 11:10, Tara Mani offers to make more tea for us, but fortunately he's not insulted when we decline with a smile. I head for the charpi.

There are only about fifty charpis in the village. The other villagers attend to their needs either in the fields or in the family pigpens. Both these solutions keep the footpaths neat and clean, free of human excrement. The water buffalo are not so fastidious, so we still have to look before we step.

The charpi at Jai's house is about fifty yards from the house and up a few stone steps to a terrace planted with corn, then up to a second terrace, also planted; so when we were there, we had to step carefully between the little green shoots. This one, at Buddi's house, is about the same distance from the house, just off a level path. The first few times I used it, I heard heavy breathing and kept thinking that someone was about to walk in on me, but I finally realized that what I heard was the snuffling of the two skinny little black baby pigs in the family's pigpen just on the other side of the family's latrine.

This is how I find the charpi in the dark: I walk down the steps from our sleeping balcony and then straight through the yard. When I see two curved white horns and two shiny round black eyes, I know I have reached my landmark—the *baisi*, the female water buffalo that Shiva milks early every morning. Holding my flashlight in one hand, I turn right and use my other hand to steady me as I climb up a slippery little embankment that's hard enough to manage by daylight. It goes up about five feet, and while going up is a challenge, coming down the zigzag scramble constitutes serious risk to life and limb—especially after a pelting rain slicks the rocks and mud even more. I wonder how the family manages; I think the answer is that they don't use it: they make other arrangements, often going out before dawn.

This charpi is simple but elegant. It affords privacy in a simple woven bamboo enclosure shaped like a French *pissoir* and open only on one side. Inside, four thick bamboo poles are tied together, lying flat on one side of a hole in the ground; on the other side of the gap, there's a flat wooden board. The user places one foot on the poles and the other on the board. Both poles and board are weighted down by a large rock, which also serves the purpose of a handhold to steady balance for those of us not used to squatting. The cover for the "glory hole" is made of a block of wood with a long stick that stands upright and protrudes through the bottom to keep the wooden block in place. After using the charpi it's easy to grab hold of the stick to bring the board over the opening.

There's no odor at all. The facility is well ventilated as fresh air comes in between the bamboo weavings. More important, the ashes from the family's cooking fire are deposited here every morning, creating a chemical substance similar to lime. When the hole fills up after about a year's use, another charpi is created in a different location and a tree is planted where the first one was. I've sent money over the years to have trees planted in Israel, but my contribution to the ones that will grow here is, to say the least, far more personal. Nice to know I'm helping in the country's desperately needed reforestation.

After coming home from my previous treks, I would happily regale my friends about sunrise over majestic Himalayan peaks, about kind and gentle people, about eastern spirituality, about the chaotic excitement that is Kathmandu. Friends would listen—at first eagerly, then politely—before their eyes inevitably glazed over. But somewhere in my recital, everyone—everyone I spoke with—would rouse themselves and ask the universal question: "But how did you—um, er, uh—go to the bathroom?" This was often closely followed by "Do the local people use toilet paper?"

This kind of charpi is a rare answer to the first question; in most places the "bathroom" is behind a tree or large boulder in someone's field. This is luxury. Aside from the privacy in the enclosure, the fact that a hole has been dug means that we westerners who can't seem to shake the habit of using toilet paper can dispose of it rather neatly. It's much easier than trying to bury it in a rocky field, or trying to burn it with matches that keep blowing out in the wind. I know. I've tried both these procedures.

The local people don't have to worry about disposing of paper because they don't use it. On the heavily trafficked tourist routes you can see what a mess this country would be in if they did. On those routes the paths are lined with shreds of the pink toilet paper imported from China, known locally as "the white man's prayer flags." Most Nepalis train themselves to defecate early in the morning while it's still dark. They take a small pitcher of water with them into the fields and afterwards, with the left hand, they wash themselves with the water. Because they squat so widely, they hardly soil their bodies. For obvious reasons, even though they wash their hands afterwards, all eating is done with the right hand.

As ingeniously constructed as the charpi is, however, my privacy is not utterly complete: while I am in here, I get company. One of the hens trots in, closely followed by three baby chicks. The hen scratches in the dirt for a couple of seconds, then leaves as unceremoniously as she arrived.

FROM MARGE'S JOURNAL:

I see these people, even the most aged, squatting comfortably as they work and eat. I struggle to get comfortable sitting on the floor, first on my knees, then cross-legged, then sticking them out in front, but being careful not to point the soles of my feet at anyone because that is taboo here. At home my granddaughter often sits on her little haunches as she plays near me, but I can no longer squat. My tendons and ligaments can never again be stretched to get back what I lost by age five.

What does all this thinking about squatting have to do with my love of the villages? It is symbolic of the way these people live, right down to the very basic needs. They live so close to the ground. Grandma sits in front of the fire, children play in the earth and everybody sleeps on mats on the floor. Everything they do either comes from the ground or is on the ground. They even walk closer to the ground than we do. I think of the bent-kneed gait of the porter hunched under his doko.

The beds Sally and I are sleeping in are a recent addition. I was disappointed to see them. Selfishly, I want nothing to change. I don't want porters and guides to come back from seeing the guest houses in Kathmandu and saying, "This is how it is done there. We must change our ways." Now some guides are even being taken to the United States for vacation by well-meaning well-to-do trekkers. Is this good? Will they be able to slip back into the rhythms of their village when they return after seeing the sights of Manhattan and San Francisco? I don't know the answer.

When we see how comfortable the Nepalis are in their bodies, we wonder who is more evolved—they, with their so-called "primitive" ways or we with our so-called "civilized" ones. They can squat comfortably on their flat feet, with no need of furniture or porcelain bathroom fixtures; we can't hold this position long, if at all. They sprint up and down the steepest hills either bare-foot or wearing the flimsiest of slippers; we slip and slide and falter even in our highest-tech heavy-lug boots. A surprising number keep their teeth into old age; we get cavities as children. They rarely wear, or seem to need, eyeglasses; beyond middle age we're rarely without them. There should be some way of marrying our two cultures—of retaining the strengths of theirs while offering them only those developments from ours that will enhance their way of life but not take away its greatest benefits.

ganga sumam Bhule looks at my Drawings

upper Rai is my cook
his wife, nirmala Rai
Son, Sunja Rai
I gave Sunja Rai
medicine. He was very sick. He is better now.

12

Mind-Body Connection: Pray to the River God

Every spring has a different taste, every man a different idea.
—Nepali proverb

One morning Buddi comes up to our balcony carrying Kusum in the fancy new taffeta dress, three sizes too big, with its flowered ruffles and white lace and pink satin roses, that he bought for her in Kathmandu and that she adores prancing around in on these dusty village footpaths. She's not prancing now, though. Kusum's little face is serious, her usually golden complexion pale and her almond-shaped eyes droopy from the upper respiratory infection she has been suffering this past week, complete with fever and a harsh hacking cough. The toddler has a charcoal smudge on her forehead the size of a silver dollar. When I ask what it is, Buddi explains: "Kusum was sick, so we took her to shaman this morning. He said she got sick because she was frightened by that fall."

Two days ago, as Kusum was playing in the middle of the downstairs veranda, Buddi, seated on a little bamboo stool,

159

scooped her up in his arms to get her out of the way so I could pass. His stool was very close to the edge of the porch, and when he leaned back with Kusum in his arms, he teetered and then fell backwards about three feet down into the chicken yard, still tightly holding his little daughter. No one was hurt except Buddi, who scratched his leg, but poor little Kusum screamed out in her fright and called out for her mother. I, feeling terribly guilty that I had, however unwittingly, been the cause of the accident, took her over to Dhana. Buddi felt stricken and was clearly shaken—as was everyone else present. And now the shaman is saying that Kusum's illness is due to that fright. His prescribed cure involves his incantations and the mark he put upon her forehead to drive away the evil spirit that entered her body when she got her scare.

"Does Buddi really believe this?" I wonder. At first, it strains my western credibility to hear this bright, savvy university graduate swallowing this explanation. Especially since Kusum has been coughing and feverish for days—ever since we got here, long before her fall.

FROM MARGE'S JOURNAL:

A few days ago I noticed Buddi giving Kusum some medicine from an old bottle with the label long worn off. In answer to my "What for?" Buddi said, "She is sick and I give her medicine from Kathmandu." Since only about a teaspoon remained of the antibiotic Buddi had bought over a year before, I thought the medicine would do no good, but probably would do no harm either. Kusum seemed healthy to me. She is active, despite her cough and runny nose, two symptoms shared by every child in Badel and a fair number of adults, including me.

When Buddi told me the shaman's diagnosis—that it was the fall on Buddi's lap that made the child sick, I hated to see the look of shame and guilt on this young father's face. I told Buddi I had been a nurse in a children's hospital, so he would respect my advice and not think I was preaching. I said it would not help to give just one dose of a medicine, that usually an antibiotic should be given for ten days in a row to cure the illness. I suggested that the next time he is in Kathmandu he talk to the doctor whom he sees when he is sick himself, and ask him what to do when Kusum does not feel well.

I could hardly say, "Take her to the doctor every time she is sick." The doctor is seven days' walk and a two-day bus ride away. I don't know that our way is better, and I want to hold to my resolution not to change anything in the village. But today I am not interfering with an old custom; I am only cautioning against the way he is introducing a new one.

Two months ago Buddi himself went to one of the ten shamans in Badel. "We have no doctors here, no medicine," he tells us with a shrug. "One time I put on those stupid army boots my uncle gave me, and I walk with my wife to my father-in-law's house in Rakha, maybe two hours. And when I come home, my ankle hurt me so bad I can't walk on that foot. The ankle was big, like this." With his graceful, long-fingered hands, he sculpts arcs in the air around his slender ankle.

"So I call the shaman, and he say, my ankle hurts because I crossed the river without praying to the river god. So the shaman chanted over the ankle and told me to go back down to the river and pray, and after a couple of days my foot feels better. That's because I believed in it then. I don't believe it anymore. In Kathmandu if I get sick I go to doctor, I get medicine. Here in Badel we don't have that."

So if he doesn't believe in it, why did he take Kusum? I guess because there was no better alternative. When in Badel, do as the Badeli. Or perhaps he does, underneath his protestations, believe, but knowing that westerners are skeptical, and abashed before Marge and me, he masks his faith, the faith that can, in fact, bring about healing. For doctors have known for centuries that such faith can often perform miracles. Contemporary western physicians and researchers are finally acknowledging the strong connection between mind and body, a connection that has always been well accepted in many societies, where shamans have long been revered for their healing powers.

How do shamans do their work? In these hill villages of Nepal, these people—almost always men—usually show their psychic powers in adolescence, and from that point on, pursue their calling. They usually follow other professions too, such as farming and cattle-raising, but when their *jhankri* self is called upon, their shamanistic duties toward their community assume the highest priority. Whether called upon to conduct a ceremony, cure an illness or foretell the future, they perform their tasks in a self-created trance. In this state, they determine the cause of illness—a fright, a dereliction toward a god or a person, some misdeed that must be righted. And under the trance they come up with the solution, which may involve herbal medicine, animal sacrifice, exorcism or hands-on manipulation of the patient.

We met our first shaman on our way to Badel. One night, when we camped in the courtyard of a home, we found ourselves observing the local clinic. There, sitting in the corner of the porch, a few yards away from our tents, the medicine man was counting out grains of rice and murmuring incantations, as the population around him grew. We watched him treat people with stomach-aches, headaches and other complaints by praying over them and sprinkling rice on the offending parts of their bodies. With no medical facilities in these remote villages, anyone with any ailment comes to see the shaman. And many of them do go away healed. Clearly, here is the mind-body connection at work—the way it works around the world, in defiance of all the efforts in all the societies that have tried to divorce the science of medicine from the art of healing.

My skeptical western mind asks, "What's the rationale? How do these cures work?" Partly, I think, because some of these shamans are effective psychotherapists. But I've also heard of scientific research suggesting biological changes in the human body in response to the belief that one is being helped—by any treatment. The placebo effect, as it's known in the west. So the part of my mind that scoffs and says, "No wonder there's such a high mortality rate for children under age five in rural Nepal if this is the extent of medical care!" is quickly overruled by the conviction that many therapies (including a number of those in the western mainstream) work for reasons we have yet to understand, and that shamanic healing may well be, in innumerable cases, more effective than aspirins or surgery. Western physicians don't know why aspirins work, either.

Of course, the major health problem in these remote villages is not the belief in shamans. It is the lack of any medical facilities to supplement shamanic remedies. During our stay, Marge and I are approached over and over again. We are westerners: ergo, we must have miraculous western cures. One woman with fluid oozing from an eye that had been tearing for months asks us for medicine, but we have nothing for her; she needs much more than our simple antibiotic opthalmic ointment. The mother of a boy who fixes us with a gaze showing one eye that turned completely white after he was hit by a hurled rock a year before also asks for our help, as do the relatives of a bedridden, long ill man.

As we continually shake our heads to these requests and others like them, saying that we have no strong medicine and are not doctors, we feel helpless and inexpressibly sad. We can do no more than the shaman—and undoubtedly much less, since he knows the well-tested household remedies for local illnesses better than we do. Furthermore, we know the danger in giving western medicines for ills they can't cure, which will then make local people distrust the kind of more advanced medical treatment that can help them—if they do manage to reach a health worker.

But since we hate to offend these welcoming villagers or to appear uncaring, we try to mitigate our inadequacies by urging the ill and their families to visit the nearest hospital or health station, even as we know how few will make the long trip. The gap between knowledge and accessibility is a chasm deeper than the gorges that pit this poor, remote region, whose people know that there are medical remedies for many of their afflictions, but find them light years beyond their reach.

Marge and I see this situation differently. She seems more concerned about the misuse of western medicine. I'm more concerned about the almost total lack of western medicine. After all, 99 percent of these villagers cannot misuse western medicine because they can't get their hands on it. We do agree, though, about what we would like to see here: health clinics within a couple of hours' walk of every village; traveling health workers to make weekly visits to villages; local staff trained in simple remedies and in the diagnosis of more serious illness; transport to hospital for complicated childbirths, injuries, and critical illnesses. And other measures startling in their simplicity, which could save countless lives.

Still, we need to be careful about introducing measures that seem sensible to us. For example, one group of health workers developed a "birthing kit" consisting of a clean cloth on which to lay a new baby, string to tie around the umbilical cord and a razor blade to cut the cord. Seems sensible, but…

FROM MARGE'S JOURNAL:

My first reaction to the birthing kits is: Oh my God! All those razor blades floating around Badel for children to cut themselves on. You know they won't be disposed of "properly" after one use. People will probably get creative for all sorts of ways to use dull rusty razor blades. Introducing razor blades to Badel is as distasteful to me as bringing in plastic toys. Since the babies and mothers do very well, by and large, in uncomplicated births, why complicate them? My guess is that few babies die from infections they get when the cord is cut. Far more die of dysentery and dehydration, and I think health efforts should focus on preventing illness by providing a clean water supply, installing latrines and dealing with dehydration caused by diarrhea by teaching people how to make and use simple rehydration solutions. So we can use what is available to the people in new ways, but save the old ways that still work.

Earlier this week Buddi took Marge and me to the Puri ethnic group's settlement on the hill overlooking Badel and showed us the water pump that had been installed as a bequest of the Kadoorie Agricultural Aid Association (KAAA). We stood on this windswept rise, gazed out at hills stretching as far as the eye could see, each one nestling a tiny village, and imagined the scene that Buddi described to us.

Then in his eighties, Sir Horace Kadoorie, a British subject living in Hong Kong, had come by helicopter to the top of this hill to celebrate the installation of the first reliable water supply in Badel. First, his engineers dismounted from the aircraft; then they helped Sir Horace into the wheelchair he had needed since breaking his hip some years before. And then, to the acclaim of the assembled villagers, they turned on the water spout up here, which gushed forth in a steady stream that was echoed in other spouts located throughout the village, and now provides a clean, convenient water supply for the villagers, who no longer need to take water jugs down the hill to the river. KAAA was also responsible for another project in Badel, a simple but sanitary toilet system next to the school—a "four-holer" with wooden doors and a cement-covered septic system. Buddi told us, "It will last 100 years."

The brothers Sir Horace and Lord Lawrence Kadoorie are now in their nineties. Active in the Jewish community of Hong Kong, they assumed the mission of sharing with needy Asian communities the fortune their father had amassed through rubber, real estate and banking. In 1880 Elly Kadoorie had come to Hong Kong from Iraq as a penniless youth, eventually building a financial empire that today includes Hong Kong's famed Peninsula Hotel. Wealth, Sir Elly taught his sons, is a sacred trust to be administered for the good of society. In recognition of this trust, the family's work has received numerous tributes, including one of the highest honors granted by the Nepal government, the Gurkha Dashin Bahu (First Class) Award, for work in helping Gurkha soldiers readjust to rural life after leaving military service.

The brothers hold in especially high esteem the Gurkha soldiers from Nepal, many of whom they met years earlier when the British had sent the Gurkhas as military police to guard Hong Kong's borders. Since so many of these soldiers come from Rai villages, these areas have been special beneficiaries of the Kadoories' philanthropy. More projects like the ones that KAAA has been undertaking could make a difference to hundreds of other small villages in Nepal without good water, without sanitary latrines. Meanwhile, people fall ill from many causes, medical help is largely out of reach and the remedies offered by local shamans deserve respect. They undoubtedly save countless lives through their still little understood healing powers and through faith— theirs and that of their suffering patients.

13

Children's Safety:
No Video-Game Seizures

It is not the tiger in the forest but the one in the mind that eats up a person.

—Nepali proverb

Yesterday, when we were sitting on the little terrace in front of Jai's house, Monos, his sister Indra's chubby 11-month-old baby, was crawling on the porch. The baby spotted and picked up a lethal-looking *khukri*, the large, curved, razor-sharp knife that Nepalis use for decapitating animals, lopping off branches, forging paths in the jungle and all manner of other agricultural tasks, as well as for a formidable weapon in battle.

"Indra!" I shouted, beside myself. "The baby—uh-uh-oh-KHUKRI!" Sputtering, I totally forgot the Nepali word for baby or the baby's name. When I finally spit out "khukri," Indra laughed merrily and, very relaxed, gently took it out of the fist he had clenched around it. Later, on the trail, Marge and I saw two tiny little boys, one six years old, his older brother, eight. Each one had a khukri, which the younger one absentmindedly stuck in his mouth as if he were cleaning his teeth.

My heart skips a beat at least several times a day for these children, but somehow they—and their parents—float through all these things that seem so menacing to us westerners. Like that incredibly narrow balcony at the school-house, which stimulates terrifying fantasies in our heads. And like the daily activities of the children that in Badel are taken for granted, but that in the minds of two western grandmas, spell constant peril.

FROM MARGE'S JOURNAL:

I catch my breath when I see the smallest children carrying their only slightly smaller siblings. Little seven-year-old Bikas, still swathed in the fuzzy pink scarf Sally brought in her bag of baby clothes, is climbing up the open-sided hard clay stairs, carrying his 11-month-old brother piggyback. Now he stands on the planks of the narrow rail-less balcony with his little bare feet right at the edge. I wait for Indra to scold her daring little son, or at least yell out a warning. She is sitting right here, so she must see this horrible accident about to happen. But she says nothing, and the bone-breaking fall happens only in my head.

Acrophobia seems to be unheard of in this world, but doesn't anyone ever fall off anything? Are they all human flies with suctioned feet? I have seen porters with 70-pound loads wearing flip-flops scurrying across slick, unstable rocks in a cascading river with the same surefootedness that I use on the flattest paved high-way.

Much to our amazement, the village youngsters don't seem to have any more accidents than our western children do, probably because they're watched more closely by mothers or other relatives, often only slightly older siblings, who are less distracted than American caregivers. These children tend to receive the kind of focused attention that I give to my baby granddaughter. When Anna and I are alone, I feel as if I am in a different world from my usual one, a world of the immediate present, a world in which every other activity fades into the background, a world in which I concentrate only on her and what she needs, a zen world. It's as if I know what I'm supposed to do: I'm carrying on an ancient tradition of grandmothering and child care and I'm totally at peace with the world and myself.

I have no memory of giving this same kind of concentration to my own children on a day-to-day basis. In those days, my mind was like a mosaic in the making, its neurons scattered like loose tiles. Part of me was so often somewhere else, as I would think about what I *had* to do or felt I had to do—the marketing, the cooking, the laundering, the chauffeuring, the cleaning, the finding of babysitters so I could be the sociable corporate wife, the shopping for children's clothes so I could dress up my little girls as I had once played with my dolls, the planning and carrying out charming little dinner parties for our friends and my husband's colleagues. Then there was all that I struggled to find snippets of time for so I could feed my soul—the writing, the civil rights activism, the part-time work for one social change agency after another.

Being a college-educated mother in suburban America in the 1960s meant feeling that you had to be the best at mothering and homemaking and wifeing—and at something else, too. Now, most of the young western mothers I know are even busier, with the new obligations to be professional-level mothers while they're soaring to the top in their careers. There are, of course, multiple satisfactions in these multiple roles, but as much as we treasure our fuller participation in the wider world, we lose an incalculable something.

We lose the calmness. We lose the focus. We lose the peace. These Nepali mothers work hard in their kitchens and their fields. But they never seem harried. We never saw a village mother rush her children to get dressed and be on time—for school, for anything. They never juggle a baby on one hip while they answer the phone. (Of course, they have no phones.) Even when they're working and baby-tending—fetching water with a baby in a sling on their backs or peeling potatoes with a toddler at their feet—they don't seem distracted.

One day, while Marge and I are staying at Jai's house, we take the ten-minute walk down the hillside to visit Gora's family. Our cook lives with his wife, Devi, and their two young daughters in a small two-story stone house with a thatched roof. As we arrive, Devi is sitting in the dark little kitchen by the fire-pit, nursing Lila, their six-month-old. On the fire sits a steaming kettle of milk tea. On the shelves lining one wall are eight shiny metal plates, eight shiny metal cups, several small pitchers—the usual assortment of dining ware. I can't get over how everything gleams. I know how much work it takes to keep it that way in these dusty hills.

Devi smiles shyly and invites us inside for tea and tiny boiled potatoes, a favorite village snack. At every home we visit here in Badel, we are welcomed warmly and hospitably. No one is ever too busy to greet us graciously. No work is ever so pressing that it can't be put off for a while. The rhythms of life here flow instead of churning, as they do back home in Port Washington and Evanston. Marge whispers to me as we sit down with Devi, "See—these women don't run around. They're not distracted, they can just sit, watch the baby, cook, work in the fields when they have to, and then have someone else watch the baby. That's why these babies hardly ever cry. They're always being held by somebody."

Despite this loving care, we do know that these children are at risk of grave illness. In these remote villages in Nepal, one in every five children dies before the fifth birthday, often a victim of dysentery and resulting dehydration, or of some other illness that, in the absence of readily available medical care, rages unchecked. [Sadly, by 2000 two of the children we came to know here had died—Indra's son, Bikas, and Gora's middle daughter.] But those who make it past the vulnerable early years grow up sturdy and healthy. And with a rising awareness of improved sanitation and a growing emphasis on health education for both parents and children, we are optimistic that this grim childhood mortality rate will improve.

We also know that accidents do, of course, befall the village children. Toddlers get burned, sometimes terribly so, when they tumble into the open fires in the center of every kitchen, and older children break limbs when they fall out of trees that they've climbed to cut firewood. But the youngsters of Badel are safe from many modern dangers. They don't get hit by cars and trucks, they don't tumble down stairs in baby-walkers, they don't fall out of supermarket carts, they don't drown in bathtubs or swimming pools, they don't get shot in gang-war crossfires. Child abuse is virtually unknown. And they're certainly not going to get brain tumors from electro-magnetic fields or epileptic seizures from playing video games, which some critics claim as the newest childhood dangers of the western world.

So in terms of accidental injury or environmental illness, the world of these children seems as sheltering, or more so, than the one inhabited by our own grandchildren.

Buddi describes the Rai marriage ceremony to Sally who gets it all on tape.

14

Marriage: "We Saw a Beautiful Flower Blooming"

The daughter from a good family is like spring water.
—Nepali proverb

On the morning that Buddi takes us up the hill to meet with the 75-year-old village midwife, Sabut Maya Mathani Rai, we assume that the slim middle-aged man working around the house is her son and that the fortyish woman who appears briefly to say hello and then goes back to her chores, is her daughter-in-law. As our interview with the senior midwife of Badel comes to an end, the man of the house, Mon Bahadur Rai, asks us to take a family photo. The photo of Mon Bahadur flanked by the two women and his youngest son turns out well. They all look straight ahead, with sober miens; Nepalis take photos seriously and rarely smile for the camera.

All the adults are barefoot. Mon Bahadur wears the typical hill village outfit of narrow beige cotton trousers with a matching tunic and jacket, and a multi-colored *topi* (traditional Nepali

173

cap). Both women are also dressed traditionally. Scarves cover their heads; gold rings dangle from septums and ears; beads wreathe their necks; bracelets encircle both wrists. Mathani, the older woman, wears a maroon velvet blouse atop her lunghi. Mon Maya, the younger one, had run into the house to wrap a beautiful yellow sari over her dusty, everyday cotton lunghi, but she kept on her simple cotton blouse. Except for his topi, twelve-year-old Madhap, in his Chinese canvas sneakers, tee shirt and western-style pants, would look at home on any school playground in America. In this one picture we can see the changes inexorably coming to even the most remote Himalayan villages.

After the photo opportunity we learn that one custom has not changed: the two women are Mon Bahadur's two wives. After Mathani bore three children, her first husband died. In a practice not uncommon in these villages, at the age of 43 she married a younger man. At 28, Mon Bahadur Matha Rai, was marrying for the first time. Since over the next several years they did not conceive any children together, Mon Bahadur was then free to take a second wife.

Even though polygamy was outlawed in Nepal in 1950, mostly as a sop to western morals, the practice is still common in rural areas, especially when a couple has not had any sons. Daughters don't count. It's ironic, of course, that a wife's failure to bear sons frees her husband to take a second wife, since it is the male contribution to conception that determines the sex of a child. But this belief is not confined to Himalayan villages. Henry VIII divorced Catherine of Aragon because she bore him a daughter rather than the son and heir he so desperately wanted. In Nepal the remedy is friendlier. The first wife is not cast aside; she and her children, daughters though they may be, remain in the home, are still part of the family and are entitled to a share of the man's property.

Mathani, as is common in these cases, actively helped Mon Bahadur arrange for his second marriage. If, however, he had sought a new wife because he had found another woman more appealing, even though his first wife had already borne him a son, Mathani would have been, to put it mildly, unsympathetic to her husband's desires. In fact, she would most likely have been as angrily opposed to the second marriage as any western woman would be—and she would have had the entire village wrathfully on her side. Husbands in cases like this are often shunned, not allowed to participate in village activities, not offered help with crops or animals. A harsh enough punishment to keep many a would-be polygamist in line.

The imperative to bear a son is not, as it first seemed to me, a question of simple sexism. It is, rather, ingrained in innumerable aspects of this culture. For one thing, when a daughter marries, she will leave her natal family and go to live in her husband's village, with his family. The son, conversely, will bring his wife home and will raise his children near, or in, his parents' home. His parents, then, can enjoy a continuity of the parent-child relationship, as well as the day-to-day pleasures from grandchildren, the son's children; the daughter's children will remain virtual strangers to their grandparents. Sons can help their fathers by doing heavy work on the land. They can bring pride to their families by following in their fathers' footsteps as Gurkha soldiers. And since men have the opportunity to earn much more than women can, they will be able to make financial contributions to the family, as, for example, Buddi did when he helped his father buy his home, and as he will do again when he helps to pay university tuition and expenses for his younger brothers. Finally, the youngest son is expected to assume responsibility for his parents in their old age; and when they die, it is a son who carries out the funeral rituals.

During our stay in the village, though, we see daughters treated lovingly, from infancy on. They are also valued for the work they can do, both in the house and in the fields, where they do the most time-consuming tasks. They hoe, they transplant millet and rice, and they harvest and thresh. And, of course, they winnow, husk, grind grain into flour, cook, wash dishes and clothes, make *chang* and *rakshi*, feed the chickens, sweep and plaster the floors, and care for children and the elderly. In fact, one Nepali saying maintains: "If a man begets only sons his lot will be a difficult one," and another promises: "Where there is a woman, there is prosperity." In all the families we've met here, little girls seem to be cherished. Still, this is Asia—and, given a preference, most parents would choose sons over daughters.

Mon Maya, Mon Bahadur's second wife, acquitted herself magnificently therefore when she fulfilled her promise by bearing him three sons. The eldest, Chhitra Bahadur, is a carpet-cutter in Kathmandu; the second, Nanda, is off trekking with Peter Owens; and Madhap is in the sixth grade at the Badel school.

Mon Bahadur's two wives seem to get along harmoniously. As we see so often during these two weeks, customs that seem so strange to our western minds can work very well indeed in other places. Just as sibling rivalry is not inevitable, neither is livid jealousy by one wife for another, provided the second marriage occurs within the approved context. As with so much in life, it's okay as long as there's common agreement that it's okay. Still, the two elements in this marriage that strike us—the greater age of the first wife and the presence of two wives—are considerably rarer even here in Badel than the more typical monogamous bond between two people of about the same age, like the one between Buddi and Dhana.

Buddi has told us with great enthusiasm and joy about his betrothal, wedding and current relationship with his wife, all of which are typical of Rai matrimony. Four years ago, when Buddi was at Tribhuvan University in Kathmandu, his parents decided that now that he was 24 years old, he should give up his bachelor status. As it happened, they knew of an eminently suitable match. A young woman from a good family in the nearby village of Rakha, a two-hour walk away, had married a man in Badel—and had a younger sister who was now of an age to wed.

Buddi had seen that younger sister, Dhana Kumari Rai, years ago at the elder sister's wedding and had glimpsed her once or twice in the next few years, but they had never spoken. When Buddi first saw her, Dhana was only 10 or 11 years old; she was still wearing a skirt, not yet having passed the rite of passage in which she graduated to a lunghi. Now Dhana was 17 and had just finished high school; her age and her educational level made her seem an especially suitable wife for Buddi.

When his parents suggested Dhana as a wife, Buddi remembered what a pretty little girl she had been. He knew that her sister's marriage had worked out well. And he was ready to get married. So he cheerfully agreed to his parents' wishes to woo her, Nepali style. First, Buddi's uncle and a friend of Buddi's father made the two-hour walk to Rakha to pay a visit to Dhana's father, taking with them two liters of good rakshi. When her father accepted the rakshi, he showed that he was accepting Buddi's proposal to his daughter. (Rakshi is the sine qua non of virtually every Rai ceremony and most social occasions, playing so integral a role in them that the Rais are known by Hindus as *matwali jat*—drinking castes. But while drunkenness occasionally results in dark episodes of fighting, wife-beating and boisterousness, alcoholism of the kind we know in the west, which consistently disrupts a person's functioning in day-to-day life, is rare.)

The second ritual meeting can occur right away, or it can be postponed for a year, depending on the couple's ages and circumstances. Buddi was away guiding a trek when the first meeting took place; when he returned home, his parents gave him the welcome news that his intended's father had accepted his proposal. One month after the meeting between his emissaries and her father, Buddi went to Dhana's house and for the first time in years set eyes on this demure sloe-eyed beauty.

Buddi did not go on this momentous visit alone. He was accompanied by several men from his family, including his father and grandfather, who arrived bearing more rakshi. The 35 liters they offered this time showed the greater seriousness of their intent. In front of about ten of Dhana's relatives and neighbors, Buddi gave his fiancée 100 rupees in a small purse, showing that (in Rai idiom) he had "bought" her and would be taking care of her. Her acceptance of the gift from this young man from a family her family approved of showed her willingness to take him as her husband.

At this meeting, prettily phrased ritual exchanges took place between the representatives of both parties to the match. They all spoke in Nachhering, one of about twelve Rai languages and the one used by the people of Badel for all important occasions. They used the most respectful terms of address, rather than the more informal words used for everyday conversation. And they couched their dialogue in poetic utterances like those used in literature, not in the simple speech of every day.

On Dhana's behalf, the older men from Rakha asked Buddi's people, "Why do you come here? Where is your house?" (They knew, of course, the answers to both questions—but, as Buddi says, over and over, as he tells us about Rai customs, "That is our way.")

Buddi's people said, "We come to ask your daughter's [or "your grand-daughter's" depending on whether they were addressing Dhana's father or grandfather] hand in marriage."

"Why do you want to marry her?"

"We saw a beautiful flower blooming in this house. We are like a butterfly come to that flower."

"We have no blooming flowers," Dhana's people said, playing the game out according to ancient tradition. More lyrical give-and-take occurred until finally Buddi's family got to the point directly, asking the bride's father: "Do you want to give your daughter to our son?"

After Dhana's father finally said yes, Buddi's kinsmen asked the young woman herself, "Do you want to go with our son?" Like most prospective Rai brides, Dhana was shy and said nothing, allowing her silence to be construed as assent. Her father then said to Buddi, "Don't beat our daughter. Take care of her. From today we give her to you to have a good life. We will miss her in our family, but from today you are our son-in-law."

After this conversation, Buddi heaved a sigh of relief. He served more rakshi all around and celebrated the fact that his marriage was now considered valid. He and Dhana could now live together and have children.

Marge and I heard the account of this courtship only from Buddi, and I keep imagining what it might have been like to have been Dhana at that crucial meeting, to imagine what tangled feelings she must have had. To look shyly at this handsome young man while he shot sideways glances at her, to hope he thought you were pretty even though you were wearing simple everyday clothes, to be wooed by poetry and to know that your suitor and his family were willing to make generous outlays to win over your family, to have the support of all your relatives and to be able to see the members of the family you were marrying into, to imagine how you would feel about leaving your family, your neighbors, the home you had known all your life, and living with those strangers.

How different all of this is from the way we do things in the western world—and how appealing it sounds in so many ways, considering our high rates of marital unhappiness, assault, separation and divorce. By all the evidence, "love marriages" in the west—or those few that are increasingly taking place now in Nepal—by and large, show little to recommend them over arranged ones.

Soon Dhana came to live at Buddi's house, where she began to help his mother with the housework. The young wife was typically bashful and reserved at first, but she and Buddi liked each other, and they eventually came to love each other. Those couples who find that they don't like each other after the first ceremony don't have to go through with the final one. The bride can go home to her family, with no prejudice, even if a child has already been born of the union.

One key to the future happiness of the marriage is how well the mother-in-law and daughter-in-law get along. Many a marriage founders because a harsh mother-in-law, perhaps making up for her own bondage so many years ago, treats the young wife like a slave, making unreasonable demands on her—or because of a stubborn daughter-in-law's refusal to perform duties in the job description of Rai wife. In Dhana's case, she and Shiva do get along, according to Buddi, our only informant on the issue. (Although both Shiva and Dhana understand some English, neither one speaks it—out of inability or shyness, we don't know which.) During our stay, we do sense an easy rapport between the two women, as they share household tasks and as Shiva helps Dhana care for Kusum. We pick up no signs of tension and are inclined to accept Buddi's report at face value, that in truth there are no quarrels, no angry words, no rifts between his two women. My mother's old maxim, "Two women in the kitchen equals three kinds of trouble," doesn't seem to apply in Badel.

Even after the wife goes to live with the husband's family, one more ceremony remains to be performed. That one can take place many years later. The only requirement is that it be conducted before the couple's children get married! The final ceremony between Buddi and Dhana took place about a year after the second one, after their daughter, Kusum, had been born.

Buddi proudly shows us a color photograph taken at the grand nuptials. Dhana, the beautiful bride, wore scarlet finery, since Nepalis consider red the prettiest and luckiest color (a belief expressed by the saying our staff taught us, "*Raato raamro, guliyo mitho*"—"Red is beautiful, sweet is delicious"). Buddi, the benedict, was all in white except for his topi, which was *rungi-chungi* (multi-colored). He put vermilion powder in Dhana's hair and gave her a gold ring and earrings, which will always be hers to keep, no matter what happens with the marriage.

The bridegroom's family spends a Nepali fortune on clothing, rakshi, food and music. Since Buddi's family is prosperous, the festivities were especially elaborate, costing the considerable sum of 32,000 rupees (about $600, in a country where the average annual income per person is less than $200). Their celebration lasted for four days: the first two in Badel, the groom's village, and two more in Rakha, home of the bride's family. Buddi's family killed two pigs for the feasting, offered such extra food as vegetables, rice, chutney and other delicacies, and hired a band. Thirteen Darje musicians played flute, horns and drums for the entire four days of dancing, eating, drinking and all-round merrymaking. Usually everyone from each spouse's entire village is invited. Buddi's wedding hosted 1,000 guests, including those from both villages, as well as other relatives from other places. As is usual, Buddi tells us, every family brought ten kilos of rice and ten bottles of rakshi. No one went hungry or thirsty.

Budd's wife, Donna, shuffling the rice, removing the
husks from the grain. It is hard work and
the arms get very tired. Hers don't mine do!

Buddi is not likely to take another wife as long as Dhana is alive. They want one more child, preferably a son, but if they have another daughter, they won't keep trying for a boy. Buddi wants to send his children to school, including university, and he feels that the only way he can do this and give them the care they should have is by having a small family. (We have seen posters in every school and health station in Nepal urging people to have only two children. In a magazine addressed to Nepali women, we also saw an ad for birth control pills, appealing to the desire to be beautiful: "Gulaf is for beauty. Yes, we care for your beauty. Gulaf Oral Pills helps to maintain your beauty by having children by choice and not by chance.") Dhana works hard in the home; and apparently she does not need to be convinced to stop at two children, even though her joy in Kusum is obvious in the radiance with which she looks at her little daughter.

Although arranged marriages are still the rule in Nepal, "love marriages" are becoming more common. In one common romantic scenario, a young couple fall in love, go off into the forest by themselves for a few days and return to present themselves to their parents as husband and wife. Faced with a fait accompli, the families are generally accepting. The marriage between Buddi's sister, Sita, and Jai, our other guide, was a love marriage that followed a route that more closely hews to the common western pattern.

Star-blessed lovers, Jai and Sita came together at the right place at the right time in the right way. Just after Jai's parents had given their 21-year-old son an ultimatum, "It's time for you to find a wife—or we'll find one for you," Jai, visiting in Badel between treks, was preparing to leave for Kathmandu. At the same time, Sita wanted to go to the capital city to look for work. Since she needed a chaperone, Jai agreed to accompany her. By the time they had walked the four or five days to the closest bus stop in Kadari and then sat together on the long bus ride to Kathmandu, they had decided to marry. And this love marriage seems to be flourishing.

Before we left Kathmandu for Badel, Jai invited Marge, Buddi and me for lunch at the small house in the outskirts of Kathmandu, where Jai and Sita and Kim live. Sita, 28, greets us at the door. She has delicately chiseled features, almond-shaped eyes, a golden honey complexion and thick black waist-length hair, caught at the back of her neck and hanging down her back. We don't see Kim today, since he attends nursery school from 8:00 to 3:00. Both Marge and I, knowing very well what three-year-olds are like, are astonished at the neatness and order in the rooms. You wouldn't know a small child lives in the house—except for a big white stuffed Snoopy from Macy's that sits on a chair, and a few other stuffed animals in a tall locked glass-fronted cabinet.

Marge and I have known Jai for a long time, have met Sita before and have ingratiated ourselves with gifts for everyone. We feel comfortable here, and they seem so with us. We show them our family photos; they show us their album. There are snapshots of Jai in Disneyland in 1984, when, through Peter's good offices and the generosity of many trekkers, he visited the United States and studied English. That was before his marriage; as in many young families, the bulk of the photos since the marriage portray Kim, from infancy to his present age of 3 ½. His round little face is just like Jai's; with his wide smile, he seems to be a happy child. Kim is likely to be an only child, since Jai and Sita say they don't want any more.

This young couple left many of their village values behind them in their move to the capital city: choosing to have only one child instead of the five or six more typical in their village, sending him to school early, living far from both families, Sita's interest in finding a job outside the home—possibly even in trekking with Jai, while she finds someone to care for Kim when she's away. Seeing this pair, Marge and I wondered whether we'd find people still living traditional lives in the village they come from. And of course, while many of the old traditions are still robust, we do see changes too, especially among the younger people. One change is apparent in Buddi's expressed attitude toward marital roles.

One day as we rest by the side of the road after having walked up to the hill above Badel, Buddi voices his strong opinions about the marriages between Brahmins, the most exalted caste in Nepal. "My goodness!" he exclaims. "Brahmin men are lazy. They sit while their women do all the work. Brahmin woman must to work very hard all day in fields and then fix food for the man. She cannot eat until he is finished, and then she must to rub her husband's back every night, three hours. Brahmin women do 80 percent, maybe 100 percent of work. Brahmin men not work.

"I don't like that. I like the American way—fifty-fifty. When I come home from Kathmandu, my wife washes my clothes for me. I always bring her something. Fifty-fifty. She takes care of Kusum and does other work in the house, and I help her a little. When I am finished with my studies, I will work more. Now I do my studies."

All of this grew out of Buddi's telling the other men sitting around with us as we rest how Marge's husband, Dwyer, makes coffee in the morning and brings it to Marge. I like the sentiments Buddi espouses, but when I see how hard Dhana works, while he accompanies us, it doesn't seem like fifty-fifty to me!

One day I go up with Buddi, Dhana and Kangsha to Gita's house, not to visit but to use her rice-beater. I start to watch—and end up actually doing some work. The apparatus is a wooden tool that works by a large, foot-operated lever, which has a wide metal-tipped peg on its end that fits into a depression in the ground. Dhana empties a basket of rice—about twenty pounds (enough to make 20 giant Nepali-sized servings, or 60 puny western ones)— on the ground around the declivity. First, she carefully sweeps the area with a small hand broom. Then making graceful motions with her hand and the broom, she keeps sweeping the mound close to the center while Buddi and Kangsha work the lever with their feet. I sit down on the other side and help Dhana smooth the mound, to the pounding rhythm of the wooden beam.

Buddi is getting more and more nervous watching me. First he stops and tells me, "When the machine goes up, you put your hand in. Otherwise you get a wound." I think I'm doing it right, but he eventually gets too nervous and presses me to change places with him. So I team up with Kangsha, as we each place one foot on the lever, hold onto the wooden posts on either side and rhythmically pump the lever up and down. When the rice is beaten enough, Dhana puts mounds of it on a straw winnowing tray and skillfully tosses it up in the air, to let the husks blow off in gentle clouds. Kangsha and I keep on pumping, Buddi keeps on swishing the mound to the center and Dhana keeps tossing. After we've all been at work for about 45 minutes, the job is done— except for a final tossing, which Dhana will do back at her own house. She does this twice a week. If Buddi isn't home to work with her, she has to hire someone and pay him, sometimes a portion of the rice. A lot of work! A far cry from buying a box of Uncle Ben's at Grand Union!

Today, besides taking care of Kusum, Dhana "shuffled" (winnowed) some twenty portions of rice. Then she got down on her hands and knees and plastered the entire first floor, including the veranda, with a mixture of earth, buffalo dung and water. She does this twice a week, to clean and purify the house, and also to fill in the fine cracks in the earthen floor and keep it from crumbling. The task is always done by the younger woman of the house. This younger woman also cooked, washed clothes, cleaned up—and who knows what else.

But we have seen Buddi helping Dhana grind rice with that heavy wooden apparatus and helping Dhana bathe Kusum. And then, of course, his accompanying us is his work, and—for Badel—it is uncommonly lucrative work. Besides, as he says, "This is our way." And as Marge and I know well, plenty of American homes are more Brahmin than Rai, and hardly any are fifty-fifty.

Sabut Maya Raj, Village midwife. She is 75 years old and has been midwife since she was 25.

15

A Midwife Speaks: "I'm Just a Helper"

A man who has not traveled and a woman who has not given birth are alike.

—Nepali proverb

Our last day in Badel has dawned, sunny and clear. It is dimmed only by the sadness Marge and I both feel at our imminent departure from this secluded and friendly haven. We are somewhat brightened, though, by Buddi's news that we won't have to leave the village without meeting with Sabut Maya Mathani Rai, the presiding village midwife. We had met her briefly a few days ago in the yard of her daughter's home, but she was busy at her loom and we were not able to talk about her profession, which we were both eager to do—and had been afraid it wouldn't come to pass.

Birthing babies is important to each of us, both professionally and personally. Marge's experiences as a pediatric nurse and my research and writing about pregnancy, breastfeeding and child-rearing keep mothers and babies uppermost in both our minds.

Aside, of course, from the fact that as fecund mothers of fertile children, each of us has borne her own babies and then has vicariously kept reentering the delivery room as our children have been bringing forth our grandchildren.

The three of us walk up a little hill soon after breakfast to visit Sabut Maya Mathani Rai. She has been helping childbearing mothers for almost 50 years, since her first delivery, of twins, now 28 years old. Buddi proudly tells us that she helped his mother at his own birth, and then helped her again eleven years ago at the birth of her youngest child, Kiran, the product of Shiva's twentieth pregnancy.

Sabut Maya appears in front of her modest stone house dressed in a plum-colored velvet long-sleeved blouse and a bright flowered lunghi—typical dress of the older village women. A string around her neck displays several keys, probably to lock her doors when she goes away on calls and another to lock her trunk holding her most precious possessions, possibly gold jewelry. Why does everyone lock everything up in this village where there is no crime? Maybe taking someone's unsecured items is not considered theft—and that has colored Buddi's statement to us that there is no stealing here?

To our eyes Sabut Maya—with her wrinkled brown skin, wrinkled and worn dirty clothes, wrinkled grimy hands and missing teeth—looks far older than her 75 years. Deep furrows line her brow from three-quarters of a century of squinting into the harsh mountain sun. No sunscreen or sunglasses here. But her posture is erect, her step is quick and she still actively practices her profession. Only three days ago she attended the birth of a baby girl. And over the past months she has been training two other women in the village (including the fortyish mother of our porter, Tara Mani) just as her own mother taught her so many years ago.

Sabut Maya brings Marge and me bamboo stools to perch on, Buddi sits on a nearby step and the old midwife sits on the ground. Her large, prominently knuckled hands hug her bent knee; a bare calloused foot protrudes from the hem of her lunghi. I turn on the tape recorder, Marge pulls out her drawing pad and the interview starts. Buddi translates. Sabut Maya had told him that she would be happy to talk to us, and she seems willing enough, but, unlike most of the villagers we've met, she neither smiles expansively nor exudes an air of enthusiastic sociability. Maybe it's her age. Or maybe just her personality. Not all Nepalis are alike.

We ask her what she does when she attends a woman about to give birth. "First I feel on the outside of the woman's belly," she says, accompanying her explanation with gestures as she touches her own body. "I look to see where is the head and the other organs. I help the mother push down when her time comes."

"Do you use forceps or anything like that to help pull the baby out?" Marge asks. This message seems hard for Buddi to translate—or for Sabut Maya to understand. Maybe because the concept of using such tools here, where childbirth is looked upon as such a normal occurrence, is so unthinkable. Finally, she jerks her head up and sideways in the Nepali gesture that means no. "I don't have any instruments. I just use my hands. If the baby is upside down, I turn it from the outside."

Looking at her hands, persistent village dust ingrained in every deep crease and wrinkle, we're relieved (despite our resolutions not to judge by our country's values) to hear her declare, "I never put my hands inside the woman."

Buddi interjects his own comments about childbirth: "Birth is easy for Nepali women. They work hard. They have good muscles. The babies are small. The village women are strong, stronger than men." Nepali hill women usually give birth right after—or in the middle of—working. The delivery may occur inside or outside of the house, depending on when the woman goes into labor. If the mother has other children, they usually watch, no matter how small they are. But the husbands, Buddi tells us, shaking his head, don't want to watch and the women don't want them around.

Most women do not avail themselves of a midwife's services; they handle the delivery and dispose of the placenta and umbilical cord themselves. Like Shiva, Buddi's mother. She gave birth to one baby on the path as she was walking back from working in the fields, and then asked her husband to give her his khukri so that she could cut the cord. After the delivery, women in better-off families rest for ten to fifteen days. The poorer ones rest for only three days before going back to work, but they will work at easier jobs than usual for a while, confining themselves to bringing water and cooking food.

Sabut Maya continues her description of her work. "The first baby usually takes a long time." We nod. "This is usually true in our country, too."

In reply to our queries about the usual delivery position, Sabut Maya nimbly rises from her crossed-legs sitting position and agilely mimes a pose to show us that women usually give birth kneeling on their knees. This position allows the mother to use her strong thigh and abdominal muscles to push the baby out.

"If the baby is not coming fast, I use special medicine. I put grasses on the mother's body and I massage her with oil from a special plant. I don't give the mother any herbs or anything like that to eat or drink, only hot water or tea. Sometimes someone in the family gives her a special strong rakshi."

"What do you give the mother for her labor pains?" we ask, thinking about all the elaborate measures in use in the United States—anesthesia given generally or epidurally in the spinal cord, analgesics for relaxation, classes where expectant mothers and fathers go to learn breathing and exercises and special birthing movements—all to allay what our culture has generally taken as God's curse to Eve and to all the women who have followed her: "In sorrow shalt thou bring forth children."

"I don't give her anything to bite down on for pain. She usually doesn't need anything like that." Nor does the midwife make any cuts to widen the vagina; this isn't necessary. Although first-time mothers take longer to give birth, they never tear. Apparently their ligaments are flexible. And since the mothers eat the typical low-fat, low-sugar diet, rich in minerals and grains, they gain little extra weight and don't have large babies.

"I'm just a helper," she says, shrugging. "I don't have the medicines or the equipment that you have in your country."

When a midwife sees that a birth is complicated—if, say, the baby isn't emerging despite all her ministrations or if the mother gets sick—she has the family call the village shaman. That's the emergency backup, the only kind of intervention available in Badel. I think of my daughter whose baby, after sixteen hours of labor, did not move into the vaginal canal; I shudder, thinking what would have happened to Nancy and little Anna if they had not had access to an emergency cesarean delivery, if the birth had occurred here in Badel.

Inevitably, some babies die and some mothers die. The fact that women still die in childbirth in these remote areas helps to explain the preponderance of males in the population of Nepal. When something goes wrong and either mother or infant dies, this is looked upon as the will of the gods. However, such deaths are treated differently from other deaths. When a baby dies, the little body is cremated, and when a mother dies, she is buried down by the river—not up by the house where most of the dead are buried, because death in childbirth, like a premature death from an accident, is not considered a "good death."

In most cases, however, all goes well. Most deliveries are easy and quick. In answer to our questions, Sabut Maya tells us how the newborn is cared for:

"After the baby is born I wash the baby. I leave this much of the cord on the baby"—she holds two fingers together to indicate about an inch—"and I tie it up with very good cotton. Then I wrap a piece of cotton cloth around the baby's tummy. This stays on for a few days until the cord falls off." Sometimes a small piece of the umbilical cord is saved and inserted into a small metal bead that will be given to the child to wear on a string around the neck. The piece of cord is thought to ward away evil spirits. Somebody in the family flings the placenta high up on a tree near the house to dry out, and eventually it is thrown away. No ritual use is made of it, and so far as anyone knows, no animal eats it.

As soon as the cord is cut, the baby is washed with warm water and then given to the mother to nurse. The baby will have nothing but breast milk for the first two to six months, depending on whether the mother's breast milk seems adequate. To assure a good milk supply, the Rai mother drinks chicken soup and buffalo milk and eats rice and butter. She will probably nurse her baby for about three years if she does not become pregnant in the meantime; if she does, she will wean the child.

No one but the mother—not even the father—is allowed to hold the baby until three days of age if it's a girl, or seven days for a boy. This is probably to protect both mother and baby from infection and disease when they are both vulnerable. (Both Marge and I are distressed by the gender difference that to us suggests that it is more important to protect the boy babies, but neither of us questions it. That is their way.) After this time a combination of purification rite and naming ceremony takes place. The mother washes the clothes she has been wearing and cleans the place in the house where she stayed with her baby. Then, in the presence of both parents' families, who have brought chickens and chang to be feasted on later, the shaman conducts a rite to exorcise any evil spirits that may have attended the birth.

We welcome Sabut Maya's question, "How are babies born in the United States?" She is the first woman to have asked us anything substantial about our culture. Maybe she is bolder because of her position in the community. Or maybe she is showing the self-confidence of age, the shedding of inhibitions, the lack of worry about observing the conventions or what others might think, that even in our society, with its denial of and lack of respect for old age, often comes with advancing years. In this society, where maturity is valued, elders— even female ones—may speak and act more freely.

Marge and I describe how women lie on their backs, a position unknown in most traditional cultures, and how the doctor sometimes breaks the woman's water. We also tell how a doctor sometimes puts on surgical gloves and reaches inside the woman to turn a baby in a breech or other position. Looking at Sabut Maya's dirt-blackened hands and fingernails, I emphasize the use of gloves so that she won't take it into her head to try western techniques in an effort to be "modern." But I vastly underestimated her good sense, and I am ashamed of myself when I see her shake her head and hear Buddi's translation of what she says: "We don't have gloves and we don't have instruments. We don't do any of those things." She repeats, "I'm just a helper."

What Sabut Maya really is is a *doula*, a woman who has had a baby herself and can provide emotional support for the childbearing mother, a role that recent research has recognized as valuable in fostering healthy deliveries. In a 1991 study of over 400 American women having their first babies, the women who had doulas with them had fewer cesarean deliveries, less use of anesthesia, shorter labors, and fewer forceps deliveries. It seems so ironic that it has taken us in America all these years to rediscover what so-called "primitive" societies have known for centuries.

Sureya kumari Rai
and
her sleeping baby.
9 month old. Parmila
Rai

So yes, in developed countries like ours, women and babies involved in complicated childbirths are a million times better off. It is chilling to realize that probably daughters of both Marge and myself would have died if they had had to give birth in Badel—and had no access to surgical deliveries. But for the great majority of births, it seems that women do better in Badel than they do in the United States. Their bodies are strong, their babies are small, their support system is known and their accomplishment is hailed. (Especially, of course, if they bear sons.) So the big question we in the western world have to ask is: "What can we learn from ancient wisdom to help our own childbearing women—without giving up the advanced medical techniques that save lives?" And what can we do to bring the best of what we have to save the lives of women around the world, without invalidating the practices that serve them well?

We have been up here an hour, it's now close to 10:00 a.m. and Buddi is impatient to start out on our three-day walk back to Lamidanda, where we'll board our flight for Kathmandu. Before we leave, we honor Sabut Maya's request to snap another family photo—of Sabut Maya, her husband, his second wife and the son of the second marriage, all of whom live together as one family. As we begin to say our goodbyes with the gesture of "namaste," Sabut Maya lifts an arm to stay us. We stand in the courtyard and watch her erect figure as she slowly walks barefoot into her little house.

A moment later she emerges holding gifts for Marge and me. They are wreaths of small red flowers, found only at high altitudes, which have been dried and strung on lengths of narrow cord. She has been wearing a similar string attached to her blouse with a safety pin. Our wreaths too come equipped with safety pins. Buddi explains that these flowers are called *marache,* and that, according to the Rai custom, a woman makes a wreath and gives them to good friends as a present, to bring good luck. The family offers us both tea and rakshi; just like the French with champagne, it's never too early in the morning for Nepalis to drink rakshi.

After I return home to the States, I often pin my marache to a blouse. Looking at it, I remember a stranger who wished me well, and a morning when I felt the familiar ambivalence between admiration for the simplicity of ancient ways and appreciation for some of the modern ones.

A horssing Rai
Old man sitting on fence with two khukris

16

Death: "Going to the Heaven Place"

We come naked, we leave naked—a life of but two days.
—Part of Nepali prayer

Kangsha, our youngest porter, had to leave school to help support his family. Marge and I understand why when, setting out for an afternoon hike about 1,000 feet above Badel, we pass the modest house where Kangsha lives with his mother and younger brother, and as we skirt the edge of the property, Buddi points to a small grassy mound a few feet from the house. "That's where Kangsha's father is," he says. Buddi then tells us how the Rai commemorate the death of someone in the community.

Unlike most Nepalis, who cremate their dead, the Rais bury theirs in the earth near the family's dwelling. After someone dies, a family member washes the body, dresses it in clean cotton garments and lays it on a bamboo mat with the head facing east. The Puri, the thinner, taller, darker people who live on top of the hill, bury their dead in a communal cemetery. As we pass the Puri

197

cemetery on the side of the hill, we see tepee-like structures over piles of stones covering freshly dug graves. The Puri put bread, salt and clothing in with their dead so that their spirits will be nourished and clad in the next world, but the departed Rai go empty-handed on their journey.

After the preparation of the Rai body, family and friends gather to help build the coffin—a sturdy stone box with a cover. Then it's time to call in the shaman to conduct the funeral rites. He arrives in full ceremonial garb, and, surrounded by the deceased's family and friends, he ignites a fire. In front of its flickering flames, the shaman chants over the body.

In Mudhum, the Rai religion, the fire holds an important spiritual significance. Mudhum has one principal god, Chula, a god of fire who lives in the fire in the center of every Rai house. Every religious ceremony begins with some obeisance to Chula. The fire assumes a vital role in villagers' lives: this is how houses are heated; this is how food is cooked; this is how meat is smoked. In the amalgam of religions that characterizes Nepal, Mudhum tenets incorporate some Buddhism and a little Hinduism, but for the most part retain ancient animistic beliefs. (As Buddi tells us about his people's religion and their sacred rites, I am struck by the fact that his full name, Buddi Kumar Rai, incorporates three different religions: the name "Buddi" honors the Buddha, "the enlightened one"; "Kumar" is the name of a Hindu warrior bachelor prince; and since the Rais observe neither Buddhism nor Hinduism, "Rai" acknowledges his people's practice of the animist religion Mudhum.)

Speaking in Nachhering, the Rai language spoken in Badel, the shaman begins the funeral ritual, telling the dead person's spirit to go. "It is time to leave this world," he intones. "Do not come back. Do not worry about your husband [or wife, or children—whoever the survivors are]. They are safe in this world."

The holy man then calls upon the gods to help him decide where the grave should be dug. Only people who have had a "good" death are buried near their house. What is a good death? One that comes of natural causes, like illness or old age. Even though any death is considered to be the will of the gods, the Rais—and presumably, the gods—make distinctions. Villagers who die in accidents (like falling out of a tree while collecting firewood) or in childbirth, and those who commit suicide (such a rare occurrence that Buddi cannot remember ever hearing about an incident in Badel) cannot be interred near the house. The souls of these "bad" death victims can wander around and make trouble for the living, so they must be buried down by the river, where the river god can prevent them from wreaking harm. Apparently, they are considered in the same category as the untouchables, since the bank of the Liding Khola is also the site where the Darjes, the village untouchables, bury their dead.

Besides helping to make the coffin, neighbors perform many other services for the family. Some bring stones to mark the grave, some dig the three-foot crater for the coffin and all bring food and drink (10 kilos of rice and 10 bottles of rakshi each). They keep the mourners company all day and eat and drink with them all night to help them overcome their sadness.

As a precaution against the dead's coming back in the guise of bad spirits and giving trouble to the villagers, the family sacrifices a chicken and, if they can afford it, a pig. Sometimes the slaughtered animal becomes the funeral meat; at other times only the old people are honored by being offered the sacrificial flesh. At the funeral, Buddi tells us with animated gestures, the shaman tells the departed, "When you die, you go to heaven place, eat good. If you want anything else to eat, we give to you now." So the funeral guests are not the only ones who'll eat well. To ensure that the dead person will not go hungry, the shaman puts rice, chang and any favorite food of the deceased's into the fire. Another reason for "feeding" the fire is to placate the spirits so that they will not return.

One year later the village shaman, sometimes accompanied by a Hindu priest from another village, returns to conduct another ceremony. This marks the formal end to the mourning period. Again, the shaman tells the spirit of the dead person to go away and not to come back. He reassures the person's spirit that there's no need to worry: the family is doing fine. "And that," says Buddi, "is the end!"

Well, not quite the end. Two years after a woman dies (three to five years for a man—presumably because their spirits are more powerful), another special ceremony takes place, this one led by a Hindu priest. Again family and friends come. Again they bring food and drink. This time they winnow the rice that they have brought, and they bring other offerings, like clothing and tools; a khukri if the dead person is a man. The family of the departed walk down the slopes to the river, where they make a bridge of flowers and hang on it some of the clothing, tools and other objects brought for this purpose. With the creation of this delicate bridge, the dead person's spirit can now cross the surging waters of the Liding Khola and go to Heaven.

After the soul of the departed is sent off, the funeral turns into a festival of gaiety that starts in the morning and goes on all night. Men dressed like women do a Rai dance called *maruni*. Clowns make the assemblage laugh. Singing and dancing and drumming resound through the hills. Eating and drinking go on the entire time.

After death, the Rais believe, you get reborn 84 times, as one of 84 animals, going up the scale from fly to bird to tiger, until being reborn as a person. If you're very lucky, or if you did many good deeds in your first life, you move up the chain very quickly, and your next life will be better than this one. A comforting belief for these people who labor long in a hardscrabble existence and who have few ways to rid their lives of the constant specter of death, which snatches away so many of their babies and young people.

"We believe this," Buddi tells us. "No experiment, but we believe."

FROM MARGE'S JOURNAL:

As I listen to Buddi describe the funeral rituals, I think that I need ceremonies like these to help me get over the grief I still feel almost six years after my mother's death. Maybe we Christians need something more after the funeral to make the death final. That way we can stop grieving the dead and move on to the living. I especially like the part where the shaman tells the spirits to go on, away to that heaven place, that we will be all right now. This must help the family, too, because to me it seems to be saying, "No more guilt or regrets about what was done or left undone in that life. It is over." I don't pretend to know what goes on in the minds of a grieving family in Badel. I know only how long and deeply I mourned my parents' deaths and that there might be a better way. Maybe the Rais have found it.

As I listen to Buddi, I regret my falling away from the funeral rituals that have comforted my own Jewish ancestors through the ages. When one brother after the other died, and my father, and then my mother, we dwindling band of survivors did not observe the week-long period of shiva, with its rituals of grief. We didn't tear our clothing, cover our mirrors, sit on hard wooden benches, eschew shoes for slippers, pray every evening. Our memorial services were brief and immediate. We didn't prepare our loved ones' bodies ourselves, nor did we preserve them. Rejecting what felt like sentimentality and a reverence for the tangible rather than for the essence of those ended lives, we donated all the bodies for scientific research. There were no graves, no urns, no cemetery to visit. One year later, we didn't follow the tradition of putting an end to the time of mourning by unveiling a headstone. There was no headstone.

The traditional practices seemed foreign to me, who had never practiced my religion. Maybe if I had, I too would have achieved closure for all these deaths, would not be left with so much guilt, so many regrets. Maybe not. In any case, I'm struck by so many of the similarities between Rai and Jewish funerary rites. I'd like to think that in one or more of the next 84 lives, I'll meet this family of mine and have new chances to say and do all that I never had time—or took time—to do in this turn of the wheel of life.

My favorite part of the Rai ritual is the party—the music, the dancing, the clowns, the eating and drinking. This is what I want for my own funereal rite: the people I love coming together in the house where I lived, among the books and the paintings and the photos that enriched my days, to enjoy the music that touched me, to talk about my foibles and my idiosyncrasies, to laugh and to cry, to eat and drink well. To celebrate my life, not grieve my death. By now, I am too old to die young and my life has been rich beyond measure. When it is time for my spirit to go to "the heaven place," I think I'll be ready. I hope I'll meet some of the Rai friends that we've met here. We haven't had nearly as much time together as Marge and I would have liked.

Village Headman
Bhakta Rai.
He spoke for a long
time about the
needs of the village
most important
are irrigation roads
electricity and
education.

17

A Headman Speaks: "What Do You Need for Your Village?"

He who answers the call must open the door.
—Nepali proverb

Tomorrow we are to leave Badel, this haven from modern life where we have been so warmly welcomed and so graciously hosted. We head down to Jai's house to say goodbye to his family. Although Indra has gone back to her home in Rakha, on the other side of the Liding Khola, Jai's parents and his sisters Kali and Mithu are there. They interrupt their work to greet us, bring out bamboo stools and offer us freshly boiled potatoes and tea, which of course we accept, even though I feel as if I'm floating as fast as the muddy streams coursing through the village, with all the liquids I've been drinking!

Several times this week Buddi has tried to set up a meeting between the three of us and Bhakta Rai, the village headman, but the headman has been out of the village and no one, including his family, has known when he would return. Marge and I are both disappointed but in our new eastern mode of acceptance, tell each other, "This is how it's supposed to be." Then, just as we are finishing the last pre-lunch lunch we'll enjoy here in Badel, a small, slender, dark gentleman with a pleasant smile and a polite manner, dressed in tan jodphurs and tunic, brown vest and topi, comes up and "namaste's" us (puts his palms together and speaks the greeting).

He is Bhakta Rai. After Buddi gives us the headman's genealogy, I realize why he looks so familiar: he is the brother of two men we've met: Dhan Bahadur Rai, Gita's husband, the English teacher and storekeeper, and Bir Bahadur Rai, one of our porters. The brothers all resemble each other.

One of the children whisks out a stool for the headman; it fits his slight, spare body better than it fits ours. To the background noises of crowing roosters, laughing children, sloshing water, and singing wind, the four of us talk in the sun-drenched courtyard.

By way of introduction, Buddi tells us a little bit about Bhakta Rai. As a soldier in the highly acclaimed Gurkha regiments of the British Army, he served in Hong Kong and fought in Indonesia. Then like most Gurkha soldiers, when he became eligible for retirement, he came back to his village and picked up the farm work that his relatives had performed for him all the years he was in the military.

But then, atypically, Bhakta Rai became convinced of the importance of the role he could play as a small cog in the government of Nepal. He ran for the office of village headman, was elected one year ago and will hold office for another four years. The headman has just returned from a circuit of the several other villages that, along with Badel, constitute the territory he is responsible for. These trips are hardly junkets, however; whatever travel he undertakes comes out of his own shallow pockets. He receives neither salary nor expense monies.

Although now Bhakta Rai must return to the farming he has again neglected, now—even in the press of his official duties—he shows great pleasure at meeting with us. We detect no sign of impatience that we are keeping him from more important activities. This is not surprising to us; we have not seen any evidence of any impatience from anyone during the entire time we've been in Badel. No one has made snide remarks when they've been behind us on the narrow paths as we cautiously make our tortoise-paced way. No parent has scolded or dragged a child to hurry her up to go somewhere. No farmer has chivvied his helper to step up the work pace. Tasks take the time they need, and no one expresses annoyance when that time is longer than usual. This morning Bhakta Rai acts like a man who has all the time in a forgiving world.

"I do not speak English well." He smiles at us as he carefully enunciates the sentence, and then turns to Buddi with a long statement in Nepali. Buddi translates: "He understands English, so you can speak in English, but he will answer in Nepali."

Fine. We open our mouths to ask him some questions, when our meeting turns into Bhakta Rai's interview of the two of us: "What do you think of the government of Nepal?"

I gulp. "I don't know enough to give an intelligent opinion," I say. With that disclaimer out of the way, I plunge in: "But I think it's very exciting that you have a democracy now and that people are so interested in the government and that you're trying to do more for the people. I was just reading the history of Nepal, and you don't have a long history of democracy, so it's good to see that it's started. Since we live in America, which has democracy, we think that's a good form of government." Actually, Nepal's government is a constitutional monarchy; its nod to democracy is its recently held election which put in office the first popularly elected prime minister in 30 years.

After this long answer to a short question, a lengthy conversation ensues between Bhakta Rai and Buddi. Buddi translates: "We have more problems with our politics than how we know. We have many ups and downs of our customs with all the people, like the Rai, the Tamang, the Newar. They don't know about each other's customs. Most of Tamang and Rai, they don't know about their own cultures and their own customs. They need to read books, learn." "Maybe," I say, engaging in wishful—and egocentric—thinking, "when our book comes out, more people will know about the Rai culture."

I remember what Buddi told us about crime in his village. In his entire life he never heard of a murder in Badel. After thinking hard, he did remember a single theft, which occurred some four years ago, when a group of French high school students camped overnight in the village during a trek up to Everest Base Camp. The thief, a member of the Puri ethnic group who live on a hill above the Rai settlement, was immediately discovered by his own people and made to return the money.

"We think it's wonderful that you have never had a murder in the village and that you don't have stealing here, because in America those are very big problems," Marge declares. "People in the big cities have guns. They kill each other. Poor people steal from even their poor neighbors." Buddi nods, recalling the news he saw on television in Kathmandu about the racial rioting in Los Angeles that tore the American west coast apart a few months back.

Trying to take enlightenment back with us, Marge asks, "So—what do you think is the reason why the Rai get along so much better with each other than people do in America?" But apparently neither man wants to undertake an answer. After another long conversation in Nepali, Buddi translates Bhakta Rai's next question: "What do you think about city and village? Many differences?"

Marge leans forward on her stool. "You have the same problems in your big cities that we have in our big cities," she says, choosing her words carefully. "I think you have a problem with dope—hashish—in Kathmandu with your young people. I think that as there is a rising educated middle class in Kathmandu, this also causes more problems because there aren't jobs for them. So I see many of the same problems in Kathmandu that we have in Chicago where I live, which is a very big city."

"What do you think about village?"

"Here in the village, it's very much like maybe America was in 1900, 1850, maybe 200 years ago, when people helped each other." Marge looks wistful for a time, a peace, a cooperative ethos that is no longer alive where we live. This void in our own country was clearly one of the strongest motivators for this quest of ours. And we still haven't grasped the secret that explains Badel's tranquillity.

"It's more like a big family here in the village," I add. "No strangers. There's a song we have that says a stranger is just a friend you haven't yet met. In America that's an ideal. But in Badel it seems to be the reality."

Bhakta Rai has more questions on his agenda. "What do you think about Nepal—we get many loans from foreign countries? For example, U.S. also give big donation. And even other countries give, too. We get a lot of donation from other countries. Nepal is poor country. Even if everybody donate to Nepal, we don't know if that's enough."

Buddi digresses from his translating to remind us of the private donations of the brothers Horace and Lawrence Kadoorie, who brought a safe, convenient water supply system to Badel, and who were also responsible for the simple but sanitary latrine next to the school. Bhakta Rai waits patiently until Buddi finishes. He then asks one brief question: "Well, what do you think about—we are poor or we are rich?"

How can I express what I feel for this culture? I laugh at the impossibility of it and then make my attempt. "Well, you're rich in your people and you're rich in the beauty of your country. I think it's good that the other countries have given donations to help you get what you need. It's a much better use for money than to spend it to go to war. Better to give to Nepal than to spend it on guns and military equipment. So I hope more money will be coming. Right now America has a financial problem. We have a big debt that we need to pay off. Our new president, Clinton, is very conscious of that deficit. But he's also very conscious of helping people who need help. So I hope America will give more money to Nepal."

FROM MARGE'S JOURNAL:

This theme—of Nepali poverty and American wealth—is one that I have been hearing, it seems like every day. I try to tell these villagers that Rais are rich in many ways that we at home could learn. The love and support among family members and their large extended family. The way they all help each other. Their tenderness and kindness to one another. I sometimes say, "You are rich in spirit in many ways that money cannot buy." I speak from the experience of both worlds.

But the people of Badel know only theirs and the fairy tales they have heard about ours. Oh, the temptation to romanticize and compare! I have done too much of this already.

Bhakta Rai nods and as he looks questioningly at us, Marge asks him the question we wanted most to pose: "What do you need most in your village?"

This is an answer he is clearly eager to give. "We have two kinds of problem right here. Because first, we need education. And other is bridge—we have no bridge over the rivers. You see the Liding Khola, you cross by the legs. Only the legs. So it is hard to bring things what we need to the village. We need drinking water—irrigation. And next, after we do that, next we need big highway, you know. So we can use trucks to bring what we need. And electricity. We need that."

Marge and I exchange a quick look. We, who have come from so far and are staying here for so short a time, have no right to judge what is best for Badel. But in that look we share our fears that with highways and electricity, the worst of the modern world will impinge upon the best of life in Badel. Our guess is that Buddi, the former (and possibly future) teacher, added the concern about education to Bhakta Rai's impassioned technical wish list. We can only hope that education will help the people of Badel keep the best of the old, along with the new.

We pursue the questions we've had about schooling. "What about the schools?" I ask. "Do you have any authority over the schools—to check to see what the program is and whether the teachers are coming to class? Is that part of your responsibility?" I'm nervous, hoping that I didn't talk out of turn and put Bhakta Rai on the defensive. But we detect neither embarrassment nor apology in Buddi's translation of the headman's response.

"Before, the time of the panchayat system, what they did, he don't know, he is not responsible," Buddi says. "Now we get democracy, democracy time, he have a lot of work to do in village and he don't have the time to go and check every month. But he have right, to go and check every school. Ready, ready, as soon as he can, he is going to go straight to the school. And if the teachers are not going to do, he is going to give report." Buddi shrugs. "What happen then we don't know. We don't have enough teachers, teachers don't make enough money, big problems in schools."

Marge switches to the other issue that has seemed to the two of us more important than electricity and highways. "The new democracy—do you think they are doing a better job with the health? Are they giving you more hospitals? Are they giving you more health workers?" After a very long conversation in Nepali, Buddi translates: "Now, you know, there is not enough money. How to finance? The people say to the headman, to the government, to everybody, what they want. The government of Nepal is thinking, we must have to make education, we must have to make clinics, we must have to do everything. But—a little bit shortage of money." Buddi gestures toward Bhakta Rai. "He is hoping for other donations from U.S., maybe next year, I don't know."

Marge and I sit quietly as Bhakta Rai and Buddi converse at even greater length than before until Buddi breaks out of the conversation to tell us he'll see us later and we realize that the interview is over.

The talk has been enlightening and unsettling at the same time. In Badel we have found people living according to ancient patterns that still work for them. Over these three weeks we kept being struck anew by how far we had traveled in making this visit to the eastern hills of Nepal. For here, unlike so many seemingly remote corners of the world, these villages' boundaries have not been breached by Coca-Cola, Marlboros, McDonald's, Michaels (either Jackson or Jordan), American movies (or movies from anywhere), videocassettes, MTV, Little League. With the Americanization creeping over most of the globe these days, it is most likely that at least some such imports will follow the few tee shirts and blue jeans brought here by trekking staff.

Late this afternoon, just before dinner, I realize that for the entire time we've been here in Badel, we haven't heard any motorized sounds. No revving motorcycles, beeping car horns, roaring jet planes, belching power lawnmowers, humming farm equipment, rasping chainsaws, truck rumblings, ambulance and fire engine sirens—all the sounds that intrude upon my daily life at home. The only sounds we've heard are the ones I am listening to now: the crack of splitting wood, the soft shuffling of husked rice, the tinkling laughter of children, the lively conversation of adults, the rhythmic chirping of birds. I wonder whether this relative quiet, free from grating buzzes, helps to explain the peaceful calm so many of these villagers display.

And I know that if Bhakta Rai gets his wishes, the coming of electricity is bound to bring the clatter and clamor of contemporary "civilization," with its television and videos and trucks rumbling in bearing all manner of western things. Will these changes bring progress to Badel? Or will they contaminate a way of life and a set of values that have endured for centuries and that even today are more valuable than the material goods that may bury them with their sacred dead?

I recall something that comedian and social critic Dick Gregory said about white people: "You gotta say this for whites, their self-confidence knows no bounds. Who else could go to a small island in the South Pacific, where there's no crime, poverty, unemployment, war or worry—and call it a 'primitive society'?" This is how Marge and I feel about Badel. Primitive, yes, in terms of electricity and highways; more civilized than any other spot on earth that we know of in terms of human values.

Sally plays a
first card game
with Feran

Go PFEES!!

18

A Boy Cries: "My Friend Name Is Sally and March"

What boils will spill over.

—Nepali proverb

Buddi has invited Marge and me to eat our last dinner here in Badel downstairs in the kitchen with him and his family. The menu will be lavish: *dal bhat*, *dhiru* (a thick gloppy paste made of millet flour and water), fried local potatoes—and a special luxury. Plucked from the yard this morning, an unlucky chicken was freshly killed and cooked in honor of the American visitors. It will feed the eight of us.

The only conversation during dinner goes on between Marge and me; for Nepalis, eating itself is the main event, one not to be interrupted by idle chatter. The family eats Nepali-style, neatly and methodically scooping up the rice and dhiru with their hands; Marge and I use the forks the staff brought from Kathmandu. As soon as Buddi and Kiran have emptied their heavily laden plates, they wash their hands and rinse their mouths

213

with a pitcher of water just outside the door. Then Kiran whips out the deck of playing cards that we gave him earlier in the day. There is no hint of the emotional storm to come.

Both Marge and I fell in love at first sight with this bright boy with an almost constant smile, now shy, now excited, now impish. At our first meeting two weeks before, Kiran had impressed us with the precise, well-articulated English with which he cheerfully answered our typically adult, less than imaginative questions: "What is your name?", "How old are you?" and "What grade are you in?"

He eagerly showed us his school books, extracting from the big blue book-bag that Buddi had brought him from Kathmandu a heavy load of eight well-worn textbooks, plus a few notebooks and workbooks, covering such subjects as Nepali, Sanskrit, English, math, history and science. As Kiran pointed out and, in English, identified pictures of kings, poets and assorted historical and governmental figures, Buddi beamed proudly. He told us, "I will see that Kiran too goes to university in Kathmandu."

Buddi had asked Peter Owens, our trek leader who had established an aid fund to help his staffers send members of their family to school, for help in sending Kiran. But Peter shook his head: "No—you're rich. This money is for the poor families who can't afford to send their children to school." Even though Buddi is far from rich by American standards, in Badel his family constitutes "the rich folk up on the hill." Peter was right. Buddi can afford to, and will, send Kiran to college, whereas the aid fund might make the crucial difference in another child's life, between going to school and staying home to work in the fields.

Our visit to Kiran's school showed us how impressive indeed are Kiran's accomplishments. It's clearly not the quality of the teaching he's received that accounts for his proficiency in English. It's him. Bright-eyed, alert, eager to learn—and to practice what he's learned—he stands out in his class.

During the week we have stayed with Buddi's family, some of our most joyous moments have been with Kiran and the other children. There was the rainy day on the terrace of "our" house when Marge and I put on our show of off-key camp songs to a giggling audience. Then Kiran decided it was time for me to dance. So he ran to get the drum, the kids all sang—and what choice did

I have? I did my best. Fortunately Marge joined me so I didn't feel too silly all by myself. The kids loved it—sat in rapt attention for about an hour. (When have I been such a center of attention?) We did get a few of them to dance, but Kiran kept urging me on. Finally I pleaded fatigue and got a little rest, but he is a hard taskmaster!

We tried to teach the children "Merrily, merrily, merrily, merrily—life is but a dream"—with limited results. They didn't join in with the chorus and had trouble saying the words. But inasmuch as our mouths have trouble twisting around to make their sounds, we understand only too well. Also, the ritual of joining in on the chorus is clearly culturally based, which I had never realized before. Only when you are immersed in a foreign culture can you realize how much we assume the universality of so many practices. As one psychologist has said, "Fish don't miss the water until it isn't there."

The children taught—or tried to teach—us a few simple words and phrases, and then Kiran, the little devil, jumped up saying "*Jummraa!*" and making little crawly motions with his fingers. He was teaching us the word for head lice! With much laughter, of course! Fortunately, we never needed his addition to our vocabulary.

Marge and I taught Kiran how to play the card games that had been favorites of our own children. In the thrall of the games, he took to coming up to our sleeping balcony morning, noon and night, saying, "I want *joghi* ["joh-ghee"]. We finally figured out that he meant he wanted to play "War." Then Buddi explained to us that "joghi" is a slang word the men use when they're gambling and slapping down a winning card. We had turned this adorable innocent into a card shark!

Now, on this last evening, Marge and I, talking as we eat, are taking longer to finish our meal than our hosts do. While we finish dinner, Kiran and Buddi begin to play "Go Fish" (which comes out of Kiran's mouth as "Go Feesh").

And then the explosion. Suddenly Kiran, sitting on his haunches on the floor next to me, is sobbing uncontrollably, his hands over his face. At first I think he is laughing, because Buddi clearly is.

"What happened?" I ask Buddi, whose laughter fast fades to an embarrassed smile. Apparently, Buddi was teasing Kiran, saying something like, "The grandmas are leaving tomorrow, and after they go, you won't be able to play cards any more." But Buddi is too embarrassed to explain clearly and Kiran too distraught. Whatever it was, Kiran is now in a state of near collapse, and Buddi looks as if he wishes he could bite off his tongue and throw it to the chickens.

It is heartbreaking watching and listening to Kiran's sobbing. When I put my arms around him, he doesn't resist, he even molds to my body, but he doesn't stop crying either. Buddi too tries to talk to him, to mend fences—with no success. The older brother tries to pull the younger one to his feet, but in the method of passive resisters the world over, Kiran sinks limply to the floor again. Then Shiva, Kiran's mother, pulls this youngest child over to her and, out of our earshot, tries to talk gently to him. But still he sobs. Through all of this, everyone in the family treats him gently. No one scolds him and no one ridicules him. And when it is clear that he is not going to bounce back into gaiety, he is allowed to be—to let his mood run its course.

I begin to cry myself, and I see Marge's eyes welling up too. I think the real problem for Kiran is not the gentle teasing from a loving older brother, but the imminent departure of that brother and the surrogate grandmothers. This appealing, affectionate boy has become very close to us in this week—and we to him. I have only to look at him, and I melt. Every day we have written notes to each other. One afternoon he carefully penned in my notebook: "Kiran Kumar Rai. My friend name is sali." After I drew a heart, pierced with an arrow, and wrote "Sally loves Kiran," he wrote back "My name is Kiran Kumar Rai. My friend name is Sally and March. I [heart, pierced with arrow] you OK Sally. My dear Sally."

Yes, we three are friends. And this youngest of the three is bright enough to know that he may never see us again as long as he lives. It's hard to believe that in one week I could become so attached to an eleven-year-old from a totally different culture who doesn't even speak my language. But there it is. And he has become attached to us.

Also, there's the indisputable fact that when we leave, so does his beloved older brother. Buddi may not come back for months. And so ends a very special week in a little boy's life. Kiran has been the center of attention this week, not only from us but also from the other children in the village, as he has worn the mantle of prestige by having us, the eminent visitors from afar, here in his home, where he can visit us any time he feels like it. But I think his upset is on a more emotional basis than that. I think of my own grandson almost Kiran's age, whom my husband and I see only once or twice a year because he and his family live an ocean away from us, and of the angry, tearful scenes so common the night before we are to leave him, not to see each other for so many months. "Separation anxiety," the psychologists call it.

Finally Kiran stops crying, jumps up and leaves the room. When he returns a few minutes later, he sits sullenly in a corner, away from us all, not speaking, not looking at anyone. This is a Kiran we have not seen before.

Buddi asks Marge and me, "You want to play cards?" "Only if Kiran plays," I say, hoping for a quick recovery. But no. And neither grandma feels like playing in the face of Kiran's sadness. Buddi tenderly gives Kiran the pack of cards the two of them had been playing with, the ones I had given to Kiran earlier in the day. Then Buddi pulls out his own deck and asks Tara Mani and a boy who popped in with him if they want to play. Patently embarrassed by the whole affair, Buddi makes some feeble joke about now making Tara and the new boy cry. They all laugh, but poor sad little Kiran sits stony-faced, staring at the wall.

Marge and I talk: can we do anything to cheer up Kiran? As the card game ends, Buddi wanders over to us, and Marge asks him to go over our schedule for the next few days. I resonate immediately to her suggestion that we stay in Badel one more day than we had planned, skipping the overnight visit to Bangdel, the village on the opposite hill. This way we can cherish one more day here, where we know so many of the people, where we can spend one more day with Kiran, where we can bask in our superb balcony view and enjoy the ease of familiar surroundings—instead of going to a place that, even by local standards, from Buddi's description of it, seems to have little to offer.

We tell Kiran we will be staying one more day, but he is too deeply mired in unhappiness to brighten up. Do we flatter ourselves by thinking that the news of our staying would in fact cheer him up? So feeling sad for Kiran, and sad for ourselves at having to leave this enclave where we have shed so many of the cares that dog our days at home, Marge and I go up to bed. Both of us, emotionally drained and exhausted, fall asleep almost as soon as our heads hit the flower-printed pillowcases.

Next morning, I awaken from a bad dream in which I have been abandoned by my mother and my daughters. Had Kiran's emotional outburst stayed with me in my sleep? Had it brought flashbacks about my own grandson whom I wouldn't be seeing for so many months? Or is something else making me feel unloved and un-nurtured? I can't think of anything. Instead, here I sit on this fine day, facing a gorgeous view of green corrugated hills, crystalline blue sky, wisps of clouds. Kangsha has brought us cookies and tea in bed, and then comes back up with warm washing water. We are being so coddled it will be hard getting used to doing for ourselves again.

When Buddi comes up the steps to our balcony, we ask, "How is Kiran this morning?" The discrepancy between the ways Marge and I hear his answer speaks volumes about the shortcomings of eyewitness testimony. Marge says Buddi said, "Nepalis love children too much"; I remember hearing him say, "Too much love is not good for children." In either case, Marge seems to put her finger on the motive underlying whichever statement he made—Buddi's embarrassment over having made his little brother cry. "I don't think Buddi really believes what he said," she says to me. "But this is his way of apologizing for Kiran's little episode."

Buddi's discomfort may also stem from the crying itself. When talking about the shaman last week, Buddi said, "Nepalis cry a lot." But we haven't seen Buddi cry, not even the time he fell, holding Kusum, and was so worried about his little daughter. Now we shoo Buddi out so we can finish our baths in our little shared basin of warm water, and the subject of Kiran's outburst seems closed.

When I pass Kiran's room after breakfast on my way to the charpi, he is sitting on his bed, doing his homework. I ask him, "Do you want to go for a walk with me later, after school?" He cheerfully assents. I had thought that the emotional storm would be over by this morning; I'm glad to see I was right. There is a universality about the dawn of a new day—and the resiliency of children.

Kiran and I take a lovely, relaxed winding walk for about an hour over a ridge, up and down a few small hills, to the Jirla Khola, a nearby river, then up to the house of his friend and back home. He insists on carrying my backpack as he leads the way—my sherpa and my friend. He asks me to take his photo en route; I happily oblige. Everyone we meet knows him and asks "*Kahaa jaane?*" ("Where are you going?") He gives them our destination—Jirla Khola—and a few salient facts about me: mostly, I think, that I'm here from America and I'm leaving tomorrow.

Back home about an hour before our dinnertime, Kiran and I play "Go Feesh," "War," and "Concentration." I wouldn't dream of stopping a second sooner than he wants to; I dread a repeat of last night. But there's nothing like that: the Kiran of today continues to be the lively, spirited boy we've known for a week. Quick with the game, excited when he wins, mock-rueful when he loses. Fortunately for my waning powers of concentration, he tires of the card-playing in just under an hour and is ready for a break. He jumps up, sings the verse of "Chitty Chitty Bang Bang" (at least all that Marge and I remembered yesterday when we taught it to him), does a couple of impromptu dance steps, climbs on the corn crib, marches in step across the courtyard to our "Hup-2-3-4," keeps singing to himself.

At dinner, while Kiran is downstairs, I laugh to Marge: "I have this recurring fantasy of kidnapping him and taking him home with me. I could send him to the best schools, he would do so well, he would learn so much more than he could here, make so much more of his life." But even if I could or really would take him, I know she's right when she says, "That would ruin him."

More card-playing after dinner (I will have had enough of cards to last me for months—I hope I'll be able to face a deck with my grandchildren), and then Kiran is ready to skip off to bed. Before he goes, I ask for—and am happy to get—a kiss and a hug. I climb into bed and look at the stars this last night.

And then it's the next morning and this time we do have to go, to allow enough time for the three-day walk back to Lamidanda and the airstrip there from which we'll fly out for Kathmandu. Marge and I won't take our leave until after Kiran leaves for school. We all had a few final rounds of "Go Feesh," he played "War" with his new deck of cards with three friends, and then with a final wave, the four of them skip off to school.

Our goodbyes bring tears to the eyes of Shiva, Dhana, Kusum, Marge and me. Marge and I are happy that ours didn't start until after Kiran left. I can still see his smiling face and hear his voice saying "Goodbye, Grandma." I wanted to put my arms around him and smother him with kisses, but I contented myself with shaking hands, afraid I'd embarrass him. One thing to sneak a kiss and hug last night alone in the hallway as he was heading off to bed; quite another to do it in front of his family and the school friends who had come to walk with him.

I did tell Kiran, "I'll never forget you. You'll always be my friend." And meant every word. I think he'll remember us too. He'll meet other western-ers—at university, maybe on treks, maybe even in Badel if Peter develops "cul-ture treks," as Marge and I will suggest to him. But we were Kiran's first westerners. And we left our mementos. We tried not to leave too much cultural pollution, nothing that would change these villagers' lives, dilute their customs any more than the twentieth century in general has done. Instead, we focused on fitting into their lives—walking their paths, eating their food, meeting on their turf.

Bombahadur Rye is a 27 year old
deaf-mute who lives in
Buddi's house and
helps his father with
the farming. Buddi brought
"Bomu" the big sweater from
a trekker.

FROM MARGE'S JOURNAL:

I think the two grandmas will be missed for a day or two. I hope we were good guests. I hope we didn't alter the village in any lasting way and will be remembered for our laughter and fun. As I descend the mountain down to the Liding Khola I think of what we left behind. About 25 bead necklaces, dozens of origami swans, 12 red bandannas, two decks of playing cards, a few servings of M&Ms and jellybeans, a couple of dozen items of clothing: tee shirts, sweaters, caps, scarves; some picture books, pens and paper. We left them hopscotch, "Go Feesh," the first verse of "Chitty Chitty Bang Bang," all the words to "Row, Row, Row Your Boat."

But all this pales in comparison to what we take away with us. In two short weeks we learned a little bit about "the Rai way," and a bit of the Rai way will become my way as I work at becoming more like them. This will be hard work in my consuming, competitive culture. Harder still will be trying to explain to the people in my country what life in Badel is like and why a part of me cannot leave it. I turn and wave to the deaf-mute farm helper Bhumi, smiling and handsome in Dwyer's good wool sweater. I had thought he might save it for special occasions, but he has had it on since the night I gave it to him. Maybe in his world every day is a special occasion.

Finally the plane arrives and we board. Again, Marge and I are the only westerners. The hostess comes around with those Royal Nepal hard candies (the worst I've ever tasted) and cotton balls for the ears. As soon as the doors are locked, the plane starts to move. No line-up here. The pilot takes two-and-a-half minutes to get into position and then taxis for a total of twenty seconds (I count) before we lift off the ground.

We fly over the bumpy hills, laced with traceries of narrow footpaths, ridged with terraces, dotted with houses, painted with small patches of velvety green forests surrounded by gaping brown splotches. Fifteen minutes out of Lamidanda the awesome jagged snow peaks appear from behind the clouds, staying in view for another fifteen minutes, before the smog of an increasingly industrialized city smothers them, hides even these behemoths from sight. As we draw close to Kathmandu, urban centers appear, twin conical towers of one brick factory after another belching black smoke. Then we're in the great bowl of the Kathmandu Valley, ringed by rounded hills and by those now invisible mountains.

Looking down at those first hills, just out of Lamidanda, I begin to cry—and cry—and cry. I feel the way Kiran might have that next-to-last night. This overwhelming sadness at leaving these hills, these people, these few weeks of a kind of Paradise well up within me. I'm ready to go home, I realize—but why then do I feel so sad?

Part III
Badel Revisited:
October 1994

19

We Return:
"Wel-Come Sally and Marge"

Love grows with acquaintance; without it, there are only strangers.

—Nepali proverb

Last year, just before we left Badel, Buddi told us, "You should come back to Badel at Dasain. My village is very beautiful then. Many flowers. All over. All colors. Every house has flowers." But as easy as Buddi made it sound for us to return, we had our considerations. Both Marge and I are fortunate: we could afford the money for another trip. But could we afford the time? Our lives are complicated. We both have husbands, children, grandchildren. We both pursue work that drives our days. We both have been amply fitted out with ever-ready supplies of guilt that spring to the surface when we take too much time from either family or labor.

When we left Badel last spring, Marge knew with a gemlike certainty that she would be back here some day, but didn't know when that day would come. I didn't know whether I would ever

227

return. We both knew that we couldn't come back in the fall of 1993. But between April 26, 1993, the day we walked down the path leading away from the village, and the following spring, both of us had begun making plans to return to Badel in the fall of 1994. We would be in the village during Dasain, when Badel would be abloom.

When we went back, we would see more than the flowers Buddi talked about with such delight. By now both Kumari and Om had had the operations to correct their cleft lips, but the outcome, at least for Kumari, sounded less than satisfactory, according to Buddi's letters and a fuzzy photo he included in one of them. We had to see with our own eyes what had happened—and to arrange for follow-up surgery if necessary. Meanwhile, our friend and trek leader Peter Owens had begun to collect books for a library we wanted to establish in Badel. We would celebrate Dasain, the most important festival of the year, when family and friends travel long distances to be with each other. Our friends in Badel would be waiting for us. And yes, there were those flowers. We looked forward to another shared adventure.

This time, the agenda for our trip involved many more arrangements than presents, packing and preventive shots. We were collecting books, buying library supplies, accepting contributions in preparation for setting up the library. Concerned that Kumari might need follow-up surgery to repair her cleft lip, we contacted Interplast and the Association of Oral and Maxillofacial Surgeons, two organizations that arrange for physician volunteers to visit and work in third world countries. And since we would be adding a twelve-day trek north of Badel to Tyangboche Monastery, the famous Buddhist sanctuary that sits in the shadow of Everest, we were taking our training more seriously than we had last time—doing more hiking and running and spending more time on the hated stair climbing machine.

The day before I left New York, a friend said, "Have a spiritual experience." "I'm sure I will," I answered. And I was sure, even as I wondered what form it would take. On every previous trip I had been blessed with remarkable spiritual experiences, new insights, transformational thoughts and emotions. This trip, though, felt as if it would be less of a mystery than my first three visits to

Nepal. This time I would be retreading familiar ground—first going back to Badel and then trekking part of the Everest route I had taken in 1991. Also, our plans were more structured this time than they had been the year before. So it all added up to more familiarity, even as I knew there would still be a large element of the unknown.

A few new anxieties had crept in. Would I be able to get both my duffel bags from Bangkok to Kathmandu? By inter-Asia rules, I would be limited to one bag and to 44 pounds—or less. I had two bags, and, stuffed with books I was bringing for the library and clothes for the villagers in addition to my own gear, they were heavy. I could hardly lift them.

Then the front pages of our newspapers were full of alarming stories about a virulent pneumonic plague in India, which borders Nepal. About four million Nepalis live in India, Indian and Nepali citizens don't need passports to visit each other's countries and there is steady traffic between the two nations. Might some travelers be carrying the deadly germs as they cross the border? Would Marge and I be in danger? Before I left the United States I bought extra supplies of antibiotics plus a new addition to the medical arsenal—face masks.

The months flew by, our arrangements came together, and Marge and I came together in Kathmandu on Wednesday, October 5th, 1994. She had come a week earlier, had obtained her trekking permit, changed her money, visited Hindu and Buddhist shrines, talked with Buddi about our plans and gone with him to book stores in Kathmandu to make a start at stocking our library. And then I arrived.

The overweight duffel bags I worried so much about getting to Kathmandu come through all the airports without even a raised eyebrow. I remember a line by the Persian mystic poet Hafez: "Don't make yourself miserable over what's to come or what's not to come." There's a lesson for me here: Live in the precious moment.

The precious moment of landing is at 12:55 p.m. The sight of the jagged snow-capped mountains ringing the wide bowl of the Kathmandu Valley is still thrilling; the presence of masked operatives at the airport screening passengers from India for evidence of plague is disquieting. I don't stop to change money, assuming that Buddi will meet me and somehow get me to the Potala Guest House. Still, just going through immigration, baggage and customs involves waiting in line after interminable line.

Finally, at about 1:30 I emerge to see the welcoming and welcome smiles of Marge and Buddi. Buddi chivvies me along: "We must have to go fast. We must be at the Immigration office to get your trekking permit. Office closes 2 o'clock. Tomorrow we have no time. Tomorrow, to get on plane for Lamidanda—a special flight to take people home for Dasain—we must have to be at the airport at 7 o'clock in morning. If no permit today, we must have to find someone to get it for you and then bring to Badel."

I'm afraid I have bad trekking-permit karma. Last year during the hours I spent at the Immigration office to get my permit, my purse was stolen. I want to stay far away from that ill-starred location. Especially since the whole time we were on the trail in 1993, no one ever asked to see the permit the getting of which had caused me so much annoyance, irritation, anxiety, lost money and wasted time. "Is it so important?" I ask Buddi now. "Do I really need it?"

Buddi rushes me into the taxi, tells the driver to go as quickly as he can, and then turns to answer me. "This time very important because we plan to trek near Everest. Many official stations on that route. If you don't have permit, they make you go back. You need." We get to the Immigration office at 2:02. The metal gates are down and locked. There is no one to admit us. There is no way to get in. But Buddi finds a way. He takes me around to the back, lays a few words (but surprisingly, no baksheesh) on the clerks, who let me inside, where I get in line and accomplish my mission.

This year's flight to Lamidanda carries Marge and me, Buddi, his pregnant wife Dhana and their daughter Kusum, and our kitchen staffers Tara Mani and Kangsha. Since we were here last, Dhana and Kusum have moved to Kathmandu with Buddi, where the whole family is now going to school. Buddi is finishing his master's degree in political science, working in trekking and making plans to open a private elementary school. Dhana is studying to be a teacher, and three-and-a-half-year-old Kusum, at a private nursery school, has already learned how to write the entire English alphabet, including one word for each letter. Buddi is bringing his family home to Badel for Dasain. This year Marge and I are not the only westerners on board the plane; four American Peace Corps volunteers are also flying from Kathmandu.

Last month's monsoons washed out most of the trails we trod last year. They'll be repaired eventually, but meanwhile we explore new territory along a different route. Today's walk out of Lamidanda takes us through paths bordered by tall lush grasses swaying gently over our heads. They'll soon be gone, gathered by children and carried home in dokos, some to be eaten by water buffalo, goats, sheep, pigs; some to be dried for new thatching on roofs. Then we walk along emerald-green wet rice fields by thigh-high rice plants, along fields where we smell the sweet-sharp fragrance of fresh wild mint, with its large velvety leaves so different from our mint at home.

Walking the long uphill climb this afternoon, I'm hot. My face is constantly wet from sweat, seconds after I've wiped it with my red bandanna. My calves and thighs are tired, and I feel every step. But I realize with an exquisite burst of gratitude that nothing hurts—no blisters, no neuroma, no knee, no sciatic nerve. I feel blessed by the absence of aches, soreness, cramps or burning—an absence we never notice unless we've first felt the pain. So pain can be a blessing, too, in helping us appreciate its nonexistence.

I also realize how much I am living in the moment, with mindfulness. With every step I am conscious of where I place my feet. I have to be. On the few occasions when I try to keep walking while looking at something else or when my mind wanders, my balance suffers. Several times I barely save myself from slipping into the watery ditches on either side of the road. Although the walk is taking longer than we had expected—three nights out instead of two, and although we are eager to reach Badel, I am enjoying this part of the trip for itself. I am not impatient to rush it. Maybe all the reading and zen-oriented thinking I've been doing are bearing luscious fruit.

Our first morning on the trail, I awake in the tent and focus on letting go of my attachment to having life fit my plans for it. In this case, to the disposition of the used but serviceable clothes I brought over in my duffel bag. I see our sweet young porter Phure with his torn shorts and shredding shirt, and I grieve because Phure got nothing from that duffel. At the airport when we were catching our flight to Lamidanda and I noticed that it had not accompanied us, I asked Buddi about it. "No room to bring clothes," he replied, explaining that he had left the duffel in his apartment in Kathmandu, to distribute its contents at some future date. I wonder how many of those clothes that I saved, collected, mended, laundered, packed and shlepped halfway around the world will get to people who need them.

I need to let go of the expectations I had for those old clothes—or it will contaminate my feelings for Buddi. What happened to all that zen-inspired thinking about letting go of attachment? Maybe I can make a specific request that Phure eventually receive some of the things. Marge seems to have let go of her expectations and attachment to the disposition of the things she brought. "With expectations, serenity dies," she said last night. "Make plans but don't get attached to them."

As soon as I realize that Marge is awake this morning, I ask her for help in letting go of my attachment to the disposition of those clothes. I feel better after we talk even though nothing has changed. Later she tells Buddi that we want to give clothes to Phure from her duffel, which has already gone to Badel. Still later Buddi volunteers that he'll donate his almost-new running shoes to Phure and that he'll give away his tee shirts and some of Kusum's clothes to villagers in Badel; they both have a fairly extensive wardrobe in Kathmandu. Later he tells me, "When give porters new clothes, they sell them." Is this a rationalization? Or a valid reason for filtering them through him first? In either case, I now feel okay with what happens. I have let go of my expectations—in this regard, at least. And I do have faith in Buddi's generosity and his feelings for his fellow villagers.

Only a year and a half after our last trip, Marge and I are both feeling our age around this walking and camping. We like the slow pace set by Kusum—perfect for preschoolers and grandmas. The camping does get a little harder "with the passage of time" (as my doctor at home so tactfully puts it). Backs and knees not so limber, crawling in and out of the tent more of a challenge, squatting a physical statement. But we can still do it!

Especially since this kind of trekking gives us the best parts of camping without the work. The sleeping outside, the fresh air, the views, the informality. And we don't have to set up or take down tents, cook and clean up, make plans. All we have to do is put one foot in front of the other and eat when we're told to. Buddi and our sweet porters help us across bridges, fetch and carry for us, do our laundry, meet our every need with a smile—before we even know we need anything. And all of this is (almost) guilt-free because we're giving employment to people who need it.

FROM MARGE'S JOURNAL:

Sometime in the middle of the night I awake to hear talking and laughing. It is 1:00 a.m. Don't these people need sleep like the rest of us? What is going on? Day breaks, and as I'm organizing my tent I hear Sally say, "A baby! Born last night? Where?" I stick my head out of my tent flap calling, "Where? Where is it? I never heard it cry. I could have helped. I've delivered babies."

The mother was so quiet. Do they suffer in silence here? Maybe they are so in tune with the birthing process that they don't suffer at all. "Is the baby okay? Let me see it!" Sally seems unnaturally calm about such an unusual event. Why isn't she writing down all the details—boy, girl, length of labor, mother's condition, baby's appearance? "Where is it?" I ask again. Sally motions toward an open area outside the house and I wonder why not inside. Is this another strange custom? Is this their way?

"Here," Sally says, with what sounds like impatience. Is this an insensitive side of my dear friend that I haven't seen before? Does she have some sort of hang-up about childbirth? I look where she is pointing, and hear her say, "Isn't it amazing how big he is—and already standing!" I look into the big black eyes of a baby water buffalo, black and thin and teetering on spindly legs. All that scraping and chopping I heard in the middle of the night was the preparation of a special soup

for the mother. No wonder I heard no crying or shouts of joy. The laugh is on me this time.

On the trail we see the four Peace Corps volunteers who were on our flight to Lamidanda from Kathmandu. Jane O'Mahoney, a tall lanky blonde from the midwest, says, "I saw your picture. The headsir at my school showed it to me." Jane is teaching at the Rakha High School. In 1993 we visited that school on our walk back to Lamidanda from Badel. We signed the guest book, gave money—and yes, posed for photos with the faculty. After we returned home, we mailed the pictures to Buddi in Kathmandu. Then months later, on the way to Badel on his next visit home, he delivered them to Rakha.

I marvel that a year and a half after our visit, the headmaster in this faraway village is showing our pictures, and someone from the United States is reading our names and making a connection. No one is an island—especially here. If, according to chaos theory which sees connections in everything, a butterfly flapping its wings in Australia can change the weather on Long Island, what can two concerned American women alter in a brief visit to these remote hills? It sounds grandiose and prideful for us even to think of bringing about change. But we do hope to leave a small legacy—a new library for the village and new smiles for two children.

Our goals are modest, especially compared with some of the work we know about, work that shows the far-reaching results that one dedicated person can accomplish. We have been in touch with one such person, Pamela Carson of Ithaca, New York. Her 1988 encounter with three begging street children in Kathmandu inspired this former restaurant owner to found Educate the Children, a nonprofit organization that now sends homeless Nepali children to school, conducts literacy and teaching training programs for rural women and sponsors health clinics.

At this point Marge and I don't know how involved we will continue to be with the lives of the people of Badel. For right now, we are focusing on the library. If we set it up—and if it endures, that will be a source of great satisfaction. And a testament to what can be done with a will and a little bit of money that in the United States wouldn't even make a dimple in the social structure, let alone a dent, but that here in Nepal may be able to create something lasting. Something that we hope won't corrupt or undermine the enduring values that have given these people their strength and world views, but that may be able to help them live better in their world.

Sunday dawns with the hills in clear profile, the sky in bands of blue, white, pink. The daily miracle, promising a bountiful day. A perfect day for reaching Badel. We set out at 7:10 right after breakfast, and for the first three hours we make our way down, down, down. Not as aerobic as yesterday's climbing, but just as slow. The paths are treacherously slippery, as we try to gain firm footing while sliding and sloshing over mud, moss, rocks, water. I fall five or six times, once into a waiting patch of stinging nettles. It feels as if a dressmaker's box of needles has come alive and is squirming under my skin. Within a few yards Buddi finds me some reliable nettle-medicine—a certain species of green leaves that he crushes between his hands and squeezes to make a brown liquid, which he pats on the fiery spots on my hand and arm. The cool and soothing tonic takes away the sting—at least until I wash my hair in a spring and the water carries off the medicine.

Somehow I don't mind the stinging. Like the leech I found on me yesterday afternoon, it's a new experience, a new sensation, an awareness of being in a foreign place, a sense of being alive. And pain is as much a part of life as pleasure is.

As impatient as we are to reach Badel, we rest often. The day is hot, the hills are steep, the grandmas are tired. And then we come to a little enclosure dug into the earth, set about with golden blossoms. This shrine to the god of the forest is the gateway to Badel's outskirts. We see how justified Buddi was in lauding the fall flowers in his village. All around us grow lush fields of golden mustard flowers, bushes of orange and yellow marigolds, little fuschia marache, tall purple and pink and fuschia irises. Some of the flowers we see today are wild, many planted year after year after year.

With new energy we forge on, and within half an hour or so, we see a small knot of children who attentively note our entry to the inhabited part of their village. But except for Laxmi Darje, who still flashes her radiant smile at us, we don't see the eager faces of the other children we came to know so well last time, the little friends who sought us out, filled our balcony, sang and danced for us, hung on our every word—and sometimes on us—until finally we would send them home. I feel a pang of disappointment. It has been a year and a half, and children's memories are short. Have they forgotten us?

Minutes later, we get our answer. We wend our way down the hill, cross behind the water spout in back of Buddi's house, head toward the gurgling creek running between his house and his neighbor's. And there we stop in astonishment, as we are gifted with the most extravagant welcome that either Marge or I have ever received in our lives—or ever expect to receive for as long as we shall live. Over the doorway to Buddi's house, just past the large flat stones we step on to cross the creek, stretches an immense yellow banner that says in bold black letters: "WEL-COME SALLY AND MARGE."

And here are those longed-for familiar faces—Muna and Meena, Dilkumari and Bikram, Kiran, Shiva, half a dozen or so other old friends. Each one smiles widely. Each one holds a fragrant lei of fresh flowers—red, yellow, orange, violet blossoms. One by one, our welcomers come up to us as we stand, stunned by emotion, in the doorway. One by one, each one reaches up to put one garland over my head, one over Marge's—till both of us are festooned by twelve wreaths apiece. Tears rush to my eyes. I see them glisten in Marge's.

FROM MARGE'S JOURNAL:

We were buried up to our eyes in flowers. Tears rolled down my cheeks but because I was afraid they would not understand the emotional tears of joy, I choked back the sobs, grateful that I did not know their language well enough to attempt a speech. Never in my life have I been treated with such ceremony. I am a very ordinary person who is important to my family and a few close friends, but my life has been, with few exceptions, without honors and awards. I have not sought them, nor have I been aware of their absence. So here in this hinterland I am suddenly treated like a rock star. The queen of England herself would hardly get a warmer welcome. There were our friends. I felt as if I had come home, really home.

What a thrill—to know that all these people—strangers in a strange land— so joyously welcome our return. Buddi has snapped our pictures as we stand collared with garlands in front of the doorway and its glorious sign. Neither Marge nor I will ever again have to explain why we come back to Nepal. All we'll have to do will be to show this photograph.

We are still concerned about another photograph—the one Buddi sent us of Kumari, in which we could see little if any improvement from her surgery. So when, late this afternoon, Buddi comes up to our balcony and summons us downstairs to tell us that Kumari and Om have arrived with other members of their families, we rush down to see the children with our own eyes.

Little Om is handsome, with his charming crooked smile, the kind of barely noticeable asymmetry of the mouth so often adored in matinée idols. And Kumari, to our relief, looks much better than she had in the photo we had seen. Her result is not as good as Om's: she can't close her mouth completely in the spot where her lip had been drawn up. But the scarf over her mouth is gone, and her eyes sparkle as she smiles—and smiles—and smiles. The first smiles we have ever seen from her. The beauty in those smiles brings tears to my eyes for the second time today.

We tell Buddi about the American doctors who will be in Kathmandu November 7, a few days after we will have left Nepal. We ask him to tell Kumari's mother that these doctors will operate on Kumari again—at no cost—if they think it necessary, and that we will pay any expenses of the trip. Marge and I confer; we agree that if she were the daughter of either of us, we would follow up. But we won't urge any course on this family, which has more obstacles to overcome than a lack of money. Mani Bhujel, Kumari's father, is off on trek; his wife has other children to care for; no one else is available to take Kumari on the five days' journey to Kathmandu and to stay with her there. Besides, we have no guarantee that the result would be better.

The miracle has already happened. No longer cursed by a grotesque defect, Kumari is now a pretty fourteen-year-old with a slightly irregular appearance. "Can she get a husband now?" I ask Buddi. "Why not?" he grins.

That night, as Marge and I lie in our beds on the balcony opposite the rounded hills, we talk about Kumari and our hopes that Buddi is right and that the change in her appearance will offer her a better life. We also think about the time and the effort that went into that joyful reception we received on our arrival. Making that banner, picking those flowers, stringing those blossoms, organizing that work. All going into such an open expression of warm feelings! How often do we in the "developed" world offer such joyous greetings—even to those we are closest to? How often do we tell ourselves we are "too busy" to allot our tightly guarded minutes and hours? What might we have lost by stifling extravagant ways of showing those we care for how glad we are to see them? What might we gain by going into ourselves and finding reserves of time, of energy?

Right before I drift into sleep, I think about how, on this first day of our return to Badel, any changes we bring here are dwarfed by the changes we'll take away in ourselves.

Dhan Bahadur, Librarian at
Our Beautiful Badel Library

20

A Library Is Born: Hamro Ramro Badel Pustekalaya

Opportunities come but do not linger.

—*Nepali proverb*

For more than an hour, Laxmi Darje has been standing almost motionless in the shimmering sunshine, just outside the open door. Behind her the hillside field is golden with mustard flowers; before her sixteen people have crowded into a 10' by 10' room. This barefoot fourteen-year-old in her worn and faded blue dress has been silently watching the whirl of activity. This small room in this two-room house, a few feet away from the main house inhabited by Dhan Bahadur Rai and his wife, Gita, is still metamorphosing. Formerly the bedroom for Uttam and Ishwor, Gita and Dhan's sons, it is being transformed into the first library in the village of Badel.

As Marge—who, with me, is largely responsible for this transfiguration—takes a children's dictionary from the shelf, I glance over at her and for a moment wonder: Are we doing the right

241

thing? Then the moment passes. I look up from the bright poster I am tacking to the wall, my eyes meet Laxmi's straw-colored ones, and I am rewarded by her radiant smile. Laxmi never considered stepping over the threshold to join the half-dozen children sitting on the one bed in the little library. From an untouchable caste, Laxmi cannot go into the home of anyone except another Darje. If this quiet girl touches someone holding water or cooked food, the water or food, now "polluted" by her touch, must be thrown out. Although the government of Nepal outlawed untouchability in 1963, laws enacted in Kathmandu don't always travel to these isolated villages.

Laxmi has never been inside a non-Darje home. She has never held a book. She has never been to school. She spends the bulk of her days caring for four younger siblings—and earning a meager handful of rupees by babysitting for other families' children, planting millet in other families' fields, collecting wood for other families' fires. If not for Laxmi's work, her widowed deaf-mute mother could not support the family. Before this day is up, Laxmi will have taken an unexpected leap. My friend and I, in effect, put her where she now is—and in the years to come, I will sometimes wonder whether we did the right thing.

As our cicerone during our two weeks in Badel during our first visit a year and a half ago, in the spring of 1993, Buddi took us all around the village. We visited the elementary school, sat in on a shaman-led ceremony to bless the first house we stayed in, and met with the 75-year-old senior midwife and the elected headman. We didn't get to meet all 1500 villagers, but every day we dropped in on two or three, all of whom stopped what they were doing to invite us in for little boiled potatoes and tea or rakshi. As we came to know the villagers, we saw many needs crying to be filled. A woman with a drooping eye asked us if we had medicine for her; we didn't. The local midwife told us that, with the nearest hospital three days away, the only backup in a complicated delivery is a hastily summoned shaman. We saw for ourselves how dark the school rooms were, how bare of furniture, how dull the books. The headman's wish list for his village included education, a bridge over the Liding Khola, irrigation, a highway, electricity.

Marge and I, conscious of how much we had, how little they did, both felt a hunger to serve these kind people in some way. But how? Neither of us was in a position to provide a health clinic, equip a school, build a hydroelectric plant, or construct a bridge. What could we do? Then one day Buddi took us on a day hike up to the highest point above the village. As we rested in an alpine meadow, fragrant with wildflowers—tiny white asterisks, blue primroses, yellow bells—he said: "Education very important. In my village, people don't have books or newspapers. If people don't have education, cannot have development. Cannot vote for good people. Cannot get health care and electricity."

He looked into our eyes and said, "Some day I will start a library in my village." Then he stood up, declared, "*Janne ho*" (time to go), and led us across the grassy lea.

Marge and I went home. Over the next couple of years, with my notes and her drawings, we completed most of the manuscript for this book. Meanwhile, with each of us back in our own affluent suburb, each with its abundantly stocked public library, thoughts of a little book house in a remote little village kept haunting us. At almost the same time she and I realized: We could help Buddi's dream come true. We needed to work out logistics, to make plans: how to get books, how to get them to Badel, where to keep them.

As that first post-Badel summer gave way to fall, we saw that our library project was do-able. We didn't tell Buddi yet, but we began to gather books and library materials, and to tap the interests of other people. Friends and relatives gave us money for our library fund. Peter Owens, the trek leader, asked all his trekkers who would be coming to Nepal the next year to bring with them one little book each. Marge bought some children's books. (Almost all of Badel's adults are illiterate, but most of the children go to school six days a week and, from fourth grade on, learn English along with Nepali.)

I bought library supplies and approached my local book shop and public library. The Dolphin Book Shop contributed *Hats for Sale* and a handful of other children's classics; the library offered boxfuls of used books. But when I looked at them, I realized that stories about bicycles and television and trains and skyscrapers would read like science fiction to the children of Badel. I didn't take these; instead, I took books about animals and farms and school.

As our excitement mounted, Marge and I resolved to return to Badel, to help midwife the library. We would help Buddi deliver it, we would serve at its birth, but we wouldn't direct or advise unless asked. This was not to be our baby.

When I faxed Buddi, asking whether he would be able to go with us to Badel in October of 1994, I also wrote: "We would like to start the library in Badel that you talked about. What kinds of books should we bring? And where can we buy books in Nepali?" He wrote back: "I can go Badel with you." And: "There are many books about stories, poems and drama in our book store in Kathmandu. We will buy some for Badel library. I hope we can get good discount." We still didn't know where these books would be housed, but we weren't worried. We knew that Buddi was a young man who makes things happen. He would find a place.

We did not expect or receive Buddi's extravagant thanks. *Dhanyabad*, the Nepali word for "thank you," is used rarely, not sprinkled liberally as in the west. In the Eastern tradition, a good deed is a happy event that will do as much for the donor's well-being in future lives as it will for the present beneficiary.

When we returned to Nepal this October, we brought with us about 100 children's picture books in English and a library fund of $400. Money goes astonishingly far in Nepal. With part of the cash, Buddi went to a bookstore in Kathmandu and carefully chose 250 books in Nepali; there was still enough money left to pay $60 for the first-year's salary of a part-time librarian, handle various expenses, and start a modest bank account. Buddi's choices were eclectic: folk tales, children's stories, songbooks (one including "We Shall Overcome"), books about women's rights and farmers' rights and the environment, novels and poetry, dictionaries and encyclopedias, books on communism, democracy, and history. We applauded most of the choices, but were privately puzzled by a few—like the weighty dictionary of legal terms. Who in this village, where few people had even graduated from high school and lawyers were as nonexistent as electric power, would need to refer to it? But we didn't presume to question Buddi's selection.

Buddi, Marge, and I would now go from Kathmandu to Badel, taking the same 35-minute flight, the same three-days' walk as before—but this time, with the added weight of 350 books. On internal flights in Nepal, passengers are limited to 33 pounds of checked baggage, and our own gear filled that. Worried we'd have to leave precious volumes behind, and grateful that carry-on baggage didn't get weighed, we scooped up as many books as we could and crammed them into our backpacks, our pockets, Marge's art bag, any place we could possibly squeeze one. Even though we ended up bulging in every conceivable place on our bodies, we still had to pay $40 in overweight charges (more than we'd paid for the books themselves) and had to hire extra porters to carry them from Lamidanda to Badel.

Every book gets to Badel, and the day after we arrive here, we get to work. The outdoor balcony in Buddi's father's house where Marge and I sleep is converted into an atelier. My bed, buried under 350 books, becomes the production site. With the help of a couple of children, Marge mends torn pages with tape she brought from home, makes new covers with construction paper bought in Evanston, reinforces spines with library tape. Dhana (Buddi's wife), Kiran (his brother), and I put plackets and cards in all 350 books. Buddi, Tara (our cook), and I write English titles on the cards and the names of donors on photocopied bookplates. Tara and Uttam (Buddi's teenage nephew) write Nepali titles on the cards. Ishwor (Uttam's brother) makes new labels to acknowledge gifts.

Uttam brings over about a dozen tattered high school textbooks that he no longer needs. The pages are dog-eared and dirty, the covers missing. In America they would have gone into the garbage, but here nothing is wasted.

After I alphabetize the English books, Hemingway's *The Old Man and the Sea* ended up next to a children's story, *One Fine Day.* Buddi gives every book a number, enters the titles in a ledger that Marge bound, and shelves the books according to those numbers. His numbering method owes nothing to the Dewey decimal system: He simply assigns a consecutive number to each book in the order in which they were stacked. I bite my tongue. It will be up to the librarian and local helpers to figure out a system for finding books. I knew they will. Nepalis have systems for everything else.

Now for a librarian. Buddi will be in Kathmandu or off trekking most of the time. Marge and I break our vow of silence to suggest his sister, Gita. In this patriarchal country, where women have few opportunities, this job seems like a natural for a village woman who went to high school and can read some English. But Buddi asks Gita's husband, Dhan Bahadur instead. Although we are disappointed, we realize that Dhan, a teacher, will be in a good position to encourage schoolchildren to use the library. And we remind ourselves that this is not *our* library. Buddi plans to form a library committee with seven people; two will be women. They will make policy decisions and spread the word through the village about the library. They'll be the trustees, and the outreach and public relations departments.

After all the books have been placed carefully on the shelves, Buddi demonstrates the checking-out procedure. A high school student named Sabate Rai, asks for a children's story, *Jinki ra Joker (Jinki and the Clown)*. Dhan looks it up in the catalog. It is #46. Buddi goes to the shelf, begins counting from the left, and pulls out the book. He withdraws the title card from the placket and writes Sabate's name and the date on the card, which he then places in the file box.

"The books, people take out for only two or three hours," Buddi says, his voice firm. "But what about the long ones?" I ask. He ponders a couple of minutes, and then reluctantly acquiesces to one or two days. He will keep close, take-no-prisoners track of the books. "If someone loses book," he states. "They must have to pay to buy a new one."

And so, on Thursday, October 13, 1994, with no ceremony, no fanfare, *Hamro Ramro Badel Pustekalaya*, "Our Beautiful Badel Library," is launched.

With the library, Marge and I may have helped to bring about a major change in the village. Even now, six years later, we don't know how much the library will change life in Badel. In 1995 Buddi wrote us: "I think this year will be around 1,000 books in our pustakalaya. The children are using." But how are they using it? And has it indeed changed their lives? If so, will this change be for the good? I think so, but I can't be sure.

The villagers of Badel live their days in concert with the same rhythms they have followed for centuries, a way of life that may not exist in another fifty years. And herein lies my own conflict: By helping Buddi found his library, I am joining those forces of change that will eventually wipe out the routines and values that have made the Nepali people who they are today. What will happen to the simplicity of this cashless life where no one goes hungry and each family helps its neighbors, when villagers begin to compete with each other for industrial jobs? What will happen to the purposeful contentment of hard-working people when electricity brings TV showing riches attained by fellow Nepalis? Will the very real gains of improved health care and education be great enough to offset the very real losses that are sure to go along with them in the underside of progress? Were my friend and I wrong in serving as agents for a home-grown dream?

On opening day, neither of us is overly troubled by any of these thoughts. We finally coax Laxmi Darje inside. She steps in hesitantly, timidly sits down with the other children, and diffidently accepts the children's dictionary Marge thrusts into her rough, calloused hands. Laxmi soon becomes entranced by the bright illustrations. Laxmi lingers in the library for an hour, fingering one book after another, looking at pictures, asking questions. She leaves only when her mother comes to the door looking for her. Laxmi shows her mother the book she was holding; but, unable to give up the old ways, the woman would not, could not yield to her daughter's urging to cross that alien threshold.

Before she leaves, Laxmi smiles buoyantly at us, the two "grandmas" from so far away. I look after her as she walks away, her slight figure in sharp relief against the fields of mustard blossoms and ripening millet, the overlapping misty hills, the azure sky. Just beyond the doorway, she turns her head and casts a backward glance toward Our Beautiful Badel Library.

Ganga Maya Rai is a very strong woman. She is very angry because her daughter is being beaten by her husband who is the headman's son.

I gave Kumar Derje this blue scarf one night when he was coughing. That was three days ago. He has been wearing it ever since.

21

A Mother's Outrage:
The Shadow Side of Paradise

*The quarrel between a man and his wife is like a straw on
fire, quick to flare up and quick to expire.*
                                          —*Nepali proverb*

We sit cross-legged on the floor, drinking tea in the kitchen of
Buddi's sister Gita and her husband, our librarian, Dhan Bahadur.
Buddi and Bhakta Rai, the village headman and Dhan Bahadur's
brother, talk with Marge and me, spinning visions of the future
for Our Beautiful Badel Library. Suddenly the air in the room
bristles as Ganga Maya Rai, Buddi's aunt, bursts in. Today this
sturdy woman is not festooned with the elaborate gold jewelry
Marge painted her wearing last year, nor is she wearing the spotless floral-printed lunghi we saw her in the other day. Today she is
wearing her worn everyday work clothes. She has left her adornments at home. Marge and I both greet Ganga Maya with the
palms-together gesture of respect and a friendly "Namaste," and
we are surprised not to receive a warm greeting in return. Last

year she was gracious and hospitable to us, and when we saw her a few days ago she smiled broadly and welcomed us back. We soon learn why she didn't greet us. This is not a social call.

Ganga Maya is angry. Furious. Enraged. Fiercely so. Pulling her faded lunghi down to cover her broad bare feet, she squats on the floor a few feet in front of Bhakta Rai and directs an impassioned protest to the headman, completely ignoring the presence of everyone else in the room. I can't begin to follow her rapid-fire Nepali well enough to know what is so distressing to Ganga Maya, but I keep hearing the Nepali words *mero chori* ("my daughter") and *tapaikko chora* ("your son").

Punctuating the long indignant outpourings from Ganga Maya, Bhakta Rai offers calm, soft-spoken, lengthy answers. He seems to be trying to reassure the angry woman, but his tranquility only fires her wrath further, sparking more and more extravagant voicings of her complaint, with what seem to be repetitions and elaborations on the same theme. Besides the many recurrences of "my daughter" and "your son," I also hear references to *mero natinatini* ("my grandchildren").

During the dispute more people drift into the kitchen—an old man, a couple of neighbor women, Gita's teenage sons Uttam and Ishwor, a cluster of children by the doorway. But for what seems an eternity no one else among the half-dozen or so people gathered here says anything. The conversation continues in head-to-head combat between Ganga Maya Rai and Bhakta Rai. And then it escalates.

As Ganga Maya becomes more and more irate and as her voice grows more and more thunderous, Bhakta finally gets excited himself. He leans forward and speaks loudly and angrily. An old man sitting behind Ganga Maya excitedly expresses his opinions to her. Buddi and Gita, brother and sister, nephew and niece, sit silently, their eyes fixed steadily on the quarreling pair, their inscrutable faces mirroring each other. Are they bored? Or discreet? Finally, Buddi cannot keep quiet a moment longer. He adds his voice to the exchange, speaking fervently to both disputants.

After what turns out to be only about half an hour, Buddi suggests that Marge and I leave with him. The argument is still in full flower, with no sign of any resolution. On our way down the hill, Buddi relates the sad story behind his aunt's righteous anger. The headman's son, who is married to Ganga Maya's daughter, Chandra Kumari, repeatedly beats her. The couple's four young children all too often see their father hitting their mother. The bad situation has gone on for far too long. What we heard the small and slender Bhakta Rai saying to Ganga Maya was: "There is nothing I can do. It is not my responsibility. My son has beaten me, too."

This marriage was a love marriage, not an arranged one, and now the husband wants to marry another woman. His wife is decidedly unenthusiastic about this idea. According to Nepali law, if a man has been married ten years and there are no children from the union, he can take a second wife—provided the first wife agrees. But this marriage has borne fruit—four times. In order for Chandra's husband to remarry, he will have to divorce her. She and her children will have to return to her parents' house. She will not be able to remarry herself.

I find the whole story terribly disturbing. It does not fit my picture of the kind, gentle Nepalis I have come to know. I know this sort of thing goes on in the United States and all over the world, but that doesn't make any instance of it less horrifying. I can't get out of my mind the image of a terrified woman being battered, bruised, thrown down, injured, humiliated in front of her frightened children. With a furrowed-brow expression of concern, Buddi says to us, "Situation very bad for women in Nepal. Hard to get justice. Men not supposed to do such things, but judges usually men, so side with husband. Also, once woman be married once, hard for her to marry again. She would have to live alone. So women stay with husbands even if they beat. Women not educated, don't know their rights. Maybe in twenty, thirty years, will be better."

FROM MARGE'S JOURNAL:

When Ganga Maya started to talk, I whispered to Sally, "We need her on our library committee. I don't know what she is saying, but I like her persistence. The way she refuses to be intimidated by the headman."

Have we just witnessed a Badel court of law? Both sides were heard, but who is the judge? Will anything be resolved? At least the young woman who was not present has a strong, fearless mother who will fight for her. Judging from Ganga Maya's size—large for a Nepali—she could probably beat up the skinny little headman. And the way she feels now, she just might. Out of love for her daughter and frustration for the situation. Women's rights here are still just a few words in an idea.

This mother is a tigress defending her cub. Ganga Maya is fighting mad. But what can she do other than take in her daughter and grandchildren to live with her? Can she move this quiet, dignified, apparently spineless headman to put on either of his hats—as father or as village leader—and take appropriate action? Can she find some other way to tame her violent son-in-law? What recourse does she have? I'll want to know how this drama turns out. Later, Buddi's brother Dilip, a high school graduate who will enroll at Tribhuvan University next month, talks to us about the abusive husband: "He is foolish man. He is educated—a teacher—but foolish. He drink too much." Dilip mimes beating with his fists. He shrugs.

This is not the first instance of wife battery we've heard of. On our walk to Badel, Tam Perry, one of the Peace Corps volunteers, told me about an incident she had seen in which a man repeatedly threw his wife to the ground. As Tam stood in anguished witness, she felt helpless to stop the beating. Wife abuse, she said, is common, especially when the men get drunk.

Of course, even if we had not learned of these individual cases, we would have known from Buddi's description of his courtship rituals that wife-beating was all too present. If it were not, there would have been no need for

Dhana's father to tell Buddi as a prospective son-in-law, "Don't beat our daughter. Take care of her." On our last visit, though, we were somewhat in denial. Not faced with direct knowledge of domestic violence, we chose to put it out of our minds, not think about it. Last time, after not hearing any voices raised in anger for the entire time we were in the village, we even thought about titling this book, *Two Weeks without Anger*. Now we know how misleading this title would be.

We had been told that Nepalis feel anger but do not show it. An American man married to a Nepali woman and living in Kathmandu told us, after my comment about the virtual absence of anger in Nepal, "It's repressed. But it comes out in other ways. People manipulate each other. You don't know what people are thinking or feeling—but there's always intrigue going on." Now, having been witness to the full face of anger we can no longer deny its existence. This "Paradise" has its earthly shadows.

After dark tonight as we get ready for bed, loud words fly up to our balcony from the house below. Ganga Maya's house. A very angry woman, who sounds like Ganga Maya, is shouting at great length to someone. The hollering goes on for about fifteen minutes. I don't hear any other voices. No one answers. No one intervenes. Then just as suddenly as it started, the shouting stops. The following morning, we ask Buddi what was going on. He tells us that the headman had managed to get his son to walk over to Ganga Maya's house to make amends. If the son said anything at all, we couldn't hear him. We did hear—although we couldn't understand—the earful he received.

Today we will celebrate Dasain with Buddi's family. At about 8 o'clock this morning Ganga Maya comes to call. Socializing begins early in Badel. Marge and I have donned our festive clothes for the occasion, she in the lunghi she bought at the Saturday market in Aiselakharka where we stopped off en route to Badel and I in my *rungi-chungi* (multi-colored) chiffon skirt I bought from a street stall in Kathmandu. We both brought jewelry from home, feeling that this would help form a bond with the village women. Today I sport silver drop earrings, the gold whistle on a gold chain that I wear almost all the time (especially when hiking and trekking), the enameled blue-and-silver bear claw I bought at an American Indian shop in New Mexico, *marachi* (dried red mountain flowers) that the village midwife, Sabut Maya, had given both of us on our last visit and a clean tee shirt. My dress-up outfit. Ganga Maya beams on both of us, takes my hand, and then Marge's. She looks us over and comments approvingly about Marge's "*ramro lunghi*" and my "*ramro*" skirt. Ganga Maya is in much better spirits than she was yesterday. Apparently venting steam at her son-in-law's father, and then at her son-in-law himself did wonders for her frame of mind.

I show my family photos to Ganga Maya and Tara Mani, and we talk about how I'm going to take Tara back with me to the U.S. to marry my youngest daughter. Much laughter, especially when I refer to him as my "*juwaai*" (son-in-law). I take Ganga Maya's ability to joke about sons-in-law as a heartening sign that her daughter's life has improved. I hope I'm not being unduly optimistic. I also hope Buddi does get Ganga Maya to serve on the library committee. She's not about to take any guff from anybody. And in a patriarchal country like Nepal, women who are not afraid to stand up to the men in their lives are a precious resource indeed. Buddi knows this.

One night our entire household goes to see a play put on by people in the Puri settlement just above Badel. In the inky darkness of a moonless night in a village without electricity, Buddi leads us by the beam of his flashlight along eight-inch-wide swaths through tall grass, up and down rocky and muddy embankments, across little streams. "Used to be better road before avalanche," Buddi apologizes.

The stage has been set up in front of the school, with a light rigged to show a curtain pieced together from three large lengths of cloth—green, red and (in this light) indeterminate; solid and printed. The hillside is thick with a couple of hundred people sitting as if in an amphitheater. In front of us another couple of hundred sit on mats or benches. Someone brings a bench for us to sit on, a kind gesture for western legs. Otherwise, we would have sat cross-legged on the straw mat Buddi borrowed along the way. Maybe not everyone is staring at us, but before the play begins, we are clearly the main attraction. "I feel like a rock star," Marge says. At least we don't have to give autographs.

The play, *My Sister-in-law's Problem,* is about the travails of an overworked wife who is ill used by her husband and his parents. An unseen narrator announces the beginning, and one by one, the four characters come out onstage—enter left, exit right—saying a few words to introduce themselves. First the father, then the mother, then the swaggering husband and finally the gentle-voiced wife. It is not until the wife's second appearance a few minutes later that we realize "she" is a man. It's easy to costume a man as a woman with these clothes—lunghi, sash and head cloth. One size fits all. Few village women will act in public, and since this principal role calls for the best acting, the producers pressed their top talent into service.

In Act One the curtain opens to show the family at home. Everyone is sitting except the wife, who's fetching water. In subsequent acts the situation steadily worsens for our heroine. Her lazy husband and in-laws sit around, lie down, eat and sleep. She, however, hitches her doko to her back and goes out to collect animal feed; she takes care of the animals; she sweeps; she cooks; she cleans up. Afterwards, she massages her husband's legs. After all, all this sitting around gives a man serious cramps! The drama ends with the wife putting an end to her troubles. She takes poison and dies.

The whole scene—the melodrama of the story, the over-emoting of the actors, the intense audience involvement—reminds me of the stories my mother used to tell me about the Yiddish theater pieces her mother used to take her to in Philadelphia. These audience members, like the ones my mother knew as a young girl, throw themselves into the action. They identify with the characters—and unfortunately, I'm sure this situation is one that many in this audience have either lived or seen, to a greater or lesser degree.

Buddi disapproves of the play's ending. He's kind toward the playwright, a recent high school graduate. "He is trying," Buddi says. But Buddi is firm in his conviction that playwrights need to do better. Buddi thinks a better ending would have the woman free herself from her situation, get money from friends and organize for women's rights. "How will Nepal improve if the good, hard-working women are dead?" he asks. I knew there was a reason Buddi became our guide and friend.

Again, it is not for strangers from foreign lands to come in and try to change this society. Change will come when concerned Nepalis bring it about. And more and more Nepalis are making changes in their personal lives, as Buddi is in sponsoring education for both his wife and his daughter. There are also more voices being raised in public to bring about better lives for women. There is Ram Kumar Khatri, for example, whom Marge and I met when he came over to our table in Narayan's restaurant in Kathmandu to sell us copies of his *Quarterly Development Review,* the magazine he struggles to put out, with its articles about the plights of Nepali women and children. There is the mushrooming growth of NGOs (non-governmental organizations) staffed by women and men who organize, raise consciousness, press for change. These are the people who will make possible new kinds of lives for all the Chandra Kumaris of Nepal, their sisters and their daughters. Meanwhile, maybe Buddi will go ahead to involve Ganga Maya with the library. He'll certainly have our blessing.

22

A Hindu Festival: Dasain in Badel

Dasain comes with a beat of drums; it leaves behind a burden of debt.

—Nepali proverb

What a great privilege my friend and I have been granted! Today we are invited to participate in the celebration of Bijaya Dashami, the ninth day of the Hindu harvest festival of Dasain. On this holy day, the oldest member of the family gives *tika* to everyone in the home (places a ritual mark on the forehead). Shiva Rai, Buddi's soft-voiced mother, will bless her foreign house guests in this way, along with all the members of her household. Buddi's father, as the oldest in the family, would ordinarily perform this rite, but 73-year-old Dhojuman Rai is in Kathmandu seeing a dentist to get a complete set of greatly needed false teeth. (I wonder whether he would still have his own teeth if he had stayed in Badel and continued to eat only *dal bhat* and *dhiru* instead of adopting foreign diets when he served in other countries as a Gurkha soldier.)

261

Sitting cross-legged on rugs or straw mats in Shiva's kitchen, we—Buddi; his wife, Dhana; their little daughter, Kusum; Buddi's younger brothers, Kiran and Dilip; Kangsha, our kitchen helper; my friend and traveling companion Margaret Roche; and I—watch Shiva making final preparations for the ceremony. Bhumi, the family's farm helper, a boy from an untouchable caste, watches from his perch outside the open door. He will receive first tika.

Shiva gracefully carries to the center of the room a small brass vase holding the bouquet of marigolds and zinnias that her youngest son, Kiran, picked this morning. She also brings an aluminum-alloy tray piled high with white grains of rice. Another tray holds bunches of *jamora*, bright yellow wheat flowers. Earlier this morning I had seen seventeen-year-old Dilip making these bundles with his all-purpose tool, the *khukri* (the curved knife better known as the favorite weapon of the Ghurka soldiers). Dilip would cut a small bundle from the flat of jamora in a large round bamboo tray, take a length of strong black thread, double it and tie the bundle, leaving a loop. He laid each bundle in a shiny metal pan. I asked to make one myself, but Dilip thought my first attempt was too small and, as tactfully as possible, he fixed it to conform with the others. I accepted my culturally based ignorance and ineptness in this skill and contented myself with watching Dilip finish his task. Finally, he looked up, flashed his bewitching smile and said, "I like this festival." So do I.

Before Shiva begins the ceremony, Buddi takes some bills from his wallet and puts them on the tray—"for Kusum." Shiva pats patches of yellow rice paste on the forehead of her eldest son, then sprinkles a few drops of water on top of his head as she murmurs a prayer for his health and a good life. Buddi throws his hands over his head in a ritual gesture. Shiva then presents him with a jamora bundle and a single marigold. Buddi kneels all the way over until his face is down at his mother's feet to pay respect to her. Then, with his hands together in the "Namaste" position, he salutes all of us and says "Happy Dashami [the Rai word for Dasain]."

Shiva comes around to each of us in turn, ending with Dhana. These people are so welcoming—making us part of their celebration, part of their household, almost part of their family. When Marge can't get my camera to work, she asks Shiva to reenact the ritual, and Shiva graciously obliges. Taking photos is fine. Receiving tika is fine. Whatever we want to do is fine. No wonder we returned to this village a year and a half after our first visit.

Another tradition marking Bijaya Dashami is the sacrifice of animals in honor of the goddess Durga's victory over demons. Buddi gives us the explanation as he tells us the story underlying this ten-day holiday celebrating the victory of Durga, the righteous, over Maikhasur, a cruel king:

"At one time the people worshipped Brahma, a god with four faces, who talked a lot, saying both good and bad things. The Nepali saying 'like a Brahma' means 'hard to trust.' Maikhasur—his name means 'smart buffalo'—was a giant. He asked a boon of Brahma: 'I want never to die in the battlefield, overcome by either a god or a strong man.' Brahma said 'Okay.' So Maikhasur fought all the kings of the land and he always won. He won three kingdoms—and he became cruel. The gods had a meeting in the Heaven place, asking each other, 'How can we preserve the earth? The only way is to kill Maikhasur. But how to do?' A very strong goddess we call by two names, Durga or Kali, said, 'Don't worry. I am here. I will save you.'

"The goddess got all her weapons and went naked into a dense forest. To lure Maikhasur there, one of the gods went up to him and whispered in his ear, 'There's a beautiful woman in the jungle.' As soon as Maikhasur saw Durga, he proposed marriage to her. He boasted, 'I am the king of three worlds. You are very lucky because I want you to marry me and be my queen.' But Durga answered, 'I do not want to marry you—I came to kill you. Fight me!' Maikhasur laughed so loud he shook the earth, and he said, 'No, beautiful lady, nobody can fight with me and win—even the king of the gods, Indra.'

"'I am no ordinary woman,' Durga said, challenging him. 'I am coming here to save the world. You are doing cruel things. I will give you one chance: go down to Hell and do good things.' But Maikhasur laughed again. He could change the form of his body into a buffalo, a goat or a pig. He became a big terrible buffalo with long horns to fight with. Durga knew that in this different form he could be conquered, so when she saw him change, she said, 'Okay—it's time for you to die. The world doesn't need you.' So they fought and she killed him with her sword. Indra got his throne back in the Heaven place and everyone was happy."

"So," concludes Buddi with a smile, "This is why we worship Kali, a very strong woman. People used to celebrate Dasain by dancing with a sword. That was what the Mongols did. But the Rai people believe that that's not good because it celebrates killing. Besides, people would get drunk, use the weapons and fight with each other. So even though many Rai people still have weapons—swords, knives, ancient guns 500 or 600 years old—the headman has some in his house—they don't do the sword dance any more. Instead, for three days they celebrate a festival of lights marked by singing and dancing. In this way they worship the goddess, and sisters and brothers honor each other.

"And when at Dasain we kill many pigs, sheep, buffalo and goats, it's like killing the bad king." I can't help being struck by the contradiction of a patriarchal society like Nepal worshipping the strength of a mighty woman. But then again, maybe that's why the men in such a culture feel the need to keep women "in their place": If such strong and powerful beings were allowed free rein, men wouldn't have a chance!

At 6 o'clock this morning I saw someone symbolically killing the bad king, and I also saw for myself for the first time what the expression "running around like a chicken without its head" means. Buddi called me down to see Tara Mani's father worshipping a god, making *puja* (an act of religious devotion). The older man put some flowers and leaves into a niche in the wall, then brought out a chicken, unsheathed his khukri and, with a lightning-quick gesture, lopped off the chicken's head. The headless fowl flapped its wings loudly and furiously, doing its dance of death in frantic dervish-like circles. After a couple of very long minutes, the poor thing collapsed on the dusty ground. Its wings fluttered briefly and piteously. Then all was still.

Meanwhile, the worshipper made a small cup from a broad green leaf, carefully wrapped the chicken's head in it, and put it into the niche in the wall, saying a few words over the offering. I knew that the rest of the chicken would be cooked and relished. When chickens are scarce, a forgiving religion accommodates the needs of worshippers.

At that time, though, I didn't know that it would be our family, who would rejoice over the killing of the evil king Maikhasur as we enjoy our celebratory lunch of that chicken. Shiva also serves us pork kidneys in blood (from the family pig that was killed yesterday), cauliflower, dal bhat and cucumber slices. Also our choice of rum, brandy or rakshi. I ask Dilip to translate my thanks to Shiva for being so welcoming and including us in their important celebration.

After lunch, since I used no utensils but instead ate with my right hand Nepali-style, I look around for the pitcher of water I've seen the family members use to wash their hands. The second Shiva sees me unbend and get to my feet, she jumps up herself, gets the pitcher and comes outside with me, where she pours it over my hands. Once again, she demonstrates how these hospitable people seem to anticipate Marge's and my every need. As usual, to my discomfort, Shiva and Dhana eat after everyone else has finished. I stay with them for a few minutes, make conversation and then go outside, for still more celebration.

FROM MARGE'S JOURNAL:

I like this ceremony. I like it better than our large holidays at home. They have gotten to be too much. Too much food, too much gifts, too much trying to make them extra-special, too much of everything. There are no holidays with gifts here. Only the one to come soon, when girls cook for their brothers and make them fancy tikas. No celebrations of birthdays. But here too, things are changing. Three-year-old Kusum asked Buddi if she could have a birthday cake at school when she turns four, as some of the other children do. "Like in America," Buddi grins.

But that is Kathmandu and I am here now in this lovely village with flowers everywhere, so I think I am living in a Renoir painting peopled with Gauguin characters. The monsoons were good this year. There will be enough food for everyone. And there will be a beautiful Badel library. Today in every Rai home a tika is pressed onto every forehead and many thanks are given because long ago

Durga killed the cruel king. Even the chickens are happy as they gather at my feet pecking at the fallen rice. Today it is good to be alive and to be in Badel.

Both Marge and I are happy that we listened to Buddi last year when he told us how sweet it is to be in Badel at Dasain. Actually, the festival is what brought us here: since the regularly scheduled flights from Kathmandu were full, Buddi booked us on a special flight scheduled specifically to bring Nepalis home to celebrate Dasain with their families. Although Dasain is rooted in Hinduism, the festival is celebrated by people all over Nepal, who integrate aspects of Hinduism, Buddhism and animism into the rich amalgam of Nepali religiosity. At Dasain Nepalis buy new clothes for themselves and their families, travel to their home villages, feast, drink, rejoice. And here in these remote farming villages shamans bless the crops in a ceremony that has been performed every year for thousands of years, the same ritual in every household.

In Badel, no one can eat anything from this year's crops until it has been so blessed. Buddi takes us to a neighbor's house for such a blessing, this one to be performed by Bhupal Singh Rai, the hunchbacked father of our little friends Dilkumari and Bikram. Bhupal Singh is of the highest order of shaman, a *Kube-Nokcho*, who is called upon for certain special rituals—those performed at marriages and funerals, as well as blessing the new crops. Unlike Gadja Bahadur Rai, Bhupal Singh uses no drums; he specializes in fire.

We are in a little house belonging to Thami Rai, a young farmer, who is here with his wife and their three young children, two daughters and a son. Thami used to go trekking with Peter—in fact, he was a kitchen boy on my first trek in 1987, but he's too busy now tending his farm and his family. Almost the entire time we are here, about an hour, Thami holds and plays with his nine-month-old daughter. When the baby starts to fuss, her father puts her in a basket and turns her over to his seven-year-old daughter, who carries the infant in a basket anchored by a tumpline around the older girl's forehead. I wonder why the mother doesn't nurse the baby to soothe her, but apparently she doesn't need to: as soon as the big sister carries the basket, the infant quiets. Besides us, the only other people here are two smiling middle-aged men—relatives or neighbors—who are as toothless as the infant. The proceedings are informal, the children talk and play, we have full permission to take photos or tape-record the proceedings.

Bhupal Singh, the shaman, squats by the back wall. He must have powerful genes because the three children of his whom we have met all have that same underslung jaw that is his dominant facial feature. None, however, are so unfortunate as to have his hunchback. (Except that what we see as a deformity may well be a sign to his fellows that he is blessed with special powers and may, therefore, be a sign of good luck.) Bhupal Singh wears the typical Rai farmer's outfit of dun-colored shorts, shirt and vest. His broad, splayed feet are bare; in his hat he has thrust a few green leaves.

The ceiling in this humble home is blackened with soot, as is everything else in the room—the cooking pots, the rice-winnowing tray, the locked chest in the corner. Even though I'm sitting near an open window, my eyes burn and tear from the smoke. A platform hangs over the fire pit in the middle of the room, and several large meaty bones hang from hooks above us. Long bundles of thatch are stored in the ceiling beams.

Bhupal Singh holds a khukri and a bottle of beer. From a wooden bowl he takes a few grains of rice, which he places on the three stones of the stove, to honor the dead. Then he scatters a few more grains around the room for the ghosts. The room erupts into a burst of laughter, and Buddi tells us that the shaman made a joke. He never translates the jokes—too hard for us to under-stand, or too bawdy for our ears? A chicken that wanders into the room for the ceremony is routed by one of the toothless neighbors. The shaman chants tunelessly over a mound of ginger leaves to bless the people in the house for one year, and keeps time to his intonations by tapping on a bamboo cylinder with his khukri. To receive blessings, the man of the house, and then his wife, kneel way down in front of the shaman, prostrate themselves and kiss his feet. Both of them go around the room, saying "Namaste" and making the accom-panying hands-together gesture to all of us.

Pork meat is also part of this ceremony, a delicacy especially important in blessing a new house or a new marriage. This house, being less than two years old, is considered new. The shaman takes a few large bones and some small chunks of raw pork and cooks them in the fire. No one but the gods will eat this sacrifice. For the gods' sake I hope the pork is cooked well enough so they won't get trichinosis. Bhupal Singh then gives the children in the family broad green banana leaves holding mounds of rice, while I sit praying that he won't give me any. My prayers are answered. To my relief, we aren't offered any of the meat that the shaman fries in an iron pan over the fire and that everyone else eats. Buddi leans over and whispers, "This meat not good for you—you might get sick." He then tells us, "The gods are happy." To keep them happy for the next three days, the family will keep the banana leaves and other ceremonial accoutrements here in their house.

The shaman's four-year-old son, Bikram, comes up to his father in the mid-dle of the ceremony, stands in front of him and asks him to take him home. "Who did you come here with?" the father asks with a teasing smile. Bikram answers, "My friend." The father laughs and says, "So go home with your friend!" He then lights a cigarette from the flaming wood from the fire. The ceremony is over, the people laugh, and we leave when the meat is about to be consumed. Marge says, "I like this better than Thanksgiving—and I like him better than any priest I've ever seen!"

Our celebrating is not over yet. At about 2 o'clock Tara and Phure take Marge and me for a long walk down to and across the rushing river at the foot of Badel. On the way we stop to visit the family of Gora, who was our cook the first time we came to Badel. Gadja Bahadur Rai, Gora's father and the shaman we met last year, greets us warmly, invites us in, brings out mats and blankets for us to sit on and shows us, with a wide smile, that he still has the red bandanna we gave him a year and a half ago. Gadja's wife, who is in her late seventies and was very sick with cancer last year, is—much to our pleased surprise—still alive. She looks ancient—like Margo in *Lost Horizon* after she left Shangri-La. She's bent over, with a face filled with so many creases that it doesn't have a centimeter of smooth skin. But last year we thought she was dying—and here she is, still among us!

Gadja brings us tall glasses of chang. I usually refuse it since I don't like beer in any guise, but I don't want to reject his hospitality, so I take a few sips—and it's the best I've ever tasted, sweet like apple cider. Still, neither Marge nor I takes more than a few sips. We don't like to be impolite, but we're getting to know our limitations. Gadja asks me to take his wife's photo, and when I take out the camera, both daughters-in-law quickly marshal their children and pose. I oblige happily. Having one's photo taken is a significant event here, and I'm glad I can make this small contribution to the villagers who are so unfailingly kind to us.

We walk farther down the hill, along a narrow line of rocks, hardly worthy of being called a path. When we come to a stream, I'm glad I'm wearing my sport sandals, so I can walk through the water instead of trying to hop from rock to rock. I have to hold up my long chiffon skirt to keep it from getting water-logged. The water feels cool and refreshing.

FROM MARGE'S JOURNAL:

We splash right through the streams. We move with the water. We are in tune with all nature. I feel safe and secure with every step. I think this way is safer than jumping from rock to slippery rock in big unwieldy boots, the lug soles slipping on the slimy boulders. Today I feel my feet mold to the crushed rock beneath them. Of course, Rahanta, in her bare feet skips and runs more easily than we do.

This walk down is beautiful—past purple asters and golden marigolds and mustard blossoms, bright green fields of rice, thick crops of pale millet. Through a bamboo forest, cool and jungly. Across the Liding Khola—and finally to our destination. Here in an open field, two young men are standing in waist-deep holes, digging the footings for the poles that will support the *ping*, a big swing like a ferris wheel that is a tradition at Nepali holidays. Another is wielding his khukri to cut lengths of wood.

The diggers use a metal soup bowl and a large metal ladle to scoop out the dirt. They keep coming up against huge rocks, which they pry loose with an iron bar and heave to the surface with slender but muscular arms. Then they disappear as they bend over in the holes to do more scooping. They have been working four hours and will have two or three more to go before they will have erected the ping. As always, a band of children closely watch the proceedings from atop one boulder. On another huge flat-topped rock, Tara and Phure join a card game in progress.

All four of the workers wear American tee shirts. Devindra, whom we met at Aiselakharka, is wearing shorts that say "Marlboro Country." "We are seeing a changing Nepal," I say to Marge. "More of these young men are moving away from village ways and Buddi talks of getting electricity and development here. Even in these remote villages, life will change." "But there will never be roads here," Marge reminds me. "So you'll always have indigenous culture." I wonder. I'm reluctant to say "never." Or "always." One never knows. The world always changes.

FROM MARGE'S JOURNAL:

Earlier, when I saw Shiva cleaning out the water buffalo pen and Dhana plastering the floor with cow dung and water while Kiran played and Buddi catalogued books, I wondered how the men managed to build the strong muscles they needed to go trekking, when they seemed to do so little work. Now I see these young men breaking their backs so the children of Badel can spin on a crude ferris wheel. I find myself falling away from my old habits of analyzing and comparing. I want to look for the truth and not judge. Today I see the truth and leave it at that. And today's truth includes beautiful, brown, gleaming bodies of men straining over their task, with skin as smooth and muscles as sinuous as those in any Rodin sculpture.

Devindra invites us to come play on the ping tomorrow morning. I plan to go, but Marge doesn't want to make this long walk again. I'll find someone to go with. Or I'll go alone—I can find the way. I just have to keep going down, down, down.

But I should have known. Our hosts would never let guests from afar go alone. Dilip picks me up at about 10 o'clock the next morning and takes me down to the field where the ping is now completed and set up. It is a ferris wheel-like structure about fifteen feet high, made of wood and bamboo, with four wooden swings. Two tree trunks, each about twelve feet high, support the works. Each trunk is surrounded by a pile of large rocks at its base, to help anchor it. A horizontal wooden pole set between the two trunks is the axis around which the swings go. Two wooden poles cross at the axis, leading to four bamboo spokes at the four corners. Where the wood and the bamboo meet, four wooden seats swing to and fro.

The ping looks amazingly sturdy, considering its simple materials and design, and the primitive tools used to build it. No electrical power tools, lathes, levels, metal nails, hammers or even measuring tapes. Measuring was done with footsteps, pounding with a rock, cutting with a khukri. And here stands the finished construction.

Before anyone can take the first ride, the ping has to be blessed. The workers have the same accoutrements Shiva had yesterday when she gave us tika—flowers, bunches of wheat grass and rice (this time pink). The young men give tikas to everyone and rupees to the children. In addition to my tika, I receive a lush garland of marigolds and asters.

I politely usher the young folk onto the ping, not so much out of courtesy as from the fervent desire to satisfy myself that the armature is sturdy and stable. Two young men and two teenage girls take the inaugural ride. I take pictures. Then I am emboldened enough to take my turn. With Dilip's help, I climb onto an upturned doko, hampered by my long skirt. Hiking it up to my knees, I manage to get one foot over the seat, where I get stuck, until, with Dilip's help, I get the other one onto the same side. And I'm off.

With every revolution the ping emits a loud creaking groan. Uh-oh. But realizing that it still feels comfortably secure, I stop listening. (Having read that all anxiety is about the future, I resolve to enjoy the ping in the present.) Round and round we go, first very slowly, then picking up a little speed as the two young men on either side of the contraption push it faster and faster. I pump my legs, feel the breeze, see the hill and blue sky rise up before me. I feel like a kid. I'm surprised that none of the real kids want to ride the ping—only teenage girls, twentyish men and me. I seem to be a source of amusement for youths, children and the few older villagers who stand by, grin and cheer me on. Well, I remember my life motto: Everyone has to grow old, but you can stay immature forever!

And now Dasain is over. Today, Sunday, we leave Badel for our trek up toward Mount Everest. It is hard to leave. I keep crying as I say goodbye to Shiva, Dhana, Kusum, Muna, Kumari—all the children who have been our constant companions. Then I weep again when one person after another—young and old, family and neighbors—places fresh golden and violet flower garlands around our necks. (Of course, walking on a hot day weighed down by eight heavy sweat-trapping garlands leaves much to be desired, so as soon as we are out of sight, Marge and I divest ourselves of the flowers on the path, wreathing everyone we meet.)

FROM MARGE'S JOURNAL:

When Sally first suggested the trek, I thought a week would be enough in Badel and I have never been to Solu Khumbu, so why not go now? But now I want to stay here. But I have given my word and we have made our plans. I know Sally would be disappointed if we changed them, and Buddi and our staff are counting on the employment. So I will go with a smile on my face and a promise to return very soon to this second home of mine.

I don't want to leave. I am happy here. I could play with the children and lie on my bed reading for another week—two weeks—a month. When would I have enough? Maybe never. But I do have a family I love at home and that is where my roots are. That is where I receive my nourishment so I can come here. It is that very connection, that very bungee cord that makes me so safe and yet so free, so I can always have a foot in both worlds.

Marge starts to sing "Auld Lang Syne," and I join in, but my voice keeps breaking. I surprise myself! I like it here in Badel, yes—but I have kept feeling that it was Marge, not I, who had the really strong emotional attachment to the village. Sometimes you don't know how you feel until you see what you do. And what I do is cry.

I shouldn't be surprised. After all, when in my life have I ever been so welcomed, so appreciated, the object of so much interest? And considering who we are, it's remarkable how little has been asked of us—to take a few pictures, bestow a few presents on the children, give some aspirin and other medicine to people who needed it. No one has asked us for money—except for that brief and disturbing encounter Marge had last night with Kumari's mother. Maybe the mother thought that since we were willing to pay for a second operation for Kumari which was not going to be performed, that the money was just sitting there with no place to go, so she might as well claim it for her family.

FROM MARGE'S JOURNAL:

After dinner the children perform for us; they dance while Uttam and Dilip play the harmonium, purchased with the money Sally and I donated to the Rungi-Chungi Children's Troupe last year. During the show Kumari's mother tugs silently at my sleeve. She wants something. Kumari becomes angry, shouts something at her mother and, in tears, runs away. A young man nearby also speaks harshly to the mother. I call Kumari back, wish her "Namaste" and tell her I will see her again.

I think that Kumari was embarrassed because her mother was asking me for money. So these are two Badel firsts: Never before have I heard a younger person raise a voice against an older one, and never in either of our visits here has anyone asked for money. But how can I be offended by this request? It is the most natural thing in the world. In this woman's eyes we are very, very rich. We paid to repair her child's face, paid to build a library, brought clothes for dozens of villagers. We are millionaires. What are a few rupees to us? She is right, but Buddi says I should not give her money, and I do what Buddi says. I respect his reasons.

I know that the rest of our stay in Nepal will be interesting and beautiful—but this bounty of love contained in one week in Badel will, I know, be the treasure that will stay with me forever—and will bring me back here still again.

Part IV
Back Again: 1996, 1998 and 2000

A Young Visitor to Our Beautiful Bandel Library

23

1996:
Letting Go Again:
Not Our Library

"Whatever you do follows wherever you go."
—Nepali proverb

Marge was right. Because of my trips to Nepal—and especially to Badel—I am a different person in more ways than I can count. I have come to think differently, feel differently, act differently, aspire differently. One sign of change has shown up in my sense of possibilities. Another in the ability to let go.

Before that first trek to Badel in 1993, I had been jogging about my Long Island neighborhood for some fourteen years, covering about three miles every morning, occasionally gearing up for a five- or six-mile local race. Then, on Marge's and my first trek to Badel I said to myself, "I am hotter and more exhausted than I have ever been in my life—if I can keep going for another two hours, I can run the New York City Marathon this fall!" I came

281

home in May, and in November I did complete all 26.2 miles—just in time to celebrate my sixtieth birthday. Thanks to my epiphany on that rocky footpath in Nepal, I did something I never before thought I could accomplish.

Then I heard of another footrace, the Everest Challenge Marathon, which would take place in November 1996 just outside Darjeeling, India, in the foothills of the Indian Himalayas. The tradition of runners, cyclists, and walkers asking for sponsorship to raise money for various worthy causes has become widespread, and this opportunity to raise money for the Badel library was the engine that led me to sign up for the Everest Challenge Marathon. My friends, my family and my colleagues in publishing proved to be amazingly generous, as did many of Marge's friends and family, largely in response to the slide shows she presented to various audiences about the library. Marge and I had talked about what the $3,000-plus that she and I had raised could accomplish. But again we reminded ourselves that this was not our decision to make. As hard as it might be to turn over the money with no strings attached, we would present it to Buddi and although we might offer our suggestions, we would leave the final disposition of the funds up to him and his fellow villagers.

After the long solitary flights from New York's John F. Kennedy Airport, through Tokyo and Bangkok—on October 6, 1996, I finally drink in my fifth arrival in the Kathmandu Valley—the green hills, the snow-capped peaks, the clusters of houses, under a brilliant azure sky barely dusted with a few wispy clouds. My eyes mist, my throat catches. I am back in Nepal! I feel an air of unreality: this emotional connection has been so unexpected I wonder where it came from. I can make up reasons—as I often do when people ask—but the truth is elusive and I don't question it. Like falling in love.

I'm the first person off the plane, down the steps; the first through Immigration, where no one collects the customs form I so carefully filled out. Activity at the airport is delightfully—and typically—chaotic. Still, I manage to get a cart, collect my duffels, get outside. I spot Buddi's beautiful smiling face, he leads me to the taxi sent by the Potala, we take the usual hair-raising ride to Thamel, and I check into Room 214 facing the street, which as usual is alive with motorcycles, hawkers of Tiger Balm, screechy players and sellers of wooden violins, barking dogs, laughing people, blaring horns, clanging shop gates. Kathmandu. I welcome the noise. Peter Owens later says to his group, whom Marge and I join for dinner, "If the dogs don't wake you, the chickens will."

Buddi comes up to my room, where we wait an hour and a half for Marge. When she comes, she apologizes and says, "I knew, though, that Buddi would be meeting you and taking care of you." I'm pleased with myself that I'm neither hurt nor angry, as I once might have been. (Another welcome change in me.) I know how this good friend of mine loses track of time, and I also know we'll have a treasure chest full of days together. I'm glad she felt she didn't have to worry about me. She didn't.

Before I left the states I sent an email to Sharad Babu Shrestha, an expert on starting libraries in Nepal. He is the director of READ (Rural Education and Development) and is on the board of ETC (Educate the Children). The heads of both those agencies suggested that Marge and I get in touch with him for advice and counsel. We make plans to meet for lunch.

Buddi comes at noon, Sharad soon after. Sharad has an appealing manner and an easy smile and looks more like a Peruvian or American Indian than a Nepali, with his aquiline nose, full lips, olive skin and straight black hair. About 5'8" (tallish for a Nepali) and a little thick around the middle (rare for a Nepali), he looks to be about 40 years old.

Buddi, Sharad, Marge and I walk over to the outdoor garden of Green Leaves. After we give our lunch orders, I describe the Badel library to Sharad, and Buddi beams as he tells Sharad, "Library going well, children like, teachers bring them from the school." Buddi estimates that 60 percent of the adults in Badel can read Nepali, and 90 percent of the children can. Although these figures sound high, neither Marge nor I contradicts. Instead, we ask, "Where do we go from here?".

Sharad speaks from his eight months' experience dealing with the people who come to READ to request libraries for their villages. Every village establishes a library committee, whose members are selected by one person, the "patron," to represent as many sectors of the community as possible. The committee then registers the library with the district government, making it eligible to receive funds from other NGOs (non-governmental organizations). Sharad agrees with our vision of a village library: to serve as a community center, empower women and offer benefits to children. Sharad explains READ's librarian training programs, and talks about the ways villagers volunteer—by giving land, building the structure, helping out in other ways.

Buddi feels sure that the village will support the library. "In Badel we have more than one hundred people who work in trekking, they can get money and books from their trekkers." He turns to Sharad. "I invite you to come to Badel, stay my father's house, maybe come in January when Peter Owens will come, to install solar energy unit in my father's house. Maybe we put solar energy in library too." Sharad seems interested, but makes no commitment. After we shake hands to take our leave, Sharad invites us all to his home tomorrow night for dinner.

As Marge, Buddi and I thread our way through the crowded streets of Thamel, we talk about Sharad's emphasis on the importance of two things: first, the community's interest and involvement in the library. The library must be the village's first priority, not something imposed by Marge and me, or even by Buddi. And second, we wonder what kind of income-producing venture the village can come up with that will sustain the library after the donated money is gone. Will the villagers come through? Buddi is full of excitement and plans. "Yes, we will have big meeting to form committee. Dhan Bahadur retires soon from teaching, will be full-time librarian. He'll get training." Sharad said he will be a resource for Buddi, whom he invited to call on him at any time. Later, Marge and I agree that the most valuable outcome of our meeting was establishing a connection between Sharad and Buddi. Networking works in Nepal, too.

Back at the Potala, before we go to breakfast I phone Buddi to tell him that we need to deposit money for the library in the bank today; and also that it's okay to leave tomorrow, as he had wanted, since we've done all our work here. Only then does Buddi say, "I want give you *my* good news—I got new baby last night." "How wonderful! How is Dhana?" "Feeling good. And baby healthy."

I hold my breath. Buddi hasn't told me the baby's sex, and I know he really wanted a boy this time, after having had two little girls. (His second daughter, Sushma, was born in 1995.) Is he terribly disappointed? Did they have another girl? "What is the baby—boy or girl?" I ask. "A boy." Jubilation. I love Buddi for not having said the sex right away, for his implication that the most important thing is a healthy baby and a healthy mom. He is surprisingly feminist, considering the patriarchal tradition he has grown up in—and lives in. "What is his name?" "Don't have name yet," he answers. "But we have grandmas here—grandmas always help pick name."

Soon after my return to the Potala, the proud father shows up with happy smiles. (Although Buddi *always* greets us with a happy smile!) I hug him; Marge, a font of spontaneity and warmth, kisses him. He is growing used to these grandmas' western ways and smilingly accepts our affection.

For the first time we tell Buddi how much money we have brought with us for the library fund. At first he takes in the information with his usual unruffled aplomb. But then he exclaims with a broad smile, "My goodness! So much money!" He asks us to give him the money so he can change it at a better rate than the bank would give—which we do gladly. We don't ask how or where he will change it; sometimes it's better not to know all the details.

Late in the afternoon Buddi comes to the Potala to fetch Marge and me for our visit to his family. It will be a short visit, after which we will accept Sharad's dinner invitation. Dhana and the baby boy are home now. "Dhana feeling good," Buddi tells us as we set out in the taxi. Thanks to his hard work and success at trekking, he and Dhana and their three children, Kusum (now 6), Sushma (1 ½) and the new baby, live in two rooms now, instead of the single room they had all been in. He has bought land near Boudnath, a suburb a few kilometers out of Kathmandu, and, as soon as he manages to save enough money, he plans to build a house for his family. He is a remarkable young man in so many ways—bright, hard-working, ingenious, loving to his wife and family, caring toward his trekkers (especially us Grandmas), honest, idealistic, with a keen sense of humor—and handsome, too, a joy to look at, especially when he flashes his open smile.

In the taxi to the airport I tell Buddi how lucky Marge and I feel to have found him, and he says how lucky he is to have found us: "It is a gift of God," he says with conviction. "When I finished school, I had no job. Peter asked, 'You want to take two grandmas to your village?' I said 'Sure.' And now I have trekking business!" "So we brought you luck?" I ask. "I think so." "Well, you've brought us so much!"

Dhana is the beautiful madonna as she lies on the bed nursing her little son (who will eventually be named Ajaya). At about eight pounds he is a good-sized baby, especially here in Nepal, but oh he looks so little. Still, he shows his strength by nursing vigorously. Neither mother nor baby needs anybody's book about breastfeeding! Dhana has good support: two of Buddi's sisters are here, along with one sister's daughter, a small round woman with a wide toothy smile. This is the kind of warm help that American women usually have to hire for pay. This is why the profession of "doula"—a woman, usually one who has given birth herself, who helps the mother during and after childbirth—has been created in the western world. In Nepal doulas come with the territory.

From Marge's Journal

Everyone seems calm and happy in this crowded little room. By U.S. standards the apartment seems cramped, but it is clean and neat. I think four families live in the building, with a communal kitchen and one bathroom for all. I think of the families I know in America living in their huge houses with bedroom and private bath for each kid and still not happy because everything isn't "perfect."

There is no perfection in this world. There is only truth to one's belief in what is right. I am carefully examining what I have held these truths to be. I may find I have been very wrong on many things. But when I look at Buddi's family I know I am seeing a truth, a commitment that is working for the happiness of all the family.

We're excited at the prospect of dining at Sharad's house, since we've taken a liking to this thoughtful, sensitive man. Also, the opportunity to visit a Nepalese home in Kathmandu is rare. Sharad picks us up in a taxi to take us to his home, which he shares with two bachelor brothers, one who will be opening a restaurant, and the other who works for an educational NGO (non-governmental organization).

Following Sharad's example, we take off our shoes. What a sensible practice, not tracking into the home all the dirt and germs picked up on the streets, after we've stepped in mud, dog poop, who knows what else. The living room has an upholstered couch and comfortable chairs, all fitted out with white cloths on armrest and headrest areas, and a big coffee table. Bookshelves hold volumes on chemistry, politics, project evaluation and other technical and professional topics—all in English—and many others on I-don't-know-what in Nepali, as well as an assortment of trinkets and souvenirs. A couple of landscape prints of no recognizable place hang on the wall; a poster of Nepal is in the hallway.

Sharad brings us Fanta and Coke, then disappears into the kitchen, leaving one brother to entertain us. Although both Marge and I have been hit with a severe attack of the sleepies—I guess we're not over our jet lag after all—we manage to make conversation about universities in Nepal, new traffic laws providing for one-way streets and other restrictions, other anti-pollution measures, and dogs.

After half an hour, Sharad emerges bearing abundantly stocked plates of food: round thick lentil bread, like a soft taco; chunks of grilled chicken (*bara*); a folded "pie" filled with chopped meat, potato and egg (*chatamari*); bean soup (*simi*); sliced cucumbers and tomatoes; little chunks of *very* spicy barbecued pork. Everything (except the meat, which is too hot for our timid western palates) is tasty. I can't finish, though I have made respectable inroads on this painstakingly prepared food.

Then to my horror, Sharad's brother the chef brings out a huge rectangular plate piled high with food, in compartments that contain bitter greens (*saag*), rice, dal, cauliflower, buffalo curry (*ragu ku masu*) and a potato, bean and bamboo-shoot soup (*aahi tama*). My alarm grows to unimaginable dimensions when Sharad brings out another identical plate, and I realize that Marge and I are each expected to polish off an entire platter. I can't do it. Marge, who by now is even sleepier than I am and almost as full, pushes her own failed appetite to new boundaries and forces herself to eat a properly polite portion.

Finally Marge bells the cat and says we'll have to be leaving because we have to get up at 4:30 tomorrow morning. Sharad sends his brother to find a taxi and says they'll go home with us, but we assure them that we can go by ourselves, that they won't need to trouble themselves. Another fifteen minutes of conversation with this kind and generous man in Marge's and my semi-somnolent states, until the taxi comes. After getting our earnest guarantee that we can indeed get home ourselves, Sharad takes us at our word and puts us into the taxi. We tumble in, sorry that we weren't better eaters, better conversationalists, better guests—but oh so happy to be going home to bed.

Next morning, Thursday, Buddi arrives at 5:30 and taxis us to the airport; we're already grossly overweight. Allowed 20 kilos of baggage each, or 60 kilos (132 pounds) total for the three of us, on this internal flight, we get the bad news that we have 150 kilos (330 pounds). So we have to pay 4,200 rupees of overweight fee ($74).

As it is, Buddi had to use every negotiating skill he had just to get us on this flight, which at this time of year is typically reserved for Nepalis only, so that they can get back to their home villages to join their families for Dasain. He told the airport official, "My travel agent made my reservations six months ago, but then the Lamidanda flight didn't open, and when it finally did, other people snapped up all the seats. I really wanted to fly on the 11th or 12th and couldn't get seats. Now, if we can't go on this flight, our program with my tourists will be ruined." Probably Buddi's most persuasive argument is the 50 rupees he presses into the official's hand. We all board the plane.

The flight is short (35 minutes) and smooth. I see snow peaks, hills, miles of lush green rice paddies, fertile terraces, hills with winding footpaths. Flying this way—low and slow—you get much more of a sense of what flying is all about than in a jet. At first the sky is clear with a few light clouds; then we're enveloped in a cloud bank; then we head down. I turn to Marge: "I think we're landing." Marge says, "You're an optimist." We do land, more or less smoothly, to find our porters and cook waiting for us. Also our sherpa, Uttam, Buddi's 19-year-old cousin, the son of his sister Gita and our librarian, Dhan Bahadur. Uttam has just completed two years of college and is waiting for the results of his examinations before knowing what he will do next. We all walk together for about an hour, then stop for lunch under the shade of a banyan tree, up a little flight of stone steps, from which I look out at overlapping green hills as far as I can see.

Our trek to Badel is hot and slippery because of the recent rains, and—what with bouts of intestinal malaise for both Marge and me (something we ate in Kathmandu? One of those delicious treats at Sharad's house?)—harder than it was in the past. Of course, we're both two years older. Still, we keep going, with the help of Buddi, Uttam, Kiran and our other faithful helpers.

Sunday morning's sky at our hilltop campsite a few hours' walk from Badel is a gift. Pinks and pale grays and the glint of a sun about to grace us with its warmth. We drink in the distant peaks of the majestic Ama Dablam range. A cool clean feel to the air. Birds sing. One of the most beautiful campsites ever. Today's walk is downhill almost all the way, in more ways than one. The path is perilously slippery mud, wet from monsoons and, in our early morning departure, not yet warmed and dried by the sun. I keep slipping and sliding as if I were on skates, until I go all the way down, bruising my thumb, creating a grotesque black blood blister and feeling as if the breath has been knocked out of me. But I don't want to stop. Buddi takes my hand and leads me along at least half of the 2600 feet down.

I hate this trail. Walking is a terrible strain. I slide and fall once again. Buddi says, "When you're afraid of falling, that's when you fall." But with me it's when

I get over-confident and forget how tricky the path is and stop being mindful and lose my attentiveness. That's when I fall. When I can't resist looking at the fascinating procedure of farmers in the act of mating their cow, I tumble over sideways. This time, Buddi says, "Three is enough. You won't fall any more." He's right; I don't.

Uttam teaches us: "*Nepal sundar tara katera*" (Nepal is beautiful but dangerous). Oh yes. Especially for a grandma who didn't check the treads on these old boots before she left home; I see how smooth they are and realize it's past time for a new pair.

Finally, three days out of Lamidanda, after going all the way down to the river and then up another 790 feet, we reach Badel. I recognize the shrine to the god at the entrance to the outer reaches of the village, then the banyan tree where we rested last time. As I pause to look out over the green hills, I alert myself: "Take a good look—you'll probably never see this view again." I have already decided that this will be my last trip to Badel.

As we enter the village proper, at about 11 a.m., a couple of boys from the untouchable Darje caste meet us with big grins, Arjun Darje's white teeth gleaming as he smiles broadly at me all the way to Badel. I am anticipating the same warm welcome from the village, with sign and flower garlands, that we received last time, but I tell myself "No expectations." If our welcome does not take this form, I won't be disappointed—I'll still know how welcome we are.

The greeting even exceeds the expectations I tried not to have. This time the sign reads a moving "WEL-COME OUR RELATIVE." So the grandmas are now family. I thought I couldn't have been more touched than I was last time, but being drawn into the embrace of family (a family that welcomes us more extravagantly than our own families have ever done) is incredibly affecting. And the smiles! And the leis! And the welcoming familiar faces! We are garlanded with so many leis that half my face is covered. I count eleven. Mostly golden marigolds, a few violet zinnias. These floral offerings must have kept the village busy all morning. They smell divine. The love they bear is even more heavenly.

It's especially good to see Shiva, Buddi's mother, whose goodness and kindness are brought home to us anew. She has taken Shyam, a fifteen-year-old Rai boy from Solu Khumbu, to live with her. After his mother died and his father remarried, Shyam, unhappy at home, made his way to Kathmandu, where Buddi met him. When Buddi saw that Shyam was living on his own, he befriended him and asked whether he'd like to live in Badel with Shiva and Dhojuman. They offered to send Shyam to school, but since he doesn't want to go, Buddi plans to teach him the trekking business. Despite his small, skinny frame, which makes him look about eleven, he was one of our porters from Lamidanda,. Strong and cheerful, he should do well in trekking.

Shiva is enjoying dressing the little children in the clothes that Marge and I brought from home, mostly from Marge's grandchildren. It's like playing with dolls. These children stand so patiently and show such pleasure as they get outfitted. Some of the children look almost the same as they did two years ago. Om, now 8, looks 5; Bikram, 5, looks 3; my granddaughter Anna, age 4, would be a giant here. Is this genetics? Or diet? One child in whom we see a dramatic change is Devi Kumari's little sister, also named Kumari. Two years ago she was so skinny, undersized and listless that we feared she would not survive the year. Now she is a fat and healthy-looking four-year-old, even though she looks two years younger. Two years ago she had terrible oozing, encrusted sores all over her face and body; today her skin is clear and beautiful. The ability of the body to heal itself is truly miraculous; in this remote country where medical help is a rare commodity, it is the clue to survival.

Devi Kumari and Om come to visit and to garland us with more flowers. Kumari, now a buxom sixteen-year-old, looks much better than she did before the surgery to repair her cleft lip, but still not the way I'd like to see her. Marge and I talk about suggesting another operation; we'll ask Buddi. I would have loved to hear that Kumari had married, but it hasn't happened yet. Laxmi is now on her second marriage; her first husband was "not good" (we never find out in what way), so she tried again and is now living in another village with her second husband, a tailor whom Laxmi's mother seems happy with.

FROM MARGE'S JOURNAL:

We ask Buddi about having Kumari's lip repaired. He says, "Oh well, Grandmas, she is sixteen and will soon be married but if you want to take picture up close I will talk to doctor in Kathmandu and see if she is too old. If not, we fix." We tell him to take whatever it will cost out of the library fund and we will reimburse him. Like the clothes and the books, we need to let go of Kumari. She too is not ours to control. I draw a picture of Kumari and her sister and I make the lip perfect.

When we arrived at Buddi's house, Dhojuman, his father, was sitting on the porch, his swollen and scratched feet stretched out straight in front of him. Two days ago while he was making the new latrine (the one reserved for Marge's and my use), he slipped and fell and cut his feet on the rocks. They are so painful he can hardly walk. He is wearing the full set of false teeth that he got two years ago in Kathmandu, but they are in constant motion as he keeps pushing his uppers in and out with his tongue. Shiva comments in wonderment on my teeth, at my age. "Are they all yours?" she asks. Oh, the wonders of modern dentistry, with all my caps and crowns. I sometimes get discouraged when I need extensive—and expensive—dental work, and then I realize how lucky I am to live in a country where this help is available—and to be able to afford it.

Little Bikram, Dilkumari's brother and the shaman's son, comes up to be outfitted. When he takes off his long trousers, I see two large and ugly sores on his leg. Marge thinks he has a staph infection that needs to be cleaned thoroughly. She will attempt the job with soap and water and the use of the surgical glove she has brought for just such contingencies. She asks Buddi to have Bikram's mother give permission for her to clean the wound, and I ask Buddi to ask the mother to come too, since it will be a painful procedure, and even these stoic little Nepali children need their mothers at times like these.

One little boy has a nasty burn on his ear and his cheek, the consequence of sizzling hot butter that spattered on him. All these medical problems are distressing. That, added to Buddi's comment that many villagers beat their children to make them work in the fields and won't send them to school, brings home once again the sad truth that we are not in Paradise. We are in a land of mostly sweet, good, kind people struggling to get by—with some people who've succumbed to the pressures of a hardscrabble life by drinking too much or abusing their wives or children. Still, I would guess there's less of that sort of thing here than there is in the U.S. I hope I'm not denying reality for the sake of a romantic view of this place where we are treated so well, but, based on the people I've met, that's my sense. Of course, the people I've met may not be a cross-section of the people of Badel—especially since we are in residence at the home of the richest man in the village.

From Marge's Journal

We give out two duffels full of clothes to the children. We pin barrettes in matted hair, give away bright yellow tennis balls. We could have brought three times as many clothes and we still would have turned children away. This is a bowl that we can never fill. But the children are all so grateful for even the smallest gift. Today from our balcony I saw two little boys about eight looking up at me. I found our last yellow ball and went down to them. I reached out and held the right hand of each boy and placed it on the ball. They knew they were meant to share it. They smiled, namaste'd and departed. After all, isn't a ball meant to be shared by two or more people? To throw you need someone to catch. Am I talking about two children and a ball or am I talking about life?

After dinner Buddi suggests our program for tomorrow: "We visit Jai's parents, visit the library, work on library books. In two, three days I call a meeting of village people to talk about the library, to get people to promise to work for it and use it, and to form a committee. He promises to translate for us, both what the people say and what we want to say to them.

By 7:30 Monday morning Buddi is eager to go visiting. We walk down along the terraces of millet, over little brooks, to Jai's parents' house, followed by our loyal retinue of dark-eyed Darje children, which Marge describes as "wagging our tail of eighteen little boys and girls." On the way we run into

Gokana Rai, Jai's father; his broad face lights up, he enthusiastically "namaste's" us, he drops his doko on the ground, and he takes a shorter route home. There we see Dilkumari, his wife, and Monos, their grandson. This slim but sturdy four-year-old was the fat little baby who played with the khukri— and survived, despite these western grandmas' fears.

Indra, Jai's eldest sister and Monos's mother, who had a life-threatening infection in her leg, was, thanks to Peter Owens's Staff Aid Fund, transported to and treated in the Teaching Hospital in Kathmandu and is now better. Her fourth son is now two years old. I express our sympathy on the death of Kali, the second eldest daughter, who died in childbirth, along with her baby. I say it half in English, half in Nepali; they understand and nod soberly. I am unsure about asking for Mithu because of the scandal surrounding her, since she bore a child with her "husband," who was already married to Ganga Maya's daughter (and beating his wife and possibly their four children). Mithu and her 19-month-old son are now living in another village. Still, she is their daughter, I do ask about her, and they respond with a smile. They invite us in and serve us huge cups of milk tea.

As we head for the library, Marge and I are both on tenterhooks. What will we find? Will it show signs that the children have been using it? Or will we find that without Buddi to oversee it, it has fallen into disuse?

It boasts a beautiful newly lettered sign: "OUR BEAUTIFUL BADEL LIBRARY," neatly printed in big block letters, white paint on a red cotton banner. But it is when we step inside that my heart catches and my doubts begin to vanish. The shelves, so sparsely stocked two years ago, are now nearly full, and may not even hold all the new books we have brought. A table with a red-and-black crocheted tablecloth sits in the middle of the room, between a long wooden bench and two wooden armchairs. The walls are covered with the posters we brought two years ago, plus fresh newspaper pages. The bed is gone. Paper shapes, made from a book we brought last time, dangle from the ceiling. What changes have taken place in this little room!

Buddi talks long and earnestly in Nepali to Dhan, apparently reporting on present circumstances and future plans for the library. Birendra Rai, a handsome young teacher with thick black hair, listens attentively. Buddi and Dhan decide to hold the library meeting on Wednesday, day after tomorrow, at 7 a.m., either in the library or the school. They'll invite the "important people" and as many others as want to come. I resolve to see that Ganga Maya, Shiva and Gita are invited. Uttam will take notes. The committee will be formed. Who knows what will happen next? Marge and I have let go. Really let go. (Or have we? We do want those women to be invited to the meeting!)

The extent of our letting go becomes especially clear after lunch, when Buddi and his crew get to work on the books, sorting them, pasting in plackets, making cards. Unlike last time, they now need no help from either grandma. What joy! What a relief! The library has a momentum of its own. We helped to get it on the track, but Buddi and his fellows have fired the engine and are speeding it on its way to undreamed-of destinations.

It is Wednesday morning, one of the most thrilling mornings of my life. Here in the dimly lit office of the village elementary school, among photos of Nepal's king and queen, national flag and map, posters of the English alphabet, and cupboards holding school supplies, Marge and I see the library acquire a life of its own. We witness an outpouring of enthusiasm that shows that this village wants this library, will work for this library, will create an enduring entity that will, I am sure, live long after these two visiting grandmas are only distant memories. The library is an idea, and a project, whose time has come. Library development is in the air throughout Nepal. Back in 1993 my friend and I sniffed that air, took a deep breath, and went from there. And now here we are.

A couple of dozen of the village's most influential citizens have come to this meeting. People began drifting in at the 7 a.m. official starting time, and the meeting is called to order at 8. Present are Bhakta Rai, the elected village headman; Mansing Rai, the former headman who had served twenty years and is now a respected elder; other politicians, teachers, students and farmers, ranging in age from 20 to 70. Most wear traditional Rai clothes—shorts or tight trousers, shirt, vest and topi. A few of the younger ones wear tee shirts and jeans. Most are barefoot; a few wear flip-flops or Chinese sneakers. All of Badel's ethnic groups are represented: Rai, Bhujel, Puri, Giri, Sherpa and Darje. But where are the two women Buddi invited, at our suggestion?

Buddi opens the meeting with a long introduction in Nepali. I recognize words for "library," "training," "Helping Hands," "librarian," "committee," "furniture," and "Kathmandu." He shows the article I wrote about the founding of the library and points out that it appeared in the publication of an important university, a magazine read by presidents of corporations. He tells how the article helped to bring in money for the library. Then he gives a full account of the library's current situation and future possibilities. He tells the gathering, "We have some money now. We can buy land, make a building, get a solar energy unit and buy more books—*if* you are interested. If not, we can give the money to some other village." Clever Buddi! Of course, these villagers are not about to let this money leave Badel.

The 22 men present give Buddi and the other speakers their rapt attention, as a free-and-easy give-and-take takes place, and some of the more outspoken men ask questions and make points. By the end of the meeting, a committee of fifteen has been named. Bhakta Rai will serve as president; Madhan Rai, a high school graduate and teacher, will be vice president; Dhan Bahadur Rai, will be the secretary; and Jhanak Rai, a politician, will act as treasurer. During the discussion in which people suggested names for committee members, I asked Buddi, "Did anyone suggest a woman's name?" "No," he said, "because women are busy—but we can suggest." He did suggest two, who won approval: Om Kumari Bhujel, a recent high school graduate about to study at university, and Buddi's sister, Gita, Dhan Bahadur's wife, a mother of three grown children and a high school graduate who has been trained as a health worker. No Darjes are on the committee now, although a couple are at the meeting. Buddi says, "Maybe in future. If present members don't work, can change."

The committee makes plans:

1) to register the library at district headquarters, so it can have a bank account and become eligible for government benefits;

2) to consider three different plots of land to erect a new two-story building with four rooms, possibly using one room for a reference room, one for a circulating library, one for a children's room, and one for a health dispensary where wounds can be cleansed and bandaged, aspirin given for fever and other simple remedies provided.

3) to buy a solar energy unit, currently being offered by Peter at a good price. This would provide light, a precious commodity for readers and a valuable one, since the village is not likely to get electricity in our lifetime.

4) to arrange for librarian training in Kathmandu. The training can be obtained free and Buddi will feed and house the librarian in his apartment during the four weeks of training.

5) to come up with a way for the village to raise money to keep the library going. Suggestions included a small furniture factory, and a nursery of fruit trees to be sold to local farmers, which would have the added plus of creating a plentiful supply of healthful fruits.

Toward the end of the meeting Buddi asks us if we want to say anything. I tell the assemblage, "We are very excited to see so much interest from the villagers for the library and the future of the village. We're very happy we were able to help." Then Mansing Rai, the former headman with the friendly, open, broad face, makes a gracious speech: "Many thanks for your help in this project. This will offer a good future for our children if they want to work. I hope we will stay friends for many years."

All of this has been accomplished in one hour. When we congratulate Buddi on getting so much done in so short a time, he says with a grin, "Meeting short—work long." Marge laughs: "In America it would have taken three meetings to get this much decided—and then all the work would still have to be done." Yes, this work will be long, but, as the Nepali proverb says: "If the beginning is good, the end will be good."

We have done what we needed to do here. We have seen the library, brought more books, witnessed the meeting and a surge in progress. Now it's time to let go—to let go of "our" library, which is not ours; to let go of the serenity of Badel, which again is not our life; to let go of the villagers, who will always be mysteries to us. I want to be on my way, on the trek by the Arun river that Buddi has planned for us. But Marge is not ready to let go of Badel. I think about my impatience to be off and do a turnaround in my thinking. What a precious opportunity this is to calm my mind: to let go of my attitude of have-to-do, to just be. I do plan to do one thing—to hold a story-hour at the library later today. And meanwhile, for myself, to read *Everyday Zen* and *Nectar in a Sieve*. And sit and think. And just sit.

I wander up to the library in the afternoon, and a throng of children materializes like the cloud of moths that swarm to our balcony as soon as the kerosene lantern is lit. I talk to them in a mixture of pidgins—English and Nepali—as I pull picture books from the shelves. Time for Grandma Sally's Story Hour. I sit on the mud step in front of the library, where I am surrounded, almost enclosed, by dark little heads and rapt little faces, who laugh broadly at my animal noises and funny faces. Arjun Rai and his friend are the only children who consistently call out the English or Nepali names of the farm animals I point to, while the others are content to listen and laugh. I have chosen picture books about farm animals, a familiar subject to these youngsters in this agricultural village. The boys eagerly shout out "cow," "horse," "goat." But when I come to a picture of a fat pink pig, they are stymied. I finally realize why. And I understand why it's so hard for test-developers to devise culture-free tests. All the pigs in these American books are fat and pink, while all the pigs in Badel are skinny and black. They are like two different species; they don't even look like relatives from the same family.

Jhukki Dorje brought her
little girl to me for medicine.
She has a bad ear infection that
I fear has gone into the mastoid
bone. I gave her aspirin and
told her to apply warm packs but
to take her to the clinic in Ausolakata
very soon.

Back at Buddi's house we are visited by a mother and her little girl, who has an immense swelling behind her ear that reveals a nasty-looking mastoid infection. Yesterday Marge (through Buddi) told the mother to take the child to the hospital in Aiselakharka, and we thought that the child's teenage brother was going to do it. But he didn't, and neither did anyone else. I feel a surge of anger: Why doesn't this mother care for her child's health? But then my anger subsides into understanding and sympathy. We know the infection could be fatal, but she does not. And this mother has other children to care for. The four-hour walk to Aiselakharka carrying her child would be hard for this slight woman. She may be afraid of going alone. Her son may not be willing to go: even though Nepali youth respect their elders, they may not always be as agreeable as their parents (and we) would like. Marge has a deep belief in the self-healing properties of the Nepali people ("They seem to have nine lives," she says). I am less optimistic. I am all too conscious of the high mortality rate in these rural areas for children under five, and I fear for this little girl's life. I hope that Marge is right and I'm wrong.

There's some basis for Marge's sanguine attitude, aside from the fact that we need to let go. We can only do what we can do in the brief time we are here—and we have to let go of the outcome. ChamarSing's daughter brought the baby boy around again, and his poor little burned hand is healing well, giving him no pain, as evinced by his easy use of it and his smiling happy disposition. And Dhojuman's injured leg is also healing well. Still, as before, the biggest shadow over this earthly Paradise is its dearth of health care. How clever of Marge to suggest—and of Buddi to immediately respond to—the idea of setting aside one room in the new library building as a health dispensary.

The next morning the mother of the little girl with the mastoid infection comes by again, and Marge gives her more aspirin. I raise my concern: "This woman thinks you're curing her child with those pills. I think you should stop giving them to her and impress upon her the seriousness of this condition—that her child might die if it goes untreated." Marge says that the aspirin would make the child feel more comfortable, but she sees my point. How can we get the woman's teenage son to take his little sister to Aiselakharka? Marge comes up with the brilliant idea of paying him 100 rupees *after* he comes back. Buddi agrees. Now we just have to hope that they come back tomorrow.

But there are other considerations: The treatment is free, but what if the doctors want to keep the child overnight? Can, or will, the brother stay? We'll deal with that when and if the question comes up. It doesn't come up, because we see neither child nor mother again. Could she tell from our conversation that no more aspirin was forthcoming, and that we would pressure her to take the child to the hospital? I still have to fight the anger that surges up against this woman who by her neglect may be endangering her child's life. And then I manage to put myself in her place. This is the shadow side of Paradise, embodied in the child's illness, the large poor family, the forces leading to the inaction of the mother and the older siblings, the specter of early death. How can I possibly say what I would do if I were that mother? Again, I need to let go—of my insistence that other people—this mother, Marge, the library committee that does not include women—do what I would have them do.

After this morning's conversation about this little girl, Marge says, "What I appreciate about our friendship is how honest we can be with each other." Yes, I treasure this too. This *is* a unique friendship. The villagers seem amazed that Marge and I live so far away from each other—as far as Pakistan is from Nepal, Uttam explains. We hardly ever see each other in the States and we don't even speak that often—and yet we live so intimately here, "like husband and wife," Marge says.

FROM MARGE'S JOURNAL:

After I carefully cleaned out all the sores on Dhojuman's toes and ankle, apply iodine and Neosporin and put on a bandage, flies still hover over the wound. I turn to Buddi: "What good are these damn flies? Certainly they have no place in reincarnation." Buddi smiles. "Flies good, Grandma. They eat dead body. When person dies, put in box and flies eat. Soon, one year maybe, body gone."

Buddi, you are wonderful! You find the good in even the most desperate of situations. Still I find a pair of white socks and give them to Dhojuman. "Put on. Keep flies away."

On our last quiet afternoon I sit alone on our beautiful balcony. I look out at the *nephara*, the graceful tree in front of Buddi's house, with its large round leaves that the villagers use to make dishes to hold rice, greens and other foods. The tree must have been here all the time—when we were here in 1993 and 1994—but it was only this morning as I was doing yoga that I really saw it. I wonder how many other beautiful treasures in my world go unnoticed? I need to pay attention, to look more, see more, do less. Tonight Marge says, "Well, I'm ready to go. Thank you for staying longer." I should thank her for giving me the opportunity to look at my life, my days here, in a different light. I'm sure I'll take some of this light home with me. I keep thinking about how I'll do things differently when I am back home with my family—let go of more responsibility, pressure, anxiety.

I keep telling people here in Badel that I'll be back, but I doubt it. I feel complete with my visits here, my work here, the people here. Yes, this place is beautiful, the people are friendly, my life here is sweet. But I feel I have had enough.

Mon Bahadur Mata Rai, Sabut Maya Mathani's husband, comes to the library to make a pretty speech of thanks and farewell. He thanks us for the library and for all the things we did for the village and says he will always remember us. Then this 65-year-old man adds, "I will die soon. The sun and the moon are up in the sky, and they will stay there, but my time will be up." He says this with great equanimity—that this is life, this is the way things go—and complete acceptance. *This* is the way to let go. He expresses gratitude that he got to know us in his lifetime. When we ask Buddi to translate, he says, "Let Uttam." But Uttam just laughs raucously. His youth shows in his embarrassment over this deeply felt poetic speech. Finally Buddi does translate.

Our last morning in Badel ends with the Dasain tika, offered on this ninth day of the festival by the elders of the household. Shiva (who now addresses me as "*timi*," the familiar form of address, which means, I guess, that she has welcomed us as intimates) has prepared the bunches of marigolds and *jamora*, the *tika* paste of rice and water. As the oldest member of the household, Dhojuman does the honors, beginning with his eldest son. When he wishes Buddi a good life, health, happiness—and that he make a lot of money, he sounds very American. He applies the tika to Buddi's forehead and they namaste each other. Then onto "*Kanchi*" (the youngest, Kiran), to whom he wishes health, happiness, a good life—and that he should study well in high school and then go on to study in America.

Dhojuman switches to English, wishing Marge and me a good and healthy and happy life—and that we should come back to Badel. With every blessing, Shiva gives flowers and a five-rupee note, and Dhojuman applies the tika. They repeat the ritual for all the staff, including the Darje helper sitting outside the door. Then it is time for a festive lunch—a small dish of buffalo meat, a huge mound of rice and a bowl of dal, plus, for Marge and me, pork cooked with green peppers, saag, and much more modest helpings of rice and lentil sauce.

After packing I come down to find the porch overflowing with people, all holding wreaths of marigolds. One by one, Shiva, Gita, Muna, Meena, faces I know but can't name, faces I don't even know, come up and garland us, until Marge and I each wear about eight leis around our necks. One tiny little girl holds up her flowers, looks at us, but is too bashful to put them on us, so we kneel down so she can reach. People smile and laugh and speak words of friendship and Uttam plays the guitar and sings. Then Marge and I sing "Auld Lang Syne," and although both our voices quaver and crack from emotion, we get through it. How can I say, after this, that I won't return?

We start to go off the porch by the back way, but Uttam stops us. "No, you go the other way—too many flowers!" I thought he meant we'd bump into something, but no, he meant something entirely different. Out in front is a tightly packed throng of thirty or forty children and adults, with *more* leis! We are soon so well garlanded that our faces are covered almost up to our eyes. Ganga Maya bustles up, resplendent in green satin blouse and heavy gold necklace, full of smiles and enthusiasm. We *namaste* all around, receive and give good wishes, take photos, and take our leave of the smiling crowd, who keep waving to us until we are out of sight. But no, they don't stop even then. Ganga Maya follows us out of town to the banyan tree where we hang most of our leis. "This is our custom," Buddi says.

I loved getting these flowers, but I couldn't see and I couldn't keep my balance, and it was so hot I didn't want one extra thing on me. As beautiful as they are, I had to let go of them—as I have had to let go of so much else. Shyam helped by climbing the tree, throwing the wreaths over branches and stalks. All the staff kept at least one garland, and then laid it on top of their doko-loads, making the procession a pretty sight.

24

1998:
Breaking New Ground:
A Building Will Rise

"After the pagoda is built, the scaffolding is dismantled."
—Burmese proverb

Here I am again. When I left Badel in 1996, I thought that was my last visit. I had done what I had planned to do; I felt that my work with the villagers and with myself had ended. But Badel would always be in my heart, and so I kept in touch with Buddi and, of course, with Marge. And when Marge and I heard that the committee had purchased land for a new building for Our Beautiful Badel Library and that work would begin soon, neither of us could stay away—especially when we learned that the library committee would wait to break ground for the new building until we could be present.

And so, on Tuesday, October 6, 1998, I land at the Kathmandu Airport, flying from Beijing (where I finished a five-week trip in

307

China with Mark—how could I not go to Nepal, when I was already in Asia?), connecting in Bangkok on the same plane as Marge's son, Brian, and his nine-year-old son, Jacob. The four of us will go together to Badel, visit old friends, be updated on the status of the library, and attend the ground-breaking ceremony at the building site.

But first we'll spend a couple of days in Kathmandu, at the Potala. I have to laugh. It seemed like such a palace in 1987 when our trekking group transferred there from the Hotel Asia, and now it has assumed a slightly seedy appearance. Still, when Marge asks me, "Does it feel like coming home?" I realize that it does.

I do have to re-orient myself to the streets and I get lost once, but then I have it all in my head and in my legs. What is it that keeps bringing me back here? The people? Yes. The remoteness? Yes. The romanticism? Yes. The feeling of belonging? Yes. The connection with the remote village of Badel? Yes. And of course, my good friend, Marge. We down beer and sodas and chat in Brian and Jacob's triple room; then I head out to the Himalayan Explorers Club to send an email, then back to Thamel to look for a tailor to embroider a dragon on my jumper, get lost (the only time) coming back, shower and shampoo. And then I know I'm in Kathmandu when the power and hot water go out, fortunately just after I rinsed the shampoo out of my hair. Tonight we meet Buddi, Dhana and their children at the Stupa Terrace Restaurant in Boudhanath, opposite the gleaming white-domed temple, where we can see the constant circumambulation of pilgrims turning the polished brass prayer wheels that ring this stupa, the largest in Nepal.

FROM MARGE'S JOURNAL:

Dhana is strikingly beautiful in her red sari. I notice a difference from the day when I first met her five years ago in Badel. She was living with Buddi's parents, as all young Nepali brides do, helping with the work in the house and on the farm. She seemed sad then, seldom smiling. Her husband was away, trekking and teaching, much of the time. Then in 1995 Buddi moved his little family to Kathmandu, where his pregnant wife could have her second baby in a hospital and little

Kusum would be enrolled in the best school. Dhana must be happy in her crowded little apartment on the outskirts of Kathmandu. I know this because she smiles a lot now. I watch and admire her gentle ways with Kusum, Sushma and Ajaya.

From midnight until 2 a.m. the next morning, I hear four separate groups of noisy Americans, singing and shouting as if it were midday instead of the middle of the night. An unpleasant change in Kathmandu: noise pollution and rudeness to go with the air pollution. Leila at the Himalayan Explorers Club says it's not just Americans, and blames it on the step-up in tourism, with a new hotel going up every day.

After a couple of days of tying up loose ends in Kathmandu, showing Brian and Jacob the sights, and preparing for our trip to Badel, we're ready to fly to Lamidanda and trek from there. On the morning of our flight, the big question still is: Will Buddi fly with us? When we first arrived in Nepal, he told us that he got our tickets confirmed but didn't know whether he would get on the plane. Since this is not a tourist flight, seats are in short supply. "Ninety percent, Grandma," Buddi smiled to me. "I am trying." I have the feeling that Buddi will make it. How can he not be there when ground is broken for his dream, our beautiful Badel library? The next question is "How?" The plane is full. First priority was given to two doctors flying in on a mission of mercy.

Every day since we arrived, we have asked Buddi whether he got his ticket. Every day he has answered, "Still trying." Big smile. "Ninety percent." He won't know until he goes to the airport this morning with us. He'll have to take his gear, not knowing whether he'll fly or whether he'll turn around and go home to Karnali Treks. He does have a ticket—the nineteenth seat on an 18-seater plane—but it is not yet confirmed. He also has a letter from the Director of Tourism, telling the airline how important it is for Buddi to accompany his tourists (us).

We arrive at the airport at 9 a.m. for a 10 a.m. flight, to find—as usual—that the flight has been delayed one hour. Buddi tells us the delay is caused by the priority given to the tourist flights to Lukla and Pokhara. "Do the Nepalis resent foreigners' getting preferential treatment?" I ask him. He doesn't seem to know what I mean, and says only, "That's our government policy." This kind of acceptance is part of the appeal the Nepalis hold for us. No complaints, no resentment. At least none visible to the naked eye of this foreigner.

Meanwhile, Buddi still doesn't know whether he will fly. He meets two men he knows: one is the M.P. (Member of Parliament) for his district. Buddi supported him in the last election, and now the M.P. is giving payback by exerting whatever influence he can bring to bear to get our boy a seat. Our boy, savvy now in the ways of politics, is pulling strings. I wonder whether he will, after all, move in this direction once he feels he has made enough money for his family?

Marge and I find a bench and sit, then get up and walk around, then stand on one foot and another, then sit again, all the time fascinated and anxious as we watch Buddi negotiating with the airport personnel. He's sober of mien. I don't want to pester him by continuing to ask "What's happening now?" We're also wondering about the clothes we've brought for the villagers. Each of us is allowed a total of 20 kilos (44 pounds)—fifteen to check and five to carry on. When all our bags (including two immense duffels, swollen fat with clothes for children and adults) are weighed, the scale reads 115 kilos (253 pounds)! Buddi and one of the airport people take the two huge bags out of the pile; Buddi will send at least one of them with a porter, to arrive while we're still in Badel. All of our personal bags will go with us, although they weigh a total of 65 kilos (143 pounds). The other 50 kilos (110 pounds) have to remain behind. I don't understand this math—until I find that Buddi does snag a seat after all and will fly with us, so divided by three, our bags are just about at the limit.

Marge and I go through the women's security line, expecting to open all our bags, but the bored young attendant just stamps our boarding passes and waves us through. I guess these two grandmas don't look like terrorists. I'm so tired that I almost fall asleep in the airport waiting room. On the airplane I offer Brian the window seat since this is his first time on this flight, and my fourth. I love that view, but I predict that I'll fall asleep, and my prediction comes true. I do miss the view—but I appreciate the rest.

Excitement bubbles up when we land, and see the crowds of young men patiently hoping for porter jobs, the passengers waiting to board our plane for the flight back to Kathmandu, and, best of all, our porters and staff: Chamarsing, Uttam, Ishwor, Bhim, Shyam, Bal Kumar, Bir Bahadur, and a few new faces. Cheerful reunions—shaking of hands, even some of that imported non-Nepali custom, hugging!

We take a new, higher route—beautiful, lush and green, and enjoy seeing it through Jacob and Brian's new eyes. It's wonderful being away from the dirt and noise and smells and vendors and beggars of Kathmandu, into clean air, quiet roads, friendly people welcoming us without importuning us to buy anything or give alms. After walking half an hour or so, we find our kitchen and the delicious lunch Chamarsing prepared for us, alongside a secondary school. While we sit on the ground waiting for food, a slender young man brings us an invitation:

> "Shree Bishwa Jyoti Secondary School—Namaste and wellcome to all
> tourists. I request you to come inside the office. I want to talk with all
> of you. Please, come here as soon as possible.
> "Binod Kumar Khadaka, Headmaster."

Of course we accept Mr. Khadaka's invitation and make our way into the stripped-down little building, considerably smaller than the elementary school in Badel. Brian asks many questions about the school, and then, in the guest book Mr. Khadaka asks us all to sign, Brian writes down some facts about Jacob's school.

We reach camp at about 10 to 5, after having trekked only three hours today. The walk was beautiful, I'm feeling good, my mostly forgotten Nepali is coming back to me, word by word—and I'm happy to be here. Jacob, tired, jet-lagged and unhappy with the food, can't stay up for dinner, not even for Brian's birthday cake. We all understand that all of this is hard for a nine-year-old, and nobody makes a big deal of it. It's a new experience having a child along on the trek—and an interesting one with this bright, interesting boy.

The next day is the hardest trekking day I can remember. Ever. If I've had worse, I have mercifully blocked them from memory. We start out happily enough—just after 7 o'clock, walking the usual up and downs, seeing the countryside and the people. And then it gets hotter. And hotter. And hotter, until the sweat is pouring off me, running down my face, my neck, my arms. I would have put back on the tee shirt I wore yesterday, but it's still damp from yesterday's sweat, so I reach into the dirty-clothes bag to pull out my only other lightweight shirt. It's good that it's dirty already, since I know that whatever I put on will be drenched within minutes.

By 10, when the heat has become almost unbearable, we cross a rickety wooden bridge and stop by a sparkling little stream. Jacob, who has been miserably uncomfortable, strips down to his shorts and immerses himself in the cool, clear water. Marge and I look on enviously, but, not being nine-year-old boys, we settle for taking off our boots and socks and dangling our feet in the welcoming runnel.

A young mother, whose name is Tulasa Devi, looks on at our little group with interest and amusement. She points to her two sons, talks in rapid-fire Nepali about a daughter in school, refers to her 86-year-old grandfather and a grandmother, up in her house. She asks me whether Jacob is my grandson. In my halting Nepali I explain the relationship, tell her about my own family and invite her down to look at my photos. As a crowd of curious onlookers gathers, my new friend stays and chats. I give her the silver earrings I'm wearing, and when she says she wants to give me something, I tell her, "This conversation is a present." Still, I am happy to accept the pair of gold hoop earrings she insists on offering me, but when she tries to put them in my ears they balk and won't go in. I try too, but my earlobes resist: the ends of the earrings are too thick for these western ears. I thank her, we "namaste" each other, and finally it's time for us to set out again.

Again the heat attacks us, more ferociously now. We go up and up and up. The sun beats down unmercifully. Buddi offers an umbrella; I turn it down. I'm having enough trouble balancing on these rocks without having to juggle an umbrella too. Brian offers a hat; but no, I resist hats—they make my head too hot. I keep wetting my bandanna to wipe my face; I dunk my head under water taps. For two hours we slog on in this heat, fiercer than I can ever remember it—although I do recall the torrid heaviness of the last trek, when I sweated so much I couldn't stand my own body odor. This time I remembered to bring deodorant—and to use it, so at least I'm not offending anyone down-wind of me—or myself.

Maybe I'm just managing to block bad memories of that earlier trek. Like childbirth. Otherwise, who would ever repeat either experience? Why, in fact, *did* I come? Because I was in "the neighborhood" already, in China? Because Marge was coming? Because of the library? Or just because? Because some mysterious magnet keeps pulling me back? Why do I have to have a reason? Because right now I'm doubting my sanity.

When the sun goes behind some clouds, the sudden relief is exhilarating. Maybe we can get to Badel, after all! I feel a few heaven-sent sprinkles of rain, which we've been expecting since the clouds of morning. Anything that relieves the sun's heat is welcome. I fish my rain jacket from my back-pack, which Buddi, Uttam and G.S. have been taking turns carrying. What a luxury! I had begun to think I wouldn't need it and shouldn't have brought it, but as the rain pours down heavily, I'm happy it's here.

Buddi, Uttam, Marge and I take shelter on the porch of a family in a village where we camped before. (Brian and Jacob have forged ahead.) This house looks like the same one we camped at, but Buddi says no. So many of these houses look alike—Levittown in the Himalayas. Another sign of the simplicity of life here is the absence of any need among the Rai to make their houses distinctive, different from their neighbors. They use little or no ornamentation; the structure is uniform from one house to another. The only difference is the size and the sturdiness, which depends on the family's finances. Maybe this is related to an absence of ego?

As I look around, I am amused to realize the difference between the necessarily simple life here—and the "voluntary simplicity" that so many Americans seek by buying books on simplifying your life, buying "plain" clothes like $400 cashmere sweaters, and hiring high-priced organizers to help them throw out unneeded possessions, while buying costly containers to keep all the stuff they hold onto.

A middle-aged woman spins black wool into yarn; an ancient bent-over woman with one eye and a pronounced shortage of teeth keeps popping out of the house; a young woman comes home, sits on the step and proceeds to card a big ball of black wool; a man steps out of the house, looks around and without a nod disappears again inside. The spinning woman brings out mats for us to sit on. We offer trail mix all around, which assures our popularity. A radio in the house alternates between blaringly loud commentary and even louder pop songs. The old woman tells the spinner to turn it off, but when Buddi asks us if it bothers us, I truthfully say no.

As soon as the rain lets up ever so slightly, Marge, who is feeling sick, heads back to the trail with Uttam. Buddi, who stays with me, has absolutely no protection from the rain, not even a coat (which he had earlier given to Marge), nor an umbrella. So he and I linger a little longer. The old woman hobbles out bearing a tray of steaming cups of tea. I take a tentative sip and ask Buddi: "Is there salt in this tea?" "Yes, Grandma. If you don't like, you don't have to drink." I have been given absolution. I lift the cup to my lips a few times as if I'm drinking and look in vain for somewhere to dump it. Feeling like a deficient guest, I just leave it in an inconspicuous corner.

When the rain lets up again Buddi and I set out. Within five minutes the skies open up once more, and Buddi maneuvers the two of us soggy souls to another house, where we take shelter on another identical porch. Again, smiling and welcoming people bring out mats and stools, though they speak less and, fortunately, offer no refreshments. Three Nepali travelers come along also seeking shelter, then another, and another. The rain stops, we set out. The rain starts, we find another refuge.

This time we are sheltered by a family Buddi knows, where a round-faced 20-month-old baby is playing on a mat. Buddi motions me to sit down next to the baby, but, afraid I'll frighten him, I sit on the bamboo stool. The baby's father went to school with Buddi, now owns an iron shop in Kathmandu, and speaks English. He sweetly tells his tiny son to "*gar namaste*" and the baby does; to "*salaam*," at which the baby salutes; and to "do bye-bye." Now the baby waves. I'm impressed. We stay here a long time as the rain pours down in loud sheets and are invited into the spotless kitchen, where the home-owner (whose name I never learn) offers us chang and snacks (bread-sticks and squash, which sounds interesting until Buddi tells me how spicy it is—so I refrain). I look around, watch the baby, and listen to Buddi talk to his friend in rapid-fire Nepali. I get the feeling that the rain will never stop and that we'll spend 40 days and 40 nights here, when Uttam shows up as our guardian angel, with an umbrella (instead of a halo) to fetch us to camp.

In view of the weather, camp is indoors. Our ever-dependable staff sets up tents for us inside the various rooms of a high school, which we're grateful for, since the roof leaks. Everything feels clammy, and I feel dirty. Why shouldn't I? I've been wearing the same clothes for three days, with no bath except for my handy baby wipes. I feel I should make more of an effort to bathe, but then I shrug, why bother? I'll get clean when I get to Badel. As Buddi says, I'm becoming Nepali, not feeling that western compulsion to change clothes every day.

It's such a relief to be here lying down in my sleeping bag. When it was so hot and we were so desperately wishing for clouds, we got torrents. "Be careful what you wish for because you may get it!" Jacob reminds us. Out of the mouths of babes.

Next morning, on our way to Badel, our path winds through the district of Bakachol, which encompasses four villages, including Badel. Bhakta Kumar Rai, 29 years old, who was elected district headman last year when he ran under the aegis of the Sun party, welcomes us with a broad smile. He will serve a five-year term. He and his fellow citizens bestow loads of leis upon us and escort us into the office of the district headquarters. The walls hold calendars, signs ("NO SMOKING") and a banner proclaiming a major meeting for the village *panchayat* (governing council), which meets twice a year. They used to meet in a private house until the owner gave it to the village to use for headquarters.

In answer to our questions, we learn that a post office, health post and new headquarters building are currently under construction, that the panchayat has nearly 4500 constituents, that Bakachol is divided into nine wards, every one of which has one representative, that the national government pays the headman 1,000 rupees a month, and that every year it can give every village 500,000 rupees for special projects, like a school. After Bhakta answers our questions, we ask whether he has any questions for us, but he gives that lopsized Nepali shake of his head and says, "No." He tells us that he's very happy about the library—and is looking forward to more help.

Bhakta's winning platform rested on his promise to help the schools and to increase their budget every year. (The Badel school operates on an annual budget of 80,000 rupees—about $1200 at current exchange rates of 67 rupees to the dollar.) Bhakta proudly tells us that over the past year three new schools were built in two districts, and he is now trying to turn the private high school here into a government school, so that more students will be able to attend. Bhakta looks at his watch—not because he wants us to leave, but because he wants us to see the high school and the headmaster is waiting.

Headmaster Ram Kumar Rai warmly welcomes us to the Shree Kalika Bal Bikash Secondary School, which was accredited by the government this year for nine classes and now has ten. The 244 students (133 boys and 111 girls—a good ratio for Nepal), ages 5 to 18, pay no fee. The school day begins at 10 a.m. and ends at 4, with playtime from 1 to 2. A Miss Nelson from Oregon brought science materials and 35,000 rupees and furniture to the school, and Buddi gave 10,000 rupees worth of needed items. We donate a modest 500 rupees, which the headmaster at first demurs at accepting. Now the children of Badel won't have to walk two hours to reach the high school in Rakha or half a day to Aiselakharka, where they would need to find lodgings for the week. It takes us less than an hour for us to reach Badel, which means that the local youngsters could do it in half that time. I can just imagine the howls from American high school students if they were told they had to walk half an hour to school.

A six-pointed star over the doorway represents education, and the stamp that the headmaster uses to stamp our notebooks shows a six-pointed star with a book inside, the symbol for a government school. So I'm confused. Is this already a government school? One more example of the confusion that results from being in a country where you don't know the language. Again, I'm humbled by how little I know, or understand.

Finally we reach Buddi's parents' house, where a large red banner stretched over the gate proclaims "WELL-COME OUR RELATIVES." Dozens of villagers come up, one by one, to drape golden garlands around our necks until our noses and mouths are completely covered. We feel the affection in the greetings from Buddi's parents, Shiva and Dhojuman, as they press their palms together and salute us with "Namaste." They don't kiss and hug or even shake hands as we would do back home, but we could not received a warmer reception from the most loving blood relatives. These welcoming traditions are addictive; maybe that's what keeps bringing us back to these adopted "relatives."

The hordes of children standing quietly in the crowd can't take their huge dark eyes off Jacob, who is the first western child to come here, and the first most of them have ever seen. He almost immediately heads into the courtyard to play ball with half a dozen kids and to give out the yoyo's he brought from home. When he comes back, he enthusiastically shouts out "Yes!" when Brian asks whether he had a good time. "We don't speak the same language, but we don't need to," he says. Like Shiva and me.

After a bite of lunch we take the ten-minute walk over to the school for the library committee meeting. Among the twelve members present is the chairman, a former headman; at first I think he is Gadja Bahadur Rai, the shaman, but Gadja is also here, and my confusion is explained when I learn that the two who look so much alike are brothers. Dhan Bahadur, our librarian; the school headmaster; and other familiar faces are also present. A torrent of conversation ensues between Buddi, the shaman and the headmaster, as both sides report on progress. We learn that the parcel of land (150 by 100 feet) next to the school, where the new library building will be constructed, cost 36,000 rupees ($537), including the cost of registering it in the district. Now no one can take it away, not even the government. Although no date is set yet, Dhan Bahadur will take the two-week librarian training course offered by READ, either in Kathmandu or Chitwan National Park.

We also learn that this school building was sponsored by the headman and by Dhojuman, Buddi's father, and that the drinking water, latrine and new bridge were jointly underwritten by the Ghurka Welfare Center and the Kadoorie Agricultural Aid Association's Ghurka Project. The committee bought the land from Mon Bahadur Rai, husband of the late Sabut Mathani Maya Rai, the midwife we met in 1993.

Tomorrow morning at 7 a.m. the ground-breaking ceremony will take place. Then Buddi will buy a map in Kathmandu to mark the spot. The building will have four rooms on two floors: a reference room, a reading and circulation room, a room for young children, and a dispensary where trained health workers can treat simple medical problems. The curriculum in the Badel elementary school will include regular weekly library visits for all classes, which will be easy to manage since the building will be erected on a parcel of land adjacent to the school. Construction on the building, which has to await the provincial registration and the end of the monsoon season, should be finished within about three months. As the meeting draws to an end, Buddi tells the four of us Americans, "The people of Badel will always remember you. For a thousand years." Brian turns to me and whispers, "This is when I wish I had a tape recorder."

We all walk over to the site where the library will be built. Now all we see is a stretch of bare land, with, in one corner, a pile of rocks, about six feet high and eight feet square. Buddi jerks his head in the direction of the rocks and tells us, "We'll need 25 more piles like that." He gave 20,000 rupees ($300) to the committee, says he'll give more when more is needed. He tells us about the long proposal he wrote to READ, applying for help.

Marge and I head back to our balcony, where we write a speech that we'll give tonight before the performance of the drama. It rains so hard that we can't believe the drama will still be performed, but show biz prevails, and the show does go on—but without us. We don't trust our footing on the muddy paths in the dark. Buddi delivers our speech:

> "We are very grateful to the people of Badel for your kindness and hospitality to us since we first came here five years ago. We are also impressed by the Badel people's appreciation of education, which we know will help your children to enjoy a happy future."

Precisely at 7 o'clock on Tuesday morning, we get the thrill of a lifetime as we take part in one more step in our library's progress, the ground-breaking ceremony for the new building. This little library that began in 1994 with 350 books in a former bedroom in the home of Dhan Bahadur Rai will soon have its own home to house the 2,000 or so books it now has, to make room for more, and to meet other community needs.

The entire committee (minus the women who we thought were members—we do have to let go of that one) assembles at the site. Everyone, including Marge and me, takes a turn using a short-handled shovel to dig the hole for the foundation. Marge carefully places a small metal canister with our statement of good wishes for the people of Badel in the opening. I read our statement, which Buddi translates into Nepali:

> "Today we are honored to be at the dedication of Our Beautiful Badel Library (Hamro Ramro Badel Pustekalaya). We hope that this library will give the people of Badel much knowledge and enjoyment, now and for many years in the future.
> "In Friendship,
> "Sally Wendkos Olds, Margaret Roche, Brian Dwyer Roche, Jacob Roche."

Then Marge and I hoist a large—and heavy—rock and place it at the bottom of the hole. One of the committee members sets a wooden post in the hole to mark the spot, and the committee members take turns shoveling the dirt back over it. To ensure that the building will never be hit by lightning nor suffer any other "bad thing," the shaman chants prayers over offerings of marigolds, rice, flour, coins, red *tika* powder, and a butter lamp, anoints all of us with a tika on the forehead, and helps us place flower petals and other offerings in the cornerstone opening.

As Marge and I watch the men shovel the dirt, filling up the hole, tears spring to both of our eyes. Marge turns to me and says, "It was worth every step." Every step on every hard trek to get here. Every step of the way to where we are now. I say to her "This is probably the best thing I have ever done." (Although later I think that maybe the cleft lip operations may have had more of an effect on individual lives.) At this powerful moment I have trouble believing what we have actually accomplished.

The committee members thank us, and then we all wander off to the business of the day—the men to their work, Buddi to Lamidanda where he has to board the plane to take him to Kathmandu where he will meet his trekkers, and we four Americans to Darje Tol.

25

1998 & 2000: A Visit to Darje Tol and a Postscript

"Coming together is a beginning, keeping together is progress, and working together is success."

—*Arabian proverb*

Marge and I have a special feeling for the residents of Darje Tol, that part of Badel where the Darje people live. Kumari and her cousin, Om, the two children whose surgery for cleft lip we arranged, live here, and the Darje families have been among the most eager recipients of the children's clothing we have brought from the States, visit after visit.

Marge, Brian, Jacob and I had a discussion yesterday about whether we're corrupting Badel by bringing all these clothes. When the villagers learn of our arrival, they come around, expecting us to give them or their children things to wear. True. But this is not developing a begging mentality. Yes, the villagers come to us because they know we bring clothes for them. I doubt that they would approach other westerners with the same expectations.

Also, they see us as special because of the library. We have been benefactors of the village in general; we're not just passing tourists. It's unlikely that many tourists will ever come through here.

I tell Marge, "We'll have to ask whether the people of Badel have approached any other westerners who came to the village." Marge bristles, "It's not important whether they ask other westerners. The important thing is that they have clothes." Also, as she points out, we *invited* the people to come to take what we brought for them, which is different from their asking for things. In any case, neither of us has any problem with the situation. We are all disappointed that the last duffel didn't arrive before we left. Brian wanted to take photos of the Badel children wearing clothes from his own children. I'm eager to show Mark's sister, Miriam, photos of children wearing the woolen caps that she knitted. So many people have opened their hearts to the people of Badel. All those who gave clothes for the villagers, money for the library, books to Peter. It's gratifying to realize how far the ripples that our little pebble started have reached.

Here in Darje Tol this morning, as on other visits to this part of Badel, musicians will play for us and young boys will dance. It seems bizarre to my western mind that musicians should come from Nepal's lowest castes, since they are an integral part of every caste's celebration and since in the culture in which I grew up anyone who makes music is held in high regard. Here is one cultural dissonance that I haven't become used to.

One man who seems to be in his thirties plays mournful melodies on the *karmal* (a horn with a big, broad base); the 55-year-old man who fingers the flute called a *sanai* has been making music for 40 years. Our young friend Arjun beats out an insistent rhythm on a big drum, and other boys clash cymbals and pound their hands upon a small drum. Little Om, whose smile has been ever-radiant since his surgery, wriggles his slim hips and dances as if he doesn't have a bone in his body.

This time, there is a new wrinkle: Uttam tells us that the dancers want some money for their performance, which of course we're happy to offer. In fact, the amount he suggests is embarrassingly little—200 rupees (about three dollars). G.S. describes what they're planning to do, but I don't get the idea until I see them do it: We place rupee-notes on a worn and faded cloth on the ground in front of the dancing boys, and after dancing for a while, the boys arch their lithe bodies into back bends, angle their heads way back and pick up the notes with their mouths. I'm uncomfortable with what smacks of sideshow enter-tainment and seems to denigrate the dancers, but apparently it is a standard part of the act. No one else seems to mind.

Darje Tol is the slum of Badel. The people are poor, the children in rags, their dark hair tangled and uncombed, their dark faces streaked with dirt, their noses dripping a thick, sometimes blood-tinged yellow mucus. Many do not go to school because their families need their work. The families are large. Buddi has enticed some of the men for vasectomies, sometimes by a sub-terfuge, which he justifies by saying it is the best thing for their families. Brian has a hard time understanding the caste system. He asks a question that both Marge and I have also puzzled over: "How do you improve the basic standard of living without destroying the indigenous culture?"

We don't know the answer to this. We're still hoping that the school and the library and an improved access to medical care will make an impact on the quality of life for these villagers, but only time will tell.

Postscript:

In November 2000 I could not make the trip to Badel because of other com-mitments. Marge did go, however, and there she saw and went into the almost-completed library building, whose use turned out to be rather different from what we had envisioned.

FROM MARGE'S JOURNAL:

There it stands. A beautiful whitewashed structure, rising from the gray dirt and rocks almost as though it were planted there, as if it had always been there, and part of the landscape. Of course it looks this way because it is part of the earth.

The walls are stones from the local ground held together by cement made from dung and river sand. It was built by men from the village with their few tools. The wood is from trees that grew in the nearby jungle. The simple two-story structure with an exposed stairway with no handrail, has a balcony circling the second floor. In front two men are planing planks of wood, about eight inches wide, to be used for shelves and furniture.

Dhan Bahadur, our part-time librarian, helps me up the narrow stairs. In the one large room with wooden walls, ceiling and floor, benches line the walls— except for the one long wall where there will be bookshelves. Sawdust and shavings carpet the floor. I expected to see the walls lined with books, but there isn't a book in sight. The books are still in the second room in Dhan's house. Two years after breaking ground Our Beautiful Badel Library is still not finished. But it is nearly so. I think my announced visit spurred the men on a bit.

I have a quiet Buddhist moment. Desire and expectation are the source of all unhappiness. Not all seeds take root; at best we can put them out there and water them and wait. Nothing happens fast in Badel. These are patient people without an agenda. They don't live by goals and deadlines. Their agenda is to feed their families. After the crops are planted and harvested there will be time to make shelves and furniture for our library. I will not wish them to live by my rules, to-do lists, and esteem-building accomplishments. I would be healthier and happier if I learned to live by theirs. I am working on it.

We leave the library building and walk about fifty meters to the school. On a small hill just beyond the school yard the children are hard at work with pick-axes—or the Nepali equivalent—swinging them at the ends of their wiry little arms to break up the rock-hard soil. They take turns at the axes, eight or ten at a time, laughing and singing as they hammer away at the rock-hard ground. "We are building new school. Students making ground ready," Dhan explains. "Old school not safe, very dangerous. Roof falling." Just then a small boy comes around the building struggling under the weight of a load of stone roof tiles. "Now using library for small children until new school is ready." This explains the rows of benches in the lower floor of the library.

Our Beautiful Badel Library

My mind does a couple of somersaults. It has been two years since we broke ground for Our Beautiful Badel Library. There seems to be no big hurry to get the new school built, and who is paying for it? I ask questions but get vague answers. It seems doubtful that the government will give the village money for a new school. They will need to finance and build this one themselves. The old school is not only unsafe but there is not enough room for all the children who want to go to school. And here sits our beautiful new library building. Have Sally and I just built a school instead of a library?

Do I dare to believe our seed has taken root? Maybe not to sprout the flower of Sally's and my dreams, but to sprout Badel's own special flower of education. More girls are going to school now and most of the Darje children go to at least third grade. In America, there is a problem with children destroying schools. In Badel children take up their pickaxes and build schools.

So in the year 2000 all the books in Our Beautiful Badel Library are still in a room in Dhan Bahadur's second house. But Badel does have a beautiful new school building. Suppose that back in 1993 Buddi had said that his dream was a new school instead of a library? We would have done all we could to make that a reality. And if Badel didn't have the library building now to house her school children, what would many of them be doing? Probably staying home and working in the fields instead of learning to read and taking step after forward step toward a brighter future.

Part V
After Badel

Muna Rai at her bath

26

Transformation: The Only Constant in Life Is Change

Nepal is here to change you; you are not here to change Nepal.
　　—Embroidered motto on tee shirts sold in Kathmandu

"If you do this thing, you will be changed forever," Marge told me when we first began talking about spending time in a village in Nepal, a year and a half before we eventually left, long before we even knew which village we would go to, or among which hills or mountains of that mystical, magnificent country it would be nestled, or how we would get there, where we would stay, what we would do. "You will never be the same."

I didn't question what Marge said. I never doubted for a nanosecond that she was right. I knew that I had been changed immeasurably, in ways both small and large, by the two treks I had already taken in Nepal. As, of course, I have been changed by every major experience in my life. And this visit, to be undertaken by two sixtyish women who barely knew each other, who would

331

be traversing dangerous narrow footpaths, living without accustomed creature comforts, in a world out of time, out of any time we knew, would certainly be major, on one exciting and anxiety-provoking level after another. But how much did I want to change? Was personal change my purpose in going? I couldn't even put my purpose into words.

The truth was that, before I left, I didn't know why I wanted so much to make this trip, felt so achingly that I needed to do it. I knew only that I felt a powerful pull that I didn't want to fight against. On the contrary, I welcomed that siren song, wanted to go with it as much as I could. And yes, I did come to realize that I was seeking a piece of myself that I didn't even know existed. I knew that I had to leave my safe, secure home and my loving family to find it. I didn't know what "it" was, what it would look like or feel like when and if I actually did find it, what or who I would be when I came back. And that was the part that filled me almost to bursting, with excitement and anxiety.

I had no idea what form my changes would take, even what realm they'd be in. Even though, early on, Marge had confided some of the myriad ways she had changed as a result of her earlier three-day visit to Tekanpur, a different Nepali village from the one we would visit.

FROM MARGE'S LETTER TO ME, January 7, 1993:

I know my life is quite different than it would have been had I never gone to Nepal. But the one experience that had the most profound effect on how I view my world back here was the village experience. Nothing has ever been the same since those three days in Tekanpur. When I sat there hour after hour, alone, watching the people in the village, the difference between them and me sank in.

"No one should ever come to Nepal for the first time," Marge said to me one day as we were picking our way along rocky paths, just after our conversation with a young American who had poured out complaint after whining complaint about the country. "You have all these judgments, all these ideas about what should be changed here." I thought about the tee shirt I had seen hanging in front of a stall on the dusty streets of Thamel, the colorful Greenwich

Village-like neighborhood of Kathmandu. The carefully embroidered letters on it had stayed with me: "NEPAL IS HERE TO CHANGE YOU, YOU ARE NOT HERE TO CHANGE NEPAL."

And so I went to Badel and came home, changed. And as I write these words, eight years after returning from the first of four visits to this remote hamlet, I am still responding to that experience, still changing. I hope to continue absorbing the lessons of Badel for the rest of my life. I think of the words written by anthropologist Nigel Barley, after he came home from spending a year in an African village: "A strange alienness grips you, not because anything has changed but rather because you no longer see things as 'natural' or 'normal.'"

I first realized one difference in the way I was seeing things on the first Sunday in May of 1993, a few days after I had come home from my first visit to Badel. My husband, Mark, my youngest daughter, Dorri, and I were celebrating Mother's Day at the home of my eldest daughter, Nancy. While Nancy and her husband went out for a short walk, Mark, Dorri and I stayed at their house with ten-month-old Anna. In the warm sunlight of this balmy afternoon, there we were: Mark was doing some sort of spring work in the yard, Dorri was catching up on lost sleep on the deck, and Anna and I were sitting on a bed sheet spread out on new grass under the shade of an old magnolia tree.

I started to get up to fetch one of the innumerable primary-color educational toys that Nancy takes such joy in buying for her little daughter. And then I remembered all those wonderful bright-eyed babies in Badel, and it suddenly hit me. No, Anna doesn't need any *thing* to play with. And indeed she didn't. She had me, she had the lawn, she had her own new motor skills to occupy and enchant her, she had a world of delights. She had no need to be entertained by anything called a toy. Instead, she kept herself busy pulling up shoots of grass, climbing onto my lap, reaching for my shiny earrings, moving from one position to another, pointing to birds overhead, feeling the breeze in her hair, taking in the big beautiful outdoors.

Over the months and years to come I was to have many such experiences when I would begin to act out of habit, custom, convention, routine, deeply entrenched ways of thinking and doing—and then I would skid to a halt. I would see life with the eyes of a beginner, with new eyes, questioning eyes. And I would pivot into a new circle of behavior.

One came about a month later, again around a little child. I had walked into the shoe store on Main Street to buy a pair of summer sneakers for my other granddaughter, Maika, the child of Jenny, my middle daughter. The salesman—cheerful, friendly, eager to help—brought out the only two pairs he had in Maika's size. One had a rounded toe, with a rubberized tip over the toe; the other had a more pointed toe, with no tip. When, in answer to his question, "How old is she?" I said, "Almost five," he pointed to the pointed ones and said, "Take them. That's the kind the kids like. She wouldn't be caught dead in the other pair." I said, "She lives in a little village in Germany. She doesn't know from fashion, she won't care about that." And I bought the round-toed ones, which seemed better for busy, growing feet.

Would I have done that if Maika lived here in the States? Or, despite my disgust at a society in which four-year-olds place so much emphasis on fashion, would I have gone along? Maybe if I hadn't gone to Badel, I would have. But after realizing that any one of the children in that little village, of any age, would be so thrilled to have a new pair of shoes—any kind—I couldn't even entertain feeding a value system that suddenly assumed such a warped aspect.

These slender little anecdotes seem so everyday, so slight. But this is how my transformation has come, little by little, inch by transfigured inch, in my everyday life. I have not sold my comfortable suburban house or either of our two cars, renounced my worldly work, given away my clothes or my computer, left my good husband, substituted meditation for movie-going, climbed a lofty mountain, entered a holy monastery, done anything classifiable as high drama. But I know that I am different in innumerable ways since those first two weeks in that little village.

Probably the biggest change that those two weeks in another place wreaked in me is the way I am now able just to *be* instead of always having to *do*. I've always been a doer, a multi-tasker, rarely content unless I was actively engaged in two or three activities at once. I also always felt that if I saw something that seemed to need fixing, I had been put here on earth to fix it. My way. But that compulsion to act, to do something, *any*thing, in any circumstance, seems to have been lifted from me.

Perhaps it was the knowledge that as a visitor for such a short time, I could get only the briefest of glimpses of the life in Badel. I couldn't "fix" anything— even if I were presumptuous enough to think that I had the right to bring my values from my society to make changes in one that was not only half a globe away geographically, but a universe away in so many less tangible ways. Whatever it was, that serenity of not feeling compelled to act on every thought stayed with me over the months to come, even after I had come home to a more complex society, a more complicated life, a life I don't want to abandon but do want to alter in countless ways, some of which I don't yet know.

After I came home, I found myself listening more and talking less. As I allowed myself to be, I found myself allowing other people to be and to accept them as they were, for who they were. I found that I have had more searching questions, fewer facile answers. I think often of the poet Rainer Maria Rilke's words, which have become a maxim for my life: "Be patient with all that is unsolved in your heart. Try to love the questions themselves like locked rooms or like books that are written in a foreign tongue. Live the questions raw."

I found myself questioning so much that I had taken for granted for years, all those things that no longer seem "natural" or "normal." Why, I asked myself, do I need to wear a watch all the time, 24 hours a day? Why do I need to eat and sleep and work and love by the clock? Why do I need to have so many belongings, to subscribe to the philosophy that "the winner is the one who dies with the most toys"? Why should I feel deprived if I don't get to see all the movies and read all the books that are well reviewed in *The New York Times*?

Looking askance at my over-involved life, I found myself simplifying it, setting new priorities, bringing in more silence, shutting out more noise, both from within and without. Some of this shedding came from a conscious decision to streamline my life, to pare it down to its core, to what really mattered. But more came unbidden, of itself, as I lost the desire to do or have so many things that had once seemed essential. I found myself erasing old social patterns and etching new ones—turning down appealing invitations, passing up interesting events, reining myself in, making efforts to keep from going off in multitudinous directions, guarding my time jealously, carving out oases of quiet and calmness and solitude.

I found myself letting go of my attachment to having the world proceed according to my blueprints. And the more I let go, the freer I have been to open myself to life and the freer to enjoy it. When something untoward has happened, I can, more often than in the past,—not always, of course, not even as often as I would like—realize how little it matters, and I can let go of it. This attitude has leached out to a greater acceptance of my daughters and their lives, my friends and their ways, even my husband, who—as close and loving as we are—does not always do or say what I would like him to do or say. I found myself listening to people, really hearing what they had to say, instead of leaping to judge them and tell them what I thought they should think, feel, do.

I found that I lost a certain arrogance shared with so many of my compatriots. I am no longer convinced that many of my most tenaciously held values are valid in all circumstances, for all people. I have come to realize that another culture, generally thought of as a primitive society by agreement in my culture, may, in innumerable newly recognized ways, be more advanced than my own.

One evening, three months after I had returned home, as I was talking with friends about Native Americans, Richard asked indignantly, "How can people not educate their children as much as possible, so they know all the technology? Otherwise, the kids are being shortchanged." And in my mind I saw the faces of Kiran and Dilkumari and Rahanta and all those other children we met in Badel, who are certainly undereducated by our western standards, but who seem to grow up with healthier attitudes and happier outlooks than our own so "well-educated" children, who, overwhelmed by our rush to teach them everything and give them everything, often fail to learn the most crucial lesson of all—who they are. Too many of our children grow up thinking that toys are essential, that love is measured by purchased gifts, that success is getting and having and winning. In their disquiet and ignorance about a well-lived life, they are the ones who are shortchanged.

Back home, away from Marge, with few exceptions I have not received a great deal of agreement on these views. She too has told me of her continual frustration in her attempts to explain to her friends and her family how she feels about Badel. Maybe it just isn't possible for people who have never visited a truly indigenous culture to imagine such a different world. One evening other friends were looking at my photo album of Badel and asking many thoughtful questions. At the end, Lily said, "I'm sure everything wasn't as rosy as it seemed to you. There must be more conflict than you heard about. People were probably putting on a good face for the visitors." So cynical, I thought. So New York. So American. Or was I being hopelessly naïve, idealizing a place I hardly knew?

The problem, of course, is that, as another friend said, "It's impossible to reproduce the experience for someone else. We can look at your photos and your friend's paintings and we can hear you talk, but we can't really be there with you." This book has been our effort to bring others there with us as much as we can and to tell what's been so for us.

I know, of course, that Badel is not Utopia. I know that the human condition involves conflict and that people are not always kind to one another. I know that Marge and I in our brief visits barely grazed an understanding of the villagers, and there has to be much that was not revealed to our western eyes, that might never be revealed to us, no matter how long we might stay. I have read about the trade in Nepali hill girls sold into prostitution, and I painfully acknowledge the grim possibility that some of those innocents may well have come from the village I fell in love with. I witnessed a mother distraught because her daughter was suffering at the hands of her husband. Still, I remain convinced that those villagers we met were not putting on a front and that, by and large, life in Badel is gentler, calmer, more peaceable, more caring, more life-affirming than it is here, with all of our technology, all of our luxury. And what I saw of that life did change mine.

FROM MARGE'S LETTER, APRIL 15, 1994:

It was one year ago that we were in Badel, and every day something happens that brings me back to our time there. I thought by now I would have integrated the experience into my daily life here and would have made some major changes in my living style. But I continue to swim among all my precious possessions, check completed tasks off my "TO DO" list, give dinner parties, babysit my grandchildren, dash off to my studio to work on a painting—and then feel guilty because I am not doing more. Did I learn nothing from that quiet time?

As I sit here at my desk and search for answers to so many questions, I wonder what it is about that magical place that won't let loose its grip on me. I know the very fact that I have so many questions and am helplessly pulled back there at odd moments is a change in me. What is the Badel life style, and is it possible to take any of it and weave it into my life here? The answer is not so simple as throwing out my possessions. That is not what simplifying is all about. It is about throwing away the clutter inside myself. The complicated way I approach everyday living, the agonizing, fretting and worrying, the over-concern of what people will think, the always trying to do more, and more, and more.

Badel has changed me. It has made me question what the good life is. And is it good if it separates children from their parents, the old from the young, the rich from the poor? Materially, I am part of the good life, but it isn't the material comforts that I need to change. Shedding those would be easy. Just give them all to the Salvation Army. No, the change has to take place inside, in my perceptions, my values, my priorities, and how I spend the finite moments left to me on this earth.

If the material things take more of these minutes than they give back, pitch them. If I can make a person's load lighter or bring a smile to a sad face, that is a good minute. If my work fulfills me and satisfies me in a way that I go out into the street in a mood of love and compassion, then that is a good minute. If what I have done or am doing makes me angry or mean-spirited, then find out why and change or pitch it, so I won't waste a precious minute.

Every time I communicate and try to understand someone, I am bringing the spirit of Badel here. After all, isn't that what the whole Badel spirit is about, caring

for others and community? Communicate, community—they both come from the
same Latin word meaning to impart, make common.

I am not ready to turn my back on the world I grew up in. But I do want to
embrace it in new ways. Not "My country right or wrong," but "How can I
make my country better?" Not a flight back to an exotic sanctuary among people whose language I don't understand, whose traditions I'm ignorant of, who
cosset me as a foreign visitor, who impose no obligations. But a commitment
to building my own safe haven here at home among my fellows, to keeping the
best of all the good that my own culture has to offer—and there is much to
cherish here—while adding to it the precious treasures gleaned from a far-off
philosophy, a way of thinking, of being that eluded me until I lived amidst it.

Throughout the year after I came home from my third trip to Nepal, I
seemed to be looking differently at everything in my life, but I still didn't feel
transformed. Until Easter Sunday 1994, exactly one year after the day Marge
and I arrived in Badel for the first time.

I am in a large meeting room in a New York City hotel, taking part in a
group seminar—one of the many self-improvement, self-enlightenment
courses available to help us obsessively self-bettering Americans change our
attitudes and become better people—because not everyone can go to Nepal to
accomplish that, and even those of us who can are still, to our discomfiture,
not nearly as good as we *know* we can be. On this, the third day of the seminar,
each of us is asked to stand up and tell the hundred or so people in the room
what our goals are for the future, how we can be the people we know ourselves
to be, and then to imagine that we have already realized those goals.

I think for a few minutes—and it all becomes as clear as those ceramic blue
skies above the Himalayas. This is my prophecy for my future that comes out of
my mouth to the listening room: "With the publication of our little book, the
book you now hold in your hand, Marge and I will introduce the English-speaking world to the good people of Badel. And—somehow, I don't yet know how—
I will work toward bringing medical care to the citizens of remote villages like

Badel." With my help, I think, women and infants won't have to die in childbirth, babies won't have to waste away from dehydration, blinded boys will get treatment for their injured eyes, and little girls born with cleft lips will not have to live out their childhoods feeling self-conscious and deformed.

In another exercise, we have to tell what we see ourselves doing ten years from now, as if it were already true. This time I completely astound myself as I announce, "I sold my house and my furniture and all the possessions I don't need any more. I kept only the things I can travel around with. I keep going back to Nepal, where I visit the medical clinics that serve the villages. I climbed a mountain." As I write these words, seven years after they left my mouth, I have only three more years to find out whether my pronouncement will have come true. Stranger things have happened.

27

A Friendship Flowers: "Love and Namaste"

Friendship with a good person is like an inscription on stone; it lasts forever.

—Nepali proverb

In Marge's and my first telephone conversation on that blustery February day in 1991, our words rushed forth like tsunamis with all that we had to talk about—our times on trek, our separate explorations of Buddhism, the book of Buddhist tales that Marge had written and illustrated and was now hand-printing, the workshop I had just signed up for on "Writing from a Zen Perspective," my adventures in the world of publishing, hers in the world of art. Now, more than ten years later, these tidal waves of shared thoughts and feelings have become even more all-encompassing to include our shared endeavors in Nepal, our families, our work and our philosophies.

But what surprises me more even now is the soil that nurtured our friendship. In these days of phone and fax and e-mail, the rich loam in which Marge's and my friendship grew, thrived and blossomed was the much maligned United States Postal Service. In some ways we feel like time travelers, like women of earlier generations who had the leisure to write long letters. But both of us, daughters of our own era, write about concerns that are very much of today. Now we both compose our often lengthy epistles on computers—and send them off to travel via email along the information superhighway. And we scissor the time for those letters out of busy lives: one thread that runs through our correspondence is a shared feeling that we have both caught the contemporary condition of being too busy.

Marge and I—both of an age when most people have already formed all the close friendships they'll ever have—came to know each other well enough through our letters that we were able to consider traveling together for a month in what were sure to be intimate circumstances in far less than luxurious conditions. We were like those soldiers and the women who wrote to them, who, after having exchanged scores of letters and an occasional photograph, resolved to marry, and then, and only then, shyly met each other in the flesh, exchanged vows, and lived together, often faring as well, if not better, than couples who had courted for years.

Before I made the commitment to travel with Marge to Nepal, I did, however, have one nagging concern. I knew that people get married on the basis of correspondence alone. I knew that when one of Marge's letters came, I dropped everything to read it—and often relished rereading it. I knew how much Marge and I liked and admired the personalities that appeared on the pages of each other's long letters, as well as the ones each of us showed during our rare telephone talks. I loved Marge's responsiveness to my feelings, my experiences, my work—as I found myself writing her about things I hadn't told friends I'd been close to for years. And I cared about her and all that she shared with me. Yes, I knew her well. But did I know her well enough to share this journey? And did she know me? The trip could turn out to be a disaster that I might be able to dine out on afterwards—but that would be good only in the retelling, not in the living. How could we do this with any certainty that we wouldn't end up hating each other with every step on every rocky trail?

When, in the fall of 1992, Marge and I decided to go together to Nepal, and spend four weeks together, most of it in a remote area in the country's isolated eastern hills where we would be the only westerners within a three-day walk, we had spent less than a day and a half in each other's company. It had been good time, close time, when Marge came to New York the previous December and stayed in our home. But it was also a little unsettling. In that short time together I had felt more than a little overwhelmed by Marge. She was so much *there*.

Not only did Marge fill more physical space than I did, as she stood half a foot taller, strong and sturdy—she also filled more of the very air itself. Marge is a talker—a wonderful talker, a colorful talker, a prolific talker. In person, words had flowed from her mouth even more vivaciously than they had poured onto her pages. I, on the other hand, had once told a friend who had asked me to speak to her women's group, "If I could speak, I wouldn't write." As with many writers, spoken words tend to come slowly to my lips, and I am comfortable with long stretches of silence. As a writer, I am used to spending long hours alone, with no sound other than the hum of my computer. Would Marge, I wondered, as much as I liked and admired her, be too much for me? Would I, more comfortable writing than talking, find my new friend too over-powering to be with for such a long time in such intense togetherness?

By now I had known Marge for a longer time than I had known my husband on our wedding day—but still we knew each other almost entirely on paper and on the phone. How would we get along in person? I had to preview this friendship. And so, on October 9th, 1992, before committing myself to airline reservations to Nepal, I scribbled a P.S. to ask Marge, "Any chance we could get together in November to talk about our trip, the book, etc.?" Tactfully (or sneakily), I didn't spell out my main agenda for this get-together: seeing how the two of us would get along in person. I didn't need to. Marge had the same unasked questions. She invited me to come to Chicago and then to drive with her to the cottage in the Michigan woods where the Roche family spends summers. In November, the weather would still be warm enough for walking on the beach and the cottage would be private enough for us to talk and talk and talk. It sounded like the perfect setting to confirm our good feelings toward each other. And so it was. And so we did.

In the cottage in Michigan we were free from Marge's outside distractions and certainly from mine. (In a departure for me, I had absolutely no interest in calling or seeing anyone from my previous life in Chicago, where I had lived for three years; I was totally focused.) We sat down, did our planning, got along beautifully. Each of us acknowledged the other's need for solitary, quiet time. When I, the "lark," was yawning and yearning for bed, I felt no compunction to stay up late to be polite. Marge, the "owl," felt equally unbound to wake up early.

I asked this new friend to let me know if I ever did anything she didn't like, asked her to tell me right away, and said I would do the same. Neither of us found anything to tell the other. Coming back to the Roches' Evanston home after those few days in the woods, I filled in a little more of Marge's life when I met her husband, two of her daughters, and five of her grandchildren, and when I saw and admired the exuberant paintings in her studio, which would illustrate a book of children's poems. My excitement about the shared journey ahead was bright, with not a cloud in sight.

Four months later, on March 30, 1993, I enter the bustling Thai Air check-in area of the Los Angeles airport, look around—and hear "Sally!" There's Marge—tall and stalwart, with her cap of chestnut hair, all smiles and enthusiasm, duffel bags in tow. With the warm welcoming embrace we give each other, our adventure has begun.

After a long plane ride (that seems to get longer every time), our friendship meets its first test in the bathroom of the Airport Hotel at the Bangkok Airport, our overnight stopover before we can board the morning flight for Kathmandu. I flunk the test—but not the course—when I forget to wash out the tub after my shower, before Marge's bath. I apologize to her; she awards me "one demerit." I shudder, hoping I didn't litter that pristine tub with my dark little pubic hairs.

Now I see the merits of Marge's suggestion, which surprised me at first, to take separate rooms at the Potala Guest House in Kathmandu. I had expected to room together, but when Marge reminded me how cheap the rooms were in this modest hotel in the Thamel district and what privacy two rooms would afford us, I saw her point. I see it even more when, in transit from one set of circadian rhythms to another on the other side of the globe, I often sit up, bolt awake, in the middle of the night and can turn on my light and take out my book, with no worry about waking a roommate. And on those couple of days when, invaded by eastern microbes, I sink into my bed and sleep much of the day away.

Two days into our first trip together, still in Kathmandu, Marge and I are getting along well. We're both conscious about giving each other space. It's a sensitive negotiation—between looking out for each other and including each other, while not leeching onto each other. Do we tell one another where we're going and when we'll be back? Wait for the other for breakfast? Plan to meet at a certain time? Or give one another total freedom outside of obligatory commitments? We'll need to talk more about how to do this.

Our first morning in Kathmandu our expectations don't mesh. I awaken early, go for a run, come back to find Marge's room locked, Marge nowhere in sight, her key in the box behind the reception desk, meaning she's out. There's no message for me. I wonder: Should I have told her I'd be going out and returning soon? Has she gone for breakfast, or is she out for the day? Is she expecting to meet me before we are to meet Buddi and Jai for our shopping trip? I go next door to Narayan's for a breakfast of fresh-squeezed orange juice, cinnamon roll, and coffee. The baked goods are delicious in Kathmandu, a remnant of the Peace Corps days when Americans taught Nepalese chefs how to please western sweet-craving palates. When Marge returns about half an hour later and finds me in the coffee shop, we talk, carefully, gingerly afraid of upsetting our delicate equilibrium. There's no blaming, no anger. We each give ourselves an "F" in communication. For the most part from here on, we make efforts—Marge, to remember she has a travel companion this time, me to remember we're not joined at the hip.

Mostly, though, we marvel that we found each other. Moments when we respond to a situation as if we were one person. There is that charged moment soon after arriving in Badel when we see the defect that has defined Kumari's life and decide to arrange for plastic surgery for her, and then for her little cousin, Om. The joint nods of assent when, in talking with Buddi about how we'll arrange our trip, we decide to stay in Badel instead of moving on as our original plan called for. When, in Kathmandu, we take under our wing Joan, the solitary American traveler who lost her three-months' worth of luggage.

Then, of course, there are those moments when we fall into paroxysms of laughter. Like the time we stop taking for granted the logistics of sharing the single small basin of warm washing water brought to us every morning and talk about it. How we take turns, first each of us washing face and hands, then sponge-bathing our bodies, and finally washing out our underpants. All in the same water. Moments when we realize there isn't one other person either of us knows who would be so attuned to each other on this kind of journey.

Then, there is the time late in our first trip, as we stop for lunch on our way back to Lamidanda and, instead of cheerily chatting as we wait for our cook to call "Lunch ready!", Marge sits under a tree to read her novel. And I, who had been afraid of too much talk, now feel abandoned in its absence. Did I do something wrong? Is she getting sick of me? Have I become dependent on her? Is this a sign that enough is enough? That it's time to go home, to our separate homes? Will we get on each other's nerves for the next week we'll be together? Is this the woman I thought I knew so well? How could she sit and bury her nose in a thriller when the scene around us, soon to be preserved only in our memories, is more thrilling than anything I can imagine?

"Enough questions," I scold myself. I look around me. An immense ancient pipal tree sheltering a well in three stone compartments, looking out over a still pool bordered by a stone wall. A porcelain blue sky speckled with clouds, mountains shaded lilac and gray, hillsides scalloped with terraces and spotted with brown patches of large eroded areas. A gentle breeze bringing a whisper of Heaven after the long hot climb. A small brown girl walks by just below us, herding a flock of over a dozen skittering goats. She is taking her job seriously—barking orders at her charges, pelting them with stones on the side when she wants them to turn, clambering barefoot over the rocks after them. Then I become absorbed in Chamar Sing's demonstration of cooking *cheru*, a sweet fried bread. He rolls out a flat circle of flour, water and baking powder; cuts it into strips; slits each strip in the middle; pulls one end through the slit; then deep-fries each piece in hot oil; and sprinkles a little sugar over the top.

By the time lunch is ready, Marge cheerfully joins us. My earlier pique has vanished. I realize she has times when she feels cramped by me—not because of anything I do or don't do, but simply because I am here—and because this woman who treasures her solitude, who almost always travels by herself, is not alone. Once I understand and accept this, I can allow her to meet her needs and to appreciate the freedom that gives me to meet mine. Today my need was to drink in the last sights and sounds and smells of the Nepali trails.

FROM MARGE'S JOURNAL:

At some time in every trek I have a crisis time when I need to completely withdraw from the experience. Some sort of overload happens and I sort of snap. With Sally I feel I could be quiet all day, and she would patiently wait me out and never ask "Why?" or say "Are you mad at me?"

There were a very few other times when we were out of sync. One happened during our second trip, when we added to our village visit a ten-day trek to the famous Buddhist temple in Tyangboche, on the route toward Mount Everest. A few days after we left Badel we spent the night in Namche Bazar, the popular launching area for trekkers and mountaineers on their way to Everest. Namche is a busy market town whose alley-streets are lined with souvenir stalls and thronged with loud-voiced trekkers and vendors bargaining in a babel of languages. The town was so crowded that instead of our usual quiet, secluded campsite, we had to pitch our tents in the yard of a completely booked inn, a yard we shared with barking dogs, snorting and bellowing yaks, and eighteen wine-drinking Italian trekkers, whose vivacity resounded long after moonrise. The night was cold, the yard was littered with piles of curly yak dung, and the latrine all of us used smelled like the bathroom from Hell.

Sharman Singh Rae
our cook Tara Mani Rae
Our young porter and
kitchen boy.

Next morning, Marge wants to escape Namche Bazar as quickly as possible. I'm exhausted and want to rest here for one day before climbing higher. We end up staying the day, and I feel guilty because I have imposed my will on my friend's, on one of the few occasions when the two of us don't agree.

The day before I had asked Marge whether she ever gets cranky, since I've seen her spirits remaining consistently (and sometimes annoyingly!) high through various tribulations that set my teeth on edge. "Oh, sure," she said. "I get what Dwyer calls the mumbly-grumblies." This morning I see the mumbly-grumblies in action. Not that I can blame my friend. She had quite a night last night, too. Worse than mine. She heard all the noises I heard—the snuffling of the animals, the laughter of the wine drinkers, the clinking of the cooking pots being washed by the staff for three groups, and, of course, the incessant barking of dogs. She was awake as often as I was—and she suffered more. Besides the two yaks tethered a couple of feet from the front opening of her tent and the numerous deposits they had left equally close to her, besides the hordes of people around us, besides the cruddy, smelly, disgusting charpi, Marge had company in her tent during the night. At dawn when she opened her tent flap, a big gray furry creature ran out ahead of her. Definitely not a mouse. A cat? A rat? Or a young yeti?

She doesn't show the mumbly-grumblies toward me today, but then she doesn't show anything toward me. She pulls a disappearing act. I have learned to accept Marge's need to be off on her own, and I relish the luxury of having my own glorious day of solitude. But what I do find disconcerting is that my companion doesn't tell me that she is taking off. I look around and she's nowhere in sight. I know she's used to traveling on her own and not answering to anyone—and I've had little experience with that. I'm a little envious of that independence. I feel too dependent, taking my cue on what to do from her inclinations. I say nothing at the time, but months later I send her my journal, in which I've expressed my feelings about this day.

FROM MARGE'S LETTER AFTER READING MY JOURNAL:

I know it took guts to leave this in and not edit it out of my copy. Thanks for being so patient and tolerant with me. I don't know what triggered my "snap" this time, except maybe the comparison between the materialism and commercialism of Namche Bazar with the peaceful simplicity we had just left in Badel. I think your talk of our relationship and perceptions of me work very well with your perceptions of Nepal. I always admire your writing, but now I admire your honesty almost as much and I value our friendship even more, if that is possible.

Ultimately, we came out of our first trip feeling even closer to each other than we had at the outset. So much so that a year and a half later, in the fall of 1994, we took our second trip back to Badel. And then in 1996, and again in 1998 we returned, together, to the village. And even in 2000, when Marge went to Badel without me, she understood the pressures in my life at that time, which kept me home—and I was happy that she went for both of us, feeling as if I were there with her, seeing the newly constructed two-story library building, visiting with our friends in Badel.

Our friendship is dynamic, a living, changing entity, in which we constantly discover new qualities about each other. I continue to be impressed by Marge and to be grateful for her place in my life. I'm sure that one reason we get along so well is that our creativity runs in different channels. We understand and empathize with each other's struggles and provide a cheering section for each other's work—but there's no competition, envy, jealousy, battling over turf.

FROM MARGE'S JOURNAL:

What a crazy team we are! It's just a good thing we are not both writers or both artists. I respect Sally and admire her talents very much, but do not need to emulate her as much as I want to use my skills, so they complement hers and we have a marriage of talents. I think we do and that is why we get along so well. I have come to believe that the combination of our talents is greater than the talents existing separately. I guess synergistic is the way I would describe it.

And then, we constitute each other's fan club—and give each other epistolary psychotherapy. In a letter responding to one in which Marge flagellated herself for being selfish, I wrote, "You are one of the least selfish people I know! I have seen your unselfishness, thoughtfulness, considerateness and kindness in action. I am tremendously impressed by the contributions I know about that you make to the lives of your husband, your children, your grandchildren and your friends. And I know that you make many more that I don't know about. So if, sometimes you feel that you need to take care of yourself in a way that's in conflict with what other people want of you, you have every right—and obligation—to do it. After all, if you're not in good shape yourself, you can't give to others. You need to have the resources to draw on!"

And after she read an article about me that appeared in our local suburban weekly, she wrote, "I could add a few more superlatives to it….Having spent a lot of time with you I can affirm that you do indeed have a life of love and humor and you made it all happen by your hard work and perseverance."

As I read reviews of two recently published books of correspondence between women writers—one containing letters between Hannah Arendt and Mary McCarthy and the other between Rachel Carson and her friend, Dorothy Freeman, I realized that Marge and I have the same kind of supportive, fulfilling friendship that these other women had. I treasure our rapport—by mail, by phone and especially in person. I value the way we can talk about so many things on so many levels—creative, emotional, social, political, and of course always—all things Nepali. Jane Austen wrote about friendship between women: "There was not a creature in the world to whom she spoke with such unreserve…with such conviction of being listened to and understood, of being always interesting and always intelligible." She could have been writing about us.

FROM MARGE'S LETTER AFTER READING MY JOURNAL:

Your journal arrived and I sat right down and read it. It is wonderful. Perfect as it is. How do you ever do it? Write so sensitively with empathy. You say all the things I think. Thank you for helping me relive our journey. I hate to see all that beautiful writing just sit in a drawer. FRAME IT AND HANG IT ON YOUR LIVING ROOM WALL. PAPER THE WALLS WITH IT AND MAKE EVERY-ONE WHO COMES INTO YOUR HOUSE READ IT BEFORE THEY GET EVEN A CUP OF COFFEE. THEN GIVE A QUIZ.

How can I not love someone who can tell me something like this!

I have been captivated by the book of Rachel Carson's and Dorothy Freeman's letters. I'm especially intrigued by the whole idea of how a relation-ship thrives on communication by mail. As ours does. I identify with Carson's need to share her feelings, her thoughts, even her day-to-day experiences. And to put it all down on paper. The curse of the writer! Which is then visited on the writer's friends!

I am struck by one passage in particular, in which Rachel tells Dorothy how wonderful it is to have someone who cares for her as a person and who also "has the capacity and the depth of understanding to share…the sometimes crushing burden of creative effort…someone who cherishes me and what I am trying to create, as well.…The few who understood the creative problem were not people to whom I felt emotionally close; those who loved the nonwriter part of me did not, by some strange paradox, understand the writer at all!" Marge and I perform this double function for one another—since we cherish each other's friendship and champion each other's work. I appreciate her sup-portiveness of my writing, and I admire, respect and respond emotionally to her painting. I remain deeply moved by her charming portrayals of the people of Nepal. I treasure the works of hers that adorn my walls and grace my book-shelf, and she has every book I have ever written—and has actually read them.

Finally, Marge and I laugh a lot together. We have a good time. We learn from each other. I know that I become more of who I can be when I am with her, either in person, on the other end of the telephone cables, or reading her words on the page. I look forward to every one of her letters and derive as much pleasure, I think, from writing my own to her. As we close each letter to one another, we express our deep currents of friendship and our shared feelings about Nepal that first brought us together. And so we end each letter—and now, each email, with "Love and Namaste."

SHREE NATH DARGE
playing Narsingha
instrument.

M Roche 10/96

Epilogue:
March 2002

Those of us who love Nepal and her people were shocked and saddened by the terrible events of June 1, 2001, which saw the violent deaths of nine members of Nepal's royal family. The complete story of what happened may never be known; the prevailing view is that at a family dinner, Crown Prince Dipendra, the son of the country's queen and king, argued with his parents about his choice of a bride, returned to his quarters after having drunk a great deal and possibly also taken drugs, and emerged, dressed in military camouflage gear, to begin firing his automatic weapon at his assembled relatives. The carnage that followed took the lives of the prince's parents, King Birendra and Queen Aiswarya, their daughter and their other son, along with five others, including a brother of the king. After these shootings, the prince turned his gun upon himself and remained in a coma for 40 hours before he also died. This version of events has not, however, been accepted by many Nepalis, who have proposed various alternate scenarios, virtually all of which blame officials of the Nepalese or Indian government, or the American C.I.A.

The killings took place against a bloody backdrop of other violence in Nepal—the Maoist uprisings that had been rocking the nation since 1996, and that have continued up to the time of this writing. Modeling their efforts on the brutal Shining Path rebels in Peru, the Nepalese revolutionaries aim to institute a communist government in place of the present constitutional monarchy,

357

which has been accused of being aloof and unresponsive to the needs of the Nepalese people, of condoning greed and corruption in the government, and of attempting to silence critics of the regime by exile, jail or death threats. Over the past five years the Maoist insurgency has been responsible for more than 2000 deaths, mostly in western Nepal. Some of those killed were officials or policemen beheaded by the Maoists. Other fatalities were suffered by the rebels themselves or the residents of remote villages where the rebels sought a stronghold. Airports that I had flown from, with Marge and with my husband, were attacked; government posts I had been inches away from were demolished; policemen I might even have spoken to during various trips were killed.

Both Marge and I had, of course, known for years about accusations of corruption in the government—claiming that foreign aid often finds its way into politicians' pockets instead of into the projects that would help the people of this poor and underdeveloped country, citing an apparent lack of interest in high places in bettering the conditions of the bulk of the population, and protesting the way the ruling classes virtually shut out anyone not of their caste for the better jobs. We suspect that Buddi, who had wanted to apply his master's degree in political science to a job in government, or in a university, was personally affected by some of these circumstances.

But still these news accounts—of both the palace slayings and the Maoist killings—were hard for us to comprehend. The people who had done these deeds were acting so very differently from the kind, gentle people we were privileged to meet, in both village and town. In fact, one argument many Nepalis cited as the reason for not believing the official version of the royal massacre was "How could a son kill his own parents? Impossible!" What a contrast this is to our own society, where our newspapers regularly report instances of patricide and matricide, and we are no longer surprised to read such accounts.

I have faith in the Nepali people. A country isn't only its government, and somehow the villagers—the ones that we came to know—seem, for the most

part, to have retained an admirable attitude about life. This is, and will doubt-
less remain, the big attraction to visitors who, like us, come at first because of
the mountains and the adventure and the foray into a past way of life, but who
return because of the people.

Nepal is not Paradise. Paradise would not contain the patriarchal system
that denies women opportunities and even access to family property; the
spousal and child abuse that exists even in the villages; the caste system that
relegates so many people to the bottom of the social and economic ladders; or
the poverty and the child mortality and the lack of medical care. But much of
this is changing, and some of these changes give some support to an optimistic
framework. The royal family ruled for so many years with apparent disregard
for the people; the new rulers may turn out to be an improvement. This
tragedy at the royal palace, coupled with the Maoist insurrection, may in the
end bring about improvements in the way of life in Nepal. And she will always
have the Himalayas. We don't know what will happen. We can only hope for
the best.

Who's Who: The People We Came to Know in Badel

JAI'S FAMILY (1993)

Father: Gokana Rai, a farmer.
Mother: Dilkumari, mother of three sons and three daughters.
Indra Maya, 30, married and living in Rakha, two hours away; mother of three sons:
Bikas, 7; Santos, 3; and Monos, 11 months.
Jai Prasad, 27, married to Buddi's sister Sita; father of Kim (& later, Jason)
Kali Maya, 25, single, living at home.
Mithu Maya, 20, single, living at home, commuting to high school in Rakha.
Prem Kumar, 14, a sixth grader in Badel school.
Kul Bahadur, 12, a fifth grader in Badel school.

BUDDI'S FAMILY (1993)

Father: Dhojuman Rai, 70, a former Gurkha soldier, now retired and working as a farmer.
Mother: Shiva, 55, originally from Darjeeling, India; mother of three sons and five daughters.
Gita, 35, married to **Dhan Bahadur Rai**, the English teacher at the Badel school and proprietor of the only store in Badel. Mother of a daughter, 17, and two sons, Ishwor, 14, and Uttam, 15.

Bina, 33, married to a man from the Terai in southern Nepal, mother of two or three children; has not seen the rest of her family in many years.

Sita Devi, 28, married to Jai; the mother of 3 1/2-year-old Kim (and later, Jason).

Buddi Kumar, 27, married to **Dhana,** 21; the father of Kusum (and later, Sushma and Ajaya).

Rita, 25, lives in Kathmandu with her husband and their small sons.

Susila, 20, living with Jai and Sita in Kathmandu while she looks for a job there.

Dilip, 17, a high school student currently off on trek, working as a porter with Peter Owens.

Kiran Kumar, 11, sixth grader in the Badel school.

Ganga Maya Rai, Buddi's aunt.

SOME OF OUR STAFF

Buddi Kumar Rai, our guide on both visits, university graduate, holder of master's degree in political science, former teacher, currently working as trek and mountaineering guide.

Jai Prasad Rai, the *sirdar* on Marge's and my previous treks; organizer of our first visit to Badel; Buddi's brother-in-law.

Gora Rai, the cook for the first week of our first visit; cook on Marge's and my previous treks; son of the shaman, Gadja Bahadur Rai.

Chamar Sing Rai, the cook for the second week of our first visit.

Tara Mani Rai, porter and kitchen helper for our first visit; cook for our second visit.

Kangsha Rai, porter for our first visit; kitchen helper for our second visit.

Mon Bahadur Darje (Mani Bhujel), porter for our first visit; father of Kumari Darje.

G.S. Rai, sherpa for our 1998 trek, son of Ganga Maya Rai.

Glossary of Nepali Words

aama mother
bahini younger sister, little girl
baksheesh under-the-table money
bango-tingo crooked, winding
basnos please sit down
bauju older brother's wife
bideshi a polite word for foreigner
bhitra aunos please come in
Bijaya Dashami ninth day of the festival of Dasain
chang homemade beer
charpi latrine
chhaina no, none, I don't have any
chola blouse
chora son; *chori* daughter
Chula god of fire who lives in the fire in the center of every Rai
house
dal bhat rice with lentil sauce
Dasain major Hindu festival celebrated in the fall throughout
Nepal
derso level ground
dhiru a thick paste made of flour (millet, corn or other grain) and
water; a staple diet among many hill people
didi older sister
doko cone-shaped woven bamboo basket
ghar home
hamro our

363

Hotar chhaina No hurry
Jaa! Go!
jamora wheat-flowers
jhankri witch-doctor, shaman
jetha first-born son; *jethi* first-born daughter
joghi a slang word used in playing cards
jummraa lice
juwaai son-in-law
kaancha youngest son; *kaanchi* youngest daughter
Kahaa bata aaeko? Where are you coming from?
Kahaa jaane? Where are you going?
Ke garne? What can you do? (very common phrase)
khola river
khukri large, curved, razor-sharp knife
Kube-Nokcho highest order of shaman in Mudhum religion
laligourans rhododendrons
lunghi ankle-length cotton saronglike skirt, usually in a bright print
maile bujhina I don't understand
marache small red flowers that grow at high altitudes and are dried and strung
on necklaces, worn for good luck
maruni Rai dance
matwali jat drinking castes
mero my, mine
Mudhum animistic religion practiced by Rai people of Badel
namaste "I salute the divine within you." Universal greeting accompanied by
putting the palms of the hands together, prayer-fashion
natinatini grandchildren
Noya barsa mani Happy New Year
Noya barsako shuba kamina Greetings for the new year
oraalo downhill
piccar chhaina no problem
ping a big swing like a ferris wheel, erected at Nepali holidays

pipal a species of fig tree that has broad shade-giving leaves and mystical qualities; the kind of tree the Buddha was born under

puja religious devotion

punjabi, or *shalwar kameez,* an Indian ensemble consisting of a graceful loose-fitting dress over matching wide pants

pustekalaya library

pustak-manche librarian

rakshi homemade liquor made by distilling millet or other grain

ramro beautiful, good

roshi teacher

rungi-chungi multi-colored

saathi friend

sherpa guide

sirdar Nepalese trek leader

suun gold

tapaikko your (polite form)

tempu a motorized tricycle-type vehicle with an enclosed cab

thangka a religious painting on silk depicting important Buddhist events and personages

tika dot placed on forehead to signify religious blessing

timro your (intimate form)

topi traditional brimless hat worn by men, shaped like an upside-down pail

ukaalo uphill

Bibliography

Allen, Michael R. (1996). *The Cult of Kumari: Virgin Worship in Nepal*, second edition. Kathmandu: Mandala Book Point.

Bezruchka, Stephen. (1991). *Trekking in Nepal: A Traveler's Guide.* 6th ed. Seattle: The Mountaineers.

Coburn, Broughton. (1995). *Nepali Aama: Life Lessons of a Himalayan Woman.* New York: Anchor (Doubleday). Previously published as *Nepali Aama: Portrait of a Nepalese Hill Woman.* 1981 (Ross-Erikson) and 1991 (Moon Publications).

Gottlieb, Alma and Graham, Philip. (1993). *Parallel Worlds: An Anthropologist and a Writer Encounter Africa.* New York: Crown.

Lall, Kesar. (1991). *The Pilgrims Proverbs of Nepal and Other Countries.* Kathmandu: R. N. Tiwari.

McDougal, Charles. (1979). *The Kulunge Rai: A Study in Kinship and Marriage Exchange.* Bibliotheca Himalayica. Kathmandu: Ratna Pustak Bhandar.

Moran, Kerry. (1991). *Nepal Handbook.* Chico, CA: Moon Publications.

Murphy, Dervla. (1968). *The Waiting Land: A Spell in Nepal.* Woodstock, NY: Overlook Press.

Niven, B. M. (1987). *The Mountain Kingdom: Portraits of Nepal and the Gurkhas.* Bombay, India: World Wide Publications. (India Book Distributors, 107/108, Arcadia, 195, Nariman Point, Bombay 400 021, India)

O. Henry (William Sidney Porter). (1953). "The Man Higher Up" in *The Complete Works of O. Henry*, vol. 1. Garden City, NY: Doubleday. Pages 315-324.

Shrestha, D. B. and Singh, C. B. (1992). *Ethnic Groups of Nepal and Their Ways of Living.* Kathmandu: Mandala Book Point

About the Author and the Artist

THE AUTHOR:

Sally Wendkos Olds has written extensively about child development, family life, human relationships, and health, and has won national awards for her book and magazine writing. She is the author or coauthor of nine books and more than 200 articles that have appeared in major national publications. Her first book, *The Complete Book of Breastfeeding*, a classic in the field, was revised in 1999 for its third edition. Her co-authored college textbooks *A Child's World* and *Human Development* are leading texts in child development and lifespan development and incorporate multi-cultural observations from Nepal and other societies. For more information, see **www.sallywendkosolds.com**.

THE ARTIST:

Margaret Roche has exhibited her award-winning artwork in numerous juried group exhibits, as well as in several one-person shows. During her treks in the Himalayas (she has made twelve so far—to Nepal, Bhutan, Tibet, Sikkim, Burma and India), she always carries her art materials, so that she can paint and sketch people as they go about their daily tasks and family life. She calls her works "narrative drawings," since she usually writes on the drawing some impression or feeling that she experiences at the time of creating it. Later, back in her studio she turns some of these drawings into limited-edition etchings.

369

0-595-24027-5